Claiming Citizenship

Claiming Citizenship is an authoritative and vital series published by Zed Books in partnership with the Citizenship Development Research Centre (CDRC).

Each high-quality volume features thoroughly peer-reviewed research from senior experts in their field, which examines the multifaceted issues of citizenship, rights, participation and accountability. The books are global in scope and packed with empirical and original case studies, largely from Southern contexts, bringing voices and materials to debates that have often been dominated by the North. While essential reading for development studies students and researchers, the series will be of interest to a broad range of scholars, activists and practitioners concerned with issues of citizenship.

Available titles

Inclusive Citizenship: Meanings and Expressions, edited by Naila Kabeer

Science and Citizens: Globalization and the Challenge of Engagement, edited by Melissa Leach, Ian Scoones and Brian Wynne

Rights, Resources and the Politics of Accountability, edited by Peter Newell and Joanna Wheeler

Spaces for Change? The Politics of Citizen Participation in New Democratic Arenas, edited by Andrea Cornwall and Vera Schattan Coelho

Citizenship and Social Movements: Perspectives from the Global South, edited by Lisa Thompson and Chris Tapscott

Forthcoming titles

Citizen Action and National Policy: Making Change Happen, edited by John Gaventa and Rosemary McGee

Mobilizing for Democracy: Citizen Action and the Politics of Public Participation, edited by Vera Schattan Coelho and Bettina von Lieres

Engaging Citizens: In a Globalizing World, edited by John Gaventa and Rajesh Tandon

About the editors

Lisa Thompson is Director of the African Centre for Citizenship and Democracy (ACCEDE) and Professor at the School of Government, University of the Western Cape. Her work focuses on issues of socio-economic development in the context of the global political economy. She has published widely on research pertaining to regional development and democratization processes in southern Africa, including her monograph, *Participatory Governance? Citizens and the State in South Africa* (ACCEDE, 2007). She serves as South African coordinator of the Development Research Centre on Citizenship, Participation and Accountability.

Chris Tapscott is Professor and Dean of the Faculty of Economic and Management Sciences at the University of the Western Cape in South Africa and was formerly the founding director of the School of Government in the same institution. His current research focus is on the local state and the political and organizational challenges which this poses to the development of substantive participatory democracy in countries of the South. He has been an active member of the Development Research Centre on Citizenship, Participation and Accountability.

Lisa Thompson and Chris Tapscott | editors

Citizenship and social movements
perspectives from the global South

Zed Books

LONDON | NEW YORK

Citizenship and social movements: perspectives from the global South was first published in 2010 by Zed Books Ltd, 7 Cynthia Street, London N1 9JF, UK and Room 400, 175 Fifth Avenue, New York, NY 10010, USA

www.zedbooks.co.uk

Editorial copyright © Lisa Thompson and Chris Tapscott 2010
Copyright in this collection © Zed Books 2010

Set in OurType Arnhem and Futura Bold by Ewan Smith, London
Index: ed.emery@thefreeuniversity.net
Cover designed by Andrew Corbett
Printed and bound in Great Britain by the MPG Books Group

Distributed in the USA exclusively by Palgrave Macmillan, a division of St Martin's Press, LLC, 175 Fifth Avenue, New York, NY 10010, USA

A catalogue record for this book is available from the British Library
Library of Congress Cataloging in Publication Data available

ISBN 978 1 84813 388 4 hb
ISBN 978 1 84813 389 1 pb
ISBN 978 1 84813 390 7 eb

Contents

Acknowledgements

This book represents a further output from the Citizenship Development Research Centre (CDRC), which, over the course of the past decade, has undertaken an extensive range of studies on the ongoing struggles for citizen rights in states of the global South. As editors, we have benefited considerably from the collective input of the CDRC team and the exhaustive debates on citizenship and social mobilization which have taken place through a succession of workshops, e-mail conferences and one-on-one discussions across three continents. In that respect we would like to acknowledge the contributions of Angela Alonso, Vera Schattan Coelho, Christopher Colvin, Valeriano Costa, Arilson Favareto, Débora Maciel, Simeen Mahmud, Lyla Mehta, Ranyjita Mohanti, Celestine Nyamu Musembi, Lubna Nadvi, Ndodana Nleya, Duncan Okello, Eghosa Osaghae, Laurence Piper, Steven Robins, Carlos Cortez Ruiz, Nardia Simpson and Linda Waldman to this book project (even the contributions that could not be accommodated in this volume helped enrich our editorial insights). We also benefited from the insights and advice of Eghosa Osaghae, Neil Stammers and John Gaventa, who reviewed various drafts of this book, as well as two anonymous reviewers of the original proposal from Zed Books. We owe a particular debt to John Gaventa, the director of the Development Research Centre on Citizenship, Participation and Accountability, not only for his inspirational leadership of the broader research team, but also for his patience and meticulous attention to detail in reviewing the chapters in this volume. We would also like to express our appreciation to the British government's Department for International Development (DfID), without whose generous support this publication would not have been possible. We are also grateful to the Flemish Inter-University Council (VLIR) for supplementary support to this undertaking.

Abbreviations and acronyms

ABM	Abahlali baseMjondolo
AFRA	Association for Rural Advancement
AGAPAN	Southern Association for the Protection of the Natural Environment
ANC	African National Congress
APPN	São Paulo Association for Natural Protection
ARD	asbestos-related disease
ASA	Serrana Institute Environmental Association
ASA	San Andrés Accords
BGMEA	Bangladesh Garment Manufacturers and Exporters Association
CBA	Brazilian Aluminum Company
CCF	Concerned Citizens Forum
CCG	Concerned Citizens Group
CDRC	Citizenship Development Research Centre
CEBRAP	Brazilian Centre for Analysis and Planning
CERU	Centre of Urban and Rural Studies of the University of São Paulo
CGRH	Committee for the Management of Water Resources
CINDI	Children in Distress Network
COCOPA	Commission for Concord and Pacification
COLACOCO	Coalition for Langa Community Concerns
COMPASS	eThekwini Municipality Community Participation and Action Support Strategy
Consad	Consortium of Food Safety and Local Development
COSATU	Congress of South African Trade Unions
CPAA	Concerned People Against Asbestos
CPASU	Community Participation and Action Support Unit
CPP	Citizen Participation Policy: Framework for eThekwini Municipality
CUT	Workers' Centre Union
DA	Democratic Alliance
DNAEE	National Department of Water and Electrical Energy
ECF	Eastwood Community Forum

EPZ	export processing zone
ERA	Environmental Rights Action
ESRAZ	Zapatista rebel autonomous secondary school
EZLN	Zapatista National Liberation Army
FBCN	Brazilian Foundation for the Conservation of Nature
FBW	free basic water
FLN	National Liberation Forces
GPCA	Green Point Common Association
IBAMA	National Institute for the Environment
ICHRP	International Council on Human Rights Policy
IDESC	Institute for Sustainable Development and Citizenship in the Vale do Ribeira
IDP	integrated development programme
IDS	Institute of Development Studies
IFI	international financial institutions
IFP	Inkatha Freedom Party
ISA	Socio-environmental Institute
ITESP	São Paulo Land Institute
IUCN	International Union for the Conservation of Nature and Natural Resources
IYC	Ijaw Youth Council
JBG	good governance council(s)
MAPE	Art and Ecological Thinking Movement
MAREZ	autonomous rebel Zapatista municipality/ies
MBOD	Medical Bureau for Occupational Diseases
MD	managing director
MEC	member of the (provincial) executive committee
MFA	Multi-Fibre Arrangement
MFMA	Municipal Finance Management Act
MOAB	Movement of Those Threatened by the Dam
MOSOP	Movement for the Survival of Ogoni People
NAFTA	North American Free Trade Agreement
NDDC	Niger Delta Development Commission
NGO	non-governmental organization
NSM	new social movement
NYCOP	National Youth Council of Ogoni People
OMPADEC	Oil Mineral Producing Area Development Commission
PMBD	Brazilian Democratic Movement Party

POS	political opportunity structure
Pronaf	National Programme for Strengthening Family Agriculture
PSDB	Brazilian Social Democracy Party
PSM	People's Social Movement
PT	Workers' Party
PV	Green Party
Rio '92	United Nations Conference on Environment and Development
Sintravale	Family Farmers' Union
SMI	Social Movements Indaba
SSPA	South-South Peoples' Assembly
UCA	environmental conservation area
UDF	United Democratic Front
UNEP	United Nations Environment Programme
WCD	World Commission on Dams
WCF	ward community forum
WWF	World Wide Fund for Nature

Foreword

In 2008, the world celebrated the sixtieth anniversary of the signing of the Universal Declaration of Human Rights, which established international commitments to civil, political, social and economic rights. Yet, for the workers and communities whose stories are recounted in this book, the struggles to make these rights real against powerful global forces continue. Deep in the heart of the oil-rich Niger Delta, youth-led ethnic minorities mobilize against the destruction of their land and livelihoods caused by careless oil extraction, as well as for a fair share of the resources which this global commodity brings. In small towns of the Northern Cape in South Africa, workers gripped by occupational disease from the extraction of asbestos pursue their claims for health rights in national and international courts, while in export processing zones of Bangladesh, the government turns a blind eye to the working conditions of young women sewing garments for international consumption. In India and South Africa, communities mobilize for their rights to water, challenging a growth model that has ripped people from their natural resources; in the southern state of Chiapas in Mexico, peasants similarly pursue their struggle for an alternative form of development in their mountainous rainforest, and in the heart of Cape Town, South Africa, residents challenge their displacement by the building of a stadium for the 2010 FIFA World Cup. What all of these cases have in common is the story of how marginalized and disenfranchised citizens mobilize to claim their rights, protect their resources, and gain recognition for their identities, usually against global odds.

This book is the fifth in the series on 'Claiming Citizenship: Rights, Participation and Accountability'. While the previous volume, *Spaces for Change*, focused largely on the dynamics of citizen engagement in 'invited' spaces of participatory governance, the chapters in this volume step outside the institutional arena to examine how citizens express their demands through social mobilization and social movements. The volume is important for several reasons.

First, while there are large literatures on citizenship and democracy, on the one hand, and social movements, on the other, these themes are often pursued separately and distinctly. Those who examine how citizens engage with the state often do so with a focus on participation in the political processes of elections, parties, deliberative spaces or occasionally protests, but not on social movements, many of which emerge outside the formal political arena, and use extra-institutional channels to express their demands. On the other hand, those who focus on social movements have concentrated largely on how and why they emerge, and on the dynamics within them, not necessarily on their contribution to realizing substantive citizenship rights or to building and deepening responsive, more democratic forms of governance. Yet, as Evelina Dagnino, a contributor to our work, consistently reminds us, citizenship is fundamentally about the 'right to have rights', and thus to be able to claim them through deep forms of social mobilization and action.[1] And, in the context of emerging democracies, where institutionalized channels to engagement have proved weak or unresponsive, social movements can be a fundamentally important vehicle for realizing rights from the state, holding it to account, and struggling for more equitable and sustainable forms of development. Citizenship without the social movements which undergird it, this volume argues, risks becoming reduced to weak forms of participation, in arenas and through channels in which citizens have little control, and with little ability to raise new issues or challenge dominant discourses.

Second, this volume is important because of whose perspective it represents. While there is an abundant literature on social movements, with a number of theoretical debates on how and when they emerge, much of this debate is dominated by Northern and Western scholars, drawing largely, though not exclusively, from the history of movements in those contexts. More recently, a growing international literature has also developed on transnational social movements. Yet with some notable exceptions (which the editors discuss), very few collections exist which are drawn from the rich history of social movements in the global South, and written through the lens of scholars who are deeply rooted in those settings. In this volume, by contrast, we have ten case studies across three continents in the southern hemisphere from countries as varied as Bangladesh, Brazil, India, Mexico, Nigeria and South Africa – all written by scholars from those countries themselves. The cases are also rich in their diversity, reflecting struggles over land and labour, water and health, political inclusion and development resources, using an array of tactics, yet all involving ordinary citizens in attempts to claim rights, to influence the development priorities of their countries and to demand more inclusive and accountable governance.

Perhaps unlike cases from richer and more powerful countries and constituencies, in these cases drawn from the global South the dynamics of grassroots movements are inextricably tied to broader issues of social and economic inequality, which are themselves linked to a global system and which require strategies and tactics that go beyond the local to achieve their results. In the past, much of the work on social movements in such countries has been on the movements for national liberation, or for achieving political and civic rights following decades of colonial or authoritarian rule. Each of the countries represented here has now achieved some level of democratic space, often after long histories of struggles for democratization, though in some cases, especially perhaps those of Nigeria and Bangladesh, that democratic space remains fragile. Nevertheless, with new democratic space, the focus of social movements in these contexts turns to how to use this space to challenge broader forms of inequality, and reflects a fundamental concern with achieving socio-economic rights, control over resources and more inclusive and responsive governance, and not with political and civil rights alone.

Future volumes in the series will continue this theme of how social mobilization contributes to claiming citizenship, deepening democracies and challenging development priorities. The next volume, *Citizen Action and National Policy* (Gaventa and McGee), focuses on how citizens mobilize to create national-level policies which are socially just and pro-poor. A subsequent volume, *Mobilizing for Democracy* (Coelho and von Lieres), narrates how mobilization from below strengthens and builds democracies themselves, going beyond more traditional institution-building approaches that dominate much of the field, while a third volume, *Engaging Citizens* (Gaventa and Tandon), will examine the challenges of linking citizen action from the local to the national and global arenas, arguing that in a globalized world, mobilization and engagement must be linked across all levels, to realize their full potential for change.

Each of these volumes is part of the work of the Development Research Centre on Citizenship, Participation and Accountability, based at the Institute of Development Studies at the University of Sussex. Now in its ninth year, this research programme represents a network of partners in each of the countries represented in the volume, as well as a number of others. The Centre has been fortunate to receive the support of the Department for International Development (DfID), as one of several centres funded over a ten-year period to conduct work on how to develop more responsive and effective states that will help to alleviate global poverty. (For further information on the Citizenship DRC, see www.drc-citizenship.org.)

This particular volume had its roots in an earlier project on science and citizens, led by Melissa Leach and Ian Scoones. In that programme, a series of case studies investigated the theme of social mobilization, focusing especially on the politics of knowledge in issues ranging from genetically modified crops, vaccines, HIV/AIDS and occupational health, to struggles over water, housing and the environment.[2]

Building on these earlier case studies, Lisa Thompson and Chris Tapscott from the University of the Western Cape, both of whom have been deeply involved throughout the Citizenship DRC, proposed this broader project. Unlike some of the other volumes in this series, which emerged through the work of formalized working groups and had dedicated institutional support, the production of this volume was itself a 'mobilization' process, in which editors and contributors formed their own links, and discussed, reviewed and submitted their work by email, through e-conferences and at the margins of other meetings. Throughout the process, they displayed the sense of partnership, collegiality and extra effort that has characterized the production of each of these volumes. As overall series editor, I would like to thank Lisa and Chris for their persistent and dedicated leadership in seeing this volume through, as well as each of the contributors for taking part. Finally, our thanks go to the team at Zed Books, who continue to make this series on 'Claiming Citizenship' possible.

John Gaventa, Director, Development Research Centre on Citizenship, Participation and Accountability

October 2009

Notes

1 See S. Alvarez, E. Dagnino and A. Escobar (1998), *Cultures of Politics/ Politics of Culture: Re-visioning Latin American Social Movements*, Westview Press, Boulder, CO, as well as the earlier contribution in this series, E. Dagnino, 'We all have rights, but ... Contesting concepts of citizenship in Brazil', in N. Kabeer, *Inclusive Citizen-ship: Meanings and Expressions*, Zed Books, London.

2 For a synthesis of this work, see Melissa Leach and Ian Scoones (2007), *Mobilising Citizens: Social Movements and the Politics of Knowledge*, IDS Working Paper 276. Available for download from: www.ntd.co.uk/idsbookshop/details.asp?id=962.

1 | Introduction: mobilization and social movements in the South – the challenges of inclusive governance[1]

LISA THOMPSON AND CHRIS TAPSCOTT

The latter half of the twentieth century witnessed an upsurge in mobilization and collective action in states of the global South, which has continued to this day. While this mobilization in its early phases comprised part of either ongoing anti-colonial struggles for national independence or struggles against despotic rule (especially in Latin America), the forms of social movement to which this has given rise have mutated over the years and they now reflect a broad array of social, political and economic concerns differentially expressed at local, national and global levels. While the literature on social movements is vast and extends back nearly a century, it remains a truism that by far the bulk of the writing and theorizing in this field has been oriented to the analysis of movements in the global North.[2] There has been little attempt to engage with the writings of Southern scholars on the topic. Where research has focused attention on transitional states, social movements have invariably been analysed in terms of criteria derived from Northern experience. While some of this comparative work retains undeniable universal validity, a good deal of it clearly does not. In the absence of historically grounded empirical research, social movements in these societies and the struggles that underpin them are not infrequently reduced to caricature. This mode of investigation, typified by long-range event analysis, denies the complexity of social formations in the South, and, ignoring any prospect of agency, portrays their members as the hapless victims of tyrannical rulers and traditional culture or the passive recipients of Northern-led actions.

While the quest for meta-theory, with its all-embracing power of explanation, remains an alluring one for social and political scientists the world over, the latent weakness in the approach remains, as always, a lack of empirical validation across different social, political and historical contexts. As Oliver et al. (2003) point out, there is a need for mainstream theory to 'continue to address a geographically and substantively broader empirical base, breaking out of a preoccupation with Anglo-America and

Europe and becoming truly global in its orientation. This broader base will open new empirical problems that will point to weaknesses in current theory and lead to the development of new theory.' They argue for a 'growing focus on mechanisms and processes that occur in many different movements, and decreasing attempts to develop universal propositions about the causes, effects or trajectories of whole movements' (ibid.).

Although this volume makes no pretence of advancing a coherent theoretical framework for understanding collective action and social movements[3] in the global South (if indeed such a project were feasible or academically useful), it does seek to present new understandings of the ways in which, and the reasons why, communities mobilize in the South. In so doing, it raises questions about the applicability of social movement theory based mainly on experiences in the North. While social movements in both the North and South have in common a desire to mobilize towards a collective goal, whether it be the attainment of rights denied or the reversal of adverse state policy, their genesis, form and orientation are likely in many, but not all, instances to be significantly different. As Stammers (2005, 2009) has pointed out, historically the attainment of rights in the North was the outcome of sustained social movement activity. In contrast, many social movements in the South have arisen as a consequence of the opportunities presented by rights entrenched in relatively recently instated constitutional democracies. In such contexts, social mobilization is, in many respects, aimed at achieving substantive citizenship which yields material gains.

This is not, however, to suggest that the extant body of social movement theory is irrelevant to experiences in the South, and the resonance of the dominant theoretical positions is to be found in virtually all of the case studies which follow in this volume. What is significantly different, however, is the departure point for an analysis of the factors that give rise to collective action and social movements in the South. On this point most Southern theorists concur, namely that the inequalities that prevail in the world political and economic order (and which have given rise to the descriptors North and South) have played and continued to play a major role in shaping relations of power and patterns of inequality within Southern states. The economic dependencies that have arisen as a consequence of the current world order, and the internal distortions that have arisen from this, however, have not been factored into analyses in the North simply because they have not been of any significance in understanding why and how social mobilization takes place in post-industrial societies.

Particularly since the end of the cold war and the emergence of the neoliberal consensus, which Castells (2003: 327), quoting Ramonet, calls *'la pensée unique'* (the only thinking), the linkages between exclusion at the level of the state and exclusion in global terms have become decidedly more pronounced. Marginalization in the South, and of the South, is a dominant characteristic of current global political and socio-economic processes. As Castells (ibid.: 325) states:

> [t]he global economy is characterised by a fundamental asymmetry between countries, in terms of their levels of integration, their competitive potential, and share of benefits from economic growth ... [t]he consequence of this is the increased segmentation of the world population ... leading to increased inequality and social exclusion ... [t]his pattern of segmentation is characterised by a double movement: on the one hand, valuable segments of territories and people are linked to global networks ... [o]n the other hand, everything, and everyone, which does not have value, according to what is valued in the networks, or ceases to have value, is switched off the networks, and ultimately discarded altogether.

The effects of global capital on development and democracy have been emphasized in the older research and literature on mobilization and social movements in the South. Scholars such as Wignaraja (1993), Amin (1976, 1993), Kothari (1993, 2005) and Mamdani et al. (1993) drew on an eclectic mix of Marxist theory to underline the importance of social movements for state transformation. According to these perspectives, the structural effects of global neoliberalism, with the emphasis on markets and the transmission of modern technology, are key to an understanding of the reasons why more unified social resistance has not taken place in states labelled Third or even Fourth World. Nevertheless, and perhaps paradoxically, in the past decade the role of popular mobilization and social movements has increasingly been seen as central in pressuring states and global organizations to reconfigure the socio-economic order both within national boundaries and beyond.

Kabeer (2005: 23) discusses the importance of understanding collective action in terms of two axes of participation, horizontal and vertical. Horizontal forms of participation are the linkages forged between mobilized citizens and communities at local, national and global levels. Such horizontal spaces of participation, which might also be called 'self-created' or 'invented' spaces, are where citizens themselves define their modes of engagement with the state and with other interest groups and resort to different forms of collective action. These linkages are not necessarily

3

stable, nor do they represent a fixed notion of citizen identity on the part of those who participate. The ways in which mobilization, collective action and social movements manifest themselves in these spaces are key to understanding the processes of collective identity formation as citizens attempt to exercise both their individual and collective rights. Vertical spaces are those created by the state and which 'invite' citizens to participate. Elaborating this point in a recent volume in this series, and flagging their limitations, Cornwall and Coelho maintain that 'the institutions of the participatory sphere are framed by those who create them, and infused with power relations and cultures of interaction carried into them from other spaces' (Cornwall and Coelho 2007: 11).

Globally, horizontal forms of networking and identity formation characterize what is discussed in the literature as 'new social movements' (hereafter NSMs). These new movements, unlike 'old' or classical social movements (SMs), tend to lack clear organizational structures and internal bureaucracies, and, effectively, function by coalescing political identities and agendas both nationally and globally. Hajer (1995) calls these 'discourse coalitions' and, in many ways, they represent the new wave of social movement organization globally (see also Leach et al. 2005). It is worth remembering, however, that NSMs represent a specific progression in civil society organization in the post-industrial North, where issues not always directly related to economic practice, but triggered by the impacts of neoliberal economic development, have given rise to social movement action (the environmental movement is a key example). The environmental movement characterizes this diversification of civil society action and organization into new forms of movement creation, organization and networking.[4] Many of these NSMs, of which the women's movement is another exemplar, have helped to bolster similar movements in Southern contexts, notwithstanding lower levels of economic development.

The degree to which mobilization and the formation of social movements at the grassroots level are necessary for the realization of fundamental rights is a question that extends back to the origins of social movement theory. As Stammers (2005) points out, struggles for rights (natural, political or socio-economic) have both shaped and been shaped by the evolution of the modern liberal democratic system. The focus of this book is precisely on the ways in which different mobilization strategies in the South, and the forms of social movements to which they give rise (or not, as the case may be), support mainstream understandings of what the predominant modes of interaction are between society and the state.

As other research from the CDRC has emphasized, notions of citizenship and of rights broadly understood are not in themselves fixed and immutable.[5] The types of identity formation and forms of collective action evident in communities in the South occur in contexts where the meanings of citizenship and rights are far more nebulous and contested, as well as globally referenced, than in the history of the North. New understandings of citizenship are perhaps most clearly understood in terms of emergent forms of collective action in the South, although of course the interplay between collective and individual identities remains crucial to democratic practices, a point that is well emphasized in the chapters by Osaghae and Cortez in this volume. The chapters explore the distinction between forms of unorganized and ad hoc mobilization and more organized forms of collective action, with more clearly developed leadership, goals and agendas, and social movements. As Alonso et al. (this volume) point out, the critical difference between ad hoc mobilization and social movements is that the latter, through a variety of means, have the capacity to develop the political and social cohesion necessary to ensure enduring (usually at least somewhat effective) concerted action on common rights.

Notwithstanding the profound disparities extant in the world political order, there is a need to broaden the case base if the universality of social movement theory in the North is to be tested in any meaningful way. The case studies presented in this volume are from countries (Bangladesh, India, Brazil, Mexico, Nigeria and South Africa) where, at least formalistically, multiparty democracy exists. As such, they present evidence of the very real challenges which exist in developing substantive forms of participatory democracy even where the requisite democratic institutions are in place. They underscore the significance of social movements in these ongoing struggles for substantive citizenship. We readily acknowledge that the case study material does not fully capture a wide diversity of other contexts, such as how movements emerge in settings with weak states, one-party states and military juntas.

As will be seen in the discussion that follows, all of the chapters in this volume stress the importance of the struggle for socio-economic rights in the emergence of social movements in the South. They also reflect on the ways in which developmental and global political economy discourses and agendas influence mobilization and social movements, both directly and indirectly. The first two sections of the book deal specifically with these two themes. The final section examines the extent to which formal channels of participation promote more inclusive citizenship and facilitate the realization of political as well as socio-economic rights.

5

The structure of the book, key themes and issues

Social movements in the South, both nationally based and those which have global linkages, tend to be much weaker than in the North, owing either to political control on the part of the state, or because understandings of citizenship do not always coalesce into clear patterns of mobilization and resistance of either the organized or unorganized variety (Amin 1993; Bond 2002; Kothari 2005). In some cases, owing to a combination of socio-economic circumstances and the lack of a strong collective political identity, groups that are systematically discriminated against do not mobilize in clearly discernible ways at all. There are, nevertheless, notable success stories in the extent to which social movements in the South have managed to assert their rights and to extract concessions from the state, and a few of these are captured in the chapters that follow.

Two key strands of mobilization emerge in the case studies presented: the dominant type can be understood as self-organized collective action around issue-based socio-economic rights. These arise, in many instances, in response to state-initiated development programmes that sacrifice individual or collective socio-economic rights in the name of national interest, and which, by forcefully suppressing protest action, also effectively trample on political rights. The other form of mobilization is by social movement groups or their representatives in spaces created by government, either for socio-economic or political rights, or to ensure and extend these rights through 'participatory democratic processes'. Both forms of mobilization, nevertheless, are directed towards the attainment of socio-economic rights in the South. This is referred to as the political economy of rights by Newell and Wheeler (2006: 9):

> in which questions of access to and distribution and production of resources are paramount. A focus on resources changes the way we think about the relationship between rights and accountability. The challenge is not to overemphasise the material dimensions of this relationship and to acknowledge instead that economic rights are in many ways indivisible from social, political and cultural rights.

The book is divided into three broad sections. Section One highlights the significance of historical context in the analysis of social movements, since the genesis of contemporary collective action can often be traced back to perceived or real discrimination or oppression stretching back into a distant past. The rationale, the framing, as it were, of such movements is that those involved have suffered from collective social and political injustice and, consequentially, that their struggle is, in the first instance, for communitarian rather than individual rights (Osaghae and Cortez, this volume). Such movements, not infrequently, are ethnically or class-based and derive their cohesion both from a sense of collective oppression and/or pre-existing sociocultural identities. The case studies in this section also include instances where mobilization has failed to take place despite severely adverse conditions (Mahmud on garment workers in Bangladesh), or where the process of mobilization, despite material gains, has failed to lead to any sense of citizen empowerment (Simpson and Waldman on transnational litigation on behalf of asbestos workers).

Osaghae, in his chapter on social activism in the Niger Delta, emphasizes that social movements in the region have built their national and international profile and support base on campaigns for collective rights based on the failure of the state to provide rights to ethnic minorities. Osaghae reminds us of the ethnic and collective dimension to many rights claims, both political and socio-economic, in the larger African context, and discusses the failure of the state to guarantee either. In the context of the Niger Delta, the question remains whether political or socio-economic rights assume precedence, since each appears to be a necessary and inseparable adjunct of the other. Osaghae also points out that while the appeal to communitarian rights serves as an important vehicle for popular mobilization, it is no guarantor of individual rights, and suggests that this might become the source of future struggles.

In their chapter, Simpson and Waldman examine the role of global partnerships and transnational litigation in the mobilization of social movements. As a case study they look at the struggles of two South African communities to extract compensation from a British mining company for health damages suffered as consequence of pollution caused by asbestos mining. Their research highlights the role that the solidarity of exogenous agents (in the form of international NGOs) can play in advancing the goals of a transnational social movement, but not necessarily in satisfying local perceptions of socio-economic entitlements by those affected by asbestos pollution. Their findings also show that different social identities in the two communities studied led to both different understandings of the nature of the struggle for compensation and different forms of engagement with, and acceptance of, their international partners. Simpson and Waldman argue that there is a need in social movement theory for a closer examination of how movements are influenced by identity struggles and in turn influence the processes through which people construct meaning and interpret cultural attitudes. In particular, they assert, there is a need for greater understanding of how the new social identities of movements may interact with, or be shaped by, other deep-rooted identities.

Mahmud's chapter demonstrates that there is nothing inevitable about the emergence of national or global social movements, even where the proximate conditions for these forms of mobilization exist. Her research on garment workers in Bangladesh seeks to explore why, despite extremely adverse labour conditions, there is so little organized opposition to the practices of the industry at the national level and virtually none at the international level. Her research reveals that a range of local factors (cultural, economic and political) act to inhibit the emergence of national or transnational social movements. In the first instance, the bulk of those employed in the factories are young women from the rural areas who have limited education and who have grown up under a patrimonial regimen that encourages subservience towards male authority. This factor, combined with poverty, a lack of awareness of labour rights, a vast pool of surplus labour, outdated labour legislation, the brutal suppression of organized labour activities by employers, and an indifferent state bureaucracy serve to further suppress prospects for social mobilization. As a result, the risks, and consequences, of losing their jobs are, for workers, high, and outweigh the perceived gains of social mobilization. Her chapter suggests that in the absence of collective action, there is a need to think in terms of 'cultural opportunity structures' or, perhaps even more broadly, 'social opportunity structures', which might serve to explain how economic, cultural and political factors impact on the prospects for mobilization and movement activism.

In the second section, the social movements under discussion focus more on actualizing the rights that have been constitutionally assigned to them. To that extent, the case studies focus on the political opportunity structures (POS) which have opened up for issue-based social movements that aim to transform civic rights into socio-economic rights. Thus environmental movements in Brazil, India and South Africa have managed to gain some national legitimacy and global (if sporadic) political influence, as the chapters by Alonso et al. and Mehta et al. discuss. Yet Mehta et al. argue that even where socio-economic rights are entrenched in both legislation and policy, in many instances this is insufficient ground to assume that these rights exist in practice. The findings of all three of the cases in this section (in Brazil, India and South Africa) demonstrate that rights need to be claimed, both through more conventional forms of participation, but often through protest action when more formal chan-

8

nels uphold the status quo. In the South African case study, for example, the national right to Free Basic Water policy is at loggerheads with other neoliberal state policies which emphasize cost recovery. The necessity of citizens emphatically claiming their rights through mobilization and activism in the South is clearly brought home by this case, as well as in the case of dam-building in India, where government macroeconomic policy, predicated on the development of major infrastructural projects, is in direct conflict with the rights of communities to their traditional livelihoods. It is clear from both cases studies that governments justify broader economic policies without necessarily deliberating on the contradictions these may bring to community or individual rights. In this sense the need for activism, and protest, is, for many poor communities in the South, not a luxury but a necessity.

Alonso et al. demonstrate that the evolution of the Brazilian environmental movement has differed in substantive ways from the evolution of social movements in more democratic contexts. This case also illustrates the importance of environmental movements in the South, and challenges the predominant focus on socio-economic rights in the literature. They emphasize that new approaches to social mobilization move beyond discussions of political opportunity structures to embrace '... symbolic and cognitive features and collective identity building processes ...' (see also Diani 1992). Central to this latter understanding is what they term 'micro-mobilization contexts' – that is, more locally based broadly organized social activism which shapes the identities of activists in relation to their struggle for political influence. The chapter traces the internal dynamics of the environmental movement to show the ways in which POS enabled the movement to flourish. In the Brazilian case, a distinct feature of this process was that, in the context of a broader process of national democratization, state institutions became more 'permeable' to lobbying by civil society groups. Significantly, environmental social movements emerged at the same time as a global environmental agenda was being set, creating a unique global precedent for environmentally sustainable practices.

Cortez's chapter on the Zapatista movement examines how deep-seated grievances over a loss of access to land in the Chiapas state in southern Mexico (aggravated by a free trade agreement with the United States) led to a sequence of protest action, military repression, armed resistance and subsequent evolution into a social movement organization. The analysis illustrates clearly the limits to protest action in the context of repressive state action – a characteristic not exclusive to states in the South, but one which is clearly made more problematic by weak democratic institutions. Cortez points out that the strength of the Zapatista movement has centred on its ability to mobilize not only local indigenous peoples, but also other social and civic association actors, both within and outside the state. As such it has grown from a movement campaigning for basic needs and resources, to an anti-state, anti-systemic, anti-capitalist movement demanding both social justice and socio-economic rights.

Section Three emphasizes the challenges faced by social movements that seek to advance their cause through government-created participatory spaces, and the often tenuous linkages between these modes of interaction and the development of more inclusive democratic processes.[6] Coelho and Favareto show the limited impact of small environmental groupings at the local level in Brazil, where participation of these groups in invited spaces is often more about building political alliances and coalitions than power sharing, and where the interests of the poor are seldom taken up in meaningful ways. Tapscott, Piper and Nadvi examine the extent to which grassroots mobilization and social movements in South Africa are able to take advantage of available political opportunity structures (Tilly 1978; Tarrow 1989), including participatory spaces created by governments to achieve both political and socio-economic rights claims.

Mohanty's chapter examines the struggles of the rural poor in India against the imposition of macroeconomic growth strategies which have led to their further impoverishment and disempowerment as citizens. In this context, she asserts, the struggles against the state's economic development policies are effectively struggles for citizen rights and for a more inclusive and deliberative form of democracy. For the state and ruling elites, 'development', broadly defined, became associated with modernity and the attendant rationality of technocratic growth. In this discourse, development has come to be seen as a component of globalization and as a necessity in the inexorable march towards a modern state. The pursuit of this form of economic development, however, has frequently led to the dispossession and displacement of the poor, leading to lost access to land, water and other resources. The social movements that have arisen to challenge this process have framed their loss in terms of three sets of meaning, namely the loss of material meaning (in terms of the expected benefits of development), the loss of social meaning (consequent to their loss of social networks following displacement) and the loss of political meaning (stemming from their exclusion from decision-making on issues affecting their livelihoods). In this context, the movements inextricably link their right to resources with their rights as citizens, and view their struggle for more equitable development policies as a struggle for a more inclusive democracy.

While the chapter documents the struggles of the rural poor against the forces of globalization and the relentless quest for foreign direct investment, it is noteworthy that these social movements are largely endogenous in nature and they have not attempted to form linkages across national boundaries. In similar vein, although their protest is directed against state policy, the movements largely eschew party political affiliation in advancing their cause. In part this is due to a disillusionment with self-interested, and often rent-seeking, political elites, but it is also due to the fact that party affiliations limit their capacity to mobilize across the varied strata of society. In that respect, the way in which these social movements define and conduct their struggle provides a basis for the formation of new and more egalitarian social identities which overcome pre-existing, and atavistic, forms of social hierarchy based on caste, class and gender.

Tapscott's chapter explores the extent to which better-educated, resource-endowed and politically adept activist groups are able to use POS in ways that less privileged groups cannot. These include an ability to shape public opinion through the media, through economic pressure, through rate-payers' associations and through a range of informal social networks which influential elites typically establish. In contrast, poor communities seeking access to state resources through formal participatory channels fare considerably worse and bring little pressure to bear on the state. It is in response to this inability to effect meaningful change through formal political channels, furthermore, that the resort to protest (and often violent protest) on the part of disempowered communities can perhaps best be understood.

Piper and Nadvi examine the ways in which ward committees were established as formal invited spaces to promote participatory democracy at the grassroots level. Their chapter speaks of a sorry tale of political co-optation and subjugation where the ward committees have become an extension of the party political battlefield. In this context, instead of addressing local concerns about service delivery, community safety and the like, ward committees have become sites of destructive intra-party and interpersonal power struggles as both social movement representatives and political and government representatives vie for greater political influence or higher political office. Confronted with the failure of these invited spaces and a consequent general disillusionment with politics at the local level, a range of social movements have arisen to provide an alternative voice for expression of popular concerns. The chapter examines how these movements have adopted a non-political standpoint as a means of forging a more inclusive agenda.

The cases described above point to the need to further explore the distinctiveness of social mobilization and social movements in the South and to consider the extent to which mainstream theory encapsulates their essence. Before doing so, we turn to a brief, and necessarily truncated, discussion of some of the central debates on social movement analysis in the literature.

Mobilization and social movements in the North and South: analytical debates and comparative understandings

In the extensive research on social movements, three central questions are dealt with – namely, what motivates groups or communities to take collective action; how do social movements coalesce around different forms of collective action; and who mobilizes within social movements? We consider each of these in turn, paying attention to the different approaches in the literature to each question while at the same time attempting to link a broad analysis of mobilization in the South to some of the key texts on mobilization and social movements in the North. In so doing we examine, in brief, some of the dominant approaches in the study of social movements, namely, resource mobilization theories, political opportunity theories and theories of political identity formation and collective action, otherwise known as frame theory.

What triggers collective action? Within the large body of thought emerging from North America and western Europe, two major strands of discussion originally predominated in analysis of the triggers of collective action, these being the grievances approach and resource mobilization theory. In the North American context, initial understandings of collective action and social movements revolved around exploring either grievance or available resources or a combination of the two as the precipitators of social mobilization. Since the early work of Park (1969 [1921]) and Smelser (1962) on grievances that serve as triggers for collective action (then portrayed mainly as irrational behaviour and mob action, especially in the context of the civil rights movement), the ongoing analytical debate has developed into a sophisticated account of the linkages between relative deprivation and the ways in which communities develop and use a variety of resources in order to effect change to their material, social and political circumstances. Instrumental in the development of the latter body of work is the analysis of McCarthy and Zald (1977), McAdam et al. (1996, 2001), Tilly (1978, 2003) and Freeman (1999), each of whom has progressively added to understandings of the importance of resources, including more intrinsic, or intangible, resources (such as social cohesion), in the process of mobilization (Jenkins 1983: 533). These scholars have also discussed the ways in which effective mobilization requires what later came to be known in the literature as political processes and their relation to 'political opportunity structures', defined as '... consistent, but not necessarily formal, permanent or national, dimensions of the political environment that provide incentives for people to undertake collective action by affecting their expectations for success or failure' (Tarrow 1994: 85, in Ballard et al. 2006: 4). A great deal of the discussion and debate that have followed has focused on the relationship between grievances, the mobilization of resources, what are referred to as 'selective incentives' (for participation) and the structural (and in some case historical) incentives for social activism and social movement behaviour.

Emerging out of a concern that the resource mobilization and political opportunity approaches had overlooked the importance of collective identities and ideology in the shaping of social movements, a group of scholars (most notably Snow and Benford 1988, 1992) emphasized the need to study the discursive and interpretive practices that 'frame' the way in which movement participants understand their circumstances and weigh alternative courses of action (Edelman 2001). According to Benford and Snow, what they term collective action frames come about 'as movement adherents negotiate a shared understanding of some problematic condition or situation they define as in need of change, make attributions regarding who or what is to blame, articulate an alternative set of arrangements, and urge others to act in concert to affect change.' (Benford and Snow 2000: 614).

While many theorists (McAdam et al. 1996, 2001; Ibarra 2003; and Tilly 2003 to name just a few) use resource mobilization theory in combination with explorations of grievance, framing and political opportunity structures, these have not always been systematically adapted to southern contexts. As Amin (1993: 88) emphasizes, historical context is essential to understanding the interplay between internal and global dynamics as 'the effectiveness of the social movement cannot be assessed by the same criteria in different periods ... periods of structural crisis are defined by uncertainty as to the rules of the game ...'. Since the South has been subject to such crises regularly, by virtue of '... unequal development engendered, reproduced and endlessly deepened by capitalist expansion', the ability of movements to coalesce into substantial political forces that can challenge the status quo has been limited. The availability of re-sources for organized action is one limiting factor, although the chapters in this volume show that even the resource-deprived mobilize, and, in fact, do so precisely because they are resource-deprived, and are claiming resources as socio-economic rights.

It is clear, nevertheless, that these (what may be termed) 'middle-range'[7] theories of social movement action do help us to understand the rise and evolution of social movements in the South. Alonso et al. in this volume demonstrate the importance of political opportunity structures and framing processes, as well as political identity and networking, to the 'dynamic and interactional character' of collective action processes and cycles of protest in the formation of a national environmental movement in Brazil. The ability of activists to develop common collective frames for environmental concerns was key to their successful engagement in three specific political opportunity structures. The significance of framing is also to be found in the Zapatista movement, where struggles for agrarian reform in the Mexican countryside were depicted as part of a global anti-capitalist struggle. Evidence of framing is also to be seen in local-level struggles in the Niger Delta, where armed struggle is rationalized as a necessary response to an anti-ethnic onslaught by the state.

There are, nevertheless, limits to the application of these theories in Southern contexts. This is because frame theorists, together with those focusing on collective political identity formation and networking, gener-ally presume levels of political identity and strategic sophistication that are often absent among movements comprised of people existing on the margins of survival. For such communities it is often merely a question of political opportunity, driven by desperation that leads to collective action rather than a conscious framing of options. Thus, for example, the immediacy of the threat posed by forced eviction is such that there is little need to persuade slum dwellers of the need for collective action. Their course of action, furthermore, is more frequently conditioned by the latitude granted to them by the state than carefully selected from an array of alternatives. At the same time, while some collective action in the South does succeed in coalescing into broader social movement organ-izations, a large proportion of these mobilizations are more localized, sporadic and discontinuous, implying that their ideological mobilization was (and sometimes stays) shallow or non-existent. This phenomenon is, of course, not unique to mobilization in the South, suggesting that these theories have analytical limitations when applied to less formalized social action in the North.

What makes a movement? Later research by Ibarra (2003) and Tilly (2003) and others argues that a combination of political opportunities and economic incentives gives rise to social movements. The work of theorists like McCarthy and Zald (1977, in McAdam et al. 1996) and Opp (1988), however, focuses on the agency of a more educated, politically conscious, normative North American or European activist, in contexts where grievances and ideology play a significant role, as opposed to the earlier understanding of social movement activism as arising from relative economic deprivation and/or the denial of political rights. The tendency to conflate social movement organizations with broader social movements has also implied that the bureaucratization of collective action emphasized by the earlier work of McCarthy and Zald (1977) has been perhaps overemphasized (Jenkins 1983).

Distinguishing between collective action and social movements, furthermore, continues to present itself as an analytical problem (Leach et al. 2005).The question that may be posed in the context of more unorganized forms of collective action is 'how many people does it take to make a movement'? Relatedly, the organizational dimensions and elite structures of both 'official' social movement organizations and broader decentred movements have been the subject of further debate. The dominance of middle-class, educated elites, or what some analysts (such as Jenkins and Wallace 1996; Norris and Cable 1994) refer to as the 'new class', is seen in some contexts as a positive development, and as opening up opportunities between the 'old working class' and the 'middle class'. Yet in both the North and the South, the danger of presuming the representativeness and legitimacy of organizations calling themselves 'social movements' lies in the overlapping structures of patronage and power that so frequently characterize the relationships between these groups and the 'the marginalized'.

Again, in the national context, while raising critical questions about how formative social movements articulate their demands to structures of political authority, and the role of political legitimacy, questions about the longevity of social movements have been framed largely within the analysis of the historical evolution of social movements in the North (Gamson 1992; Jenkins 1983). The ways in which social movements have continued to evolve collective agendas and forge enduring relationships within the polity has to be seen in the much longer historical context of societal challenges to the state and the evolution of democratic practices, and these formative contexts certainly differ considerably in the North and South as a result of the impact of accelerated globalization (Held and McGrew 2003; Castells 2003; Karns and Mingst 2004; Amin 1993; Kothari 1993, 2005). Thus, while more fluid forms of social mobilization organized across local and global contexts, such as those described by Offe (1985), Melucci (1995) and Touraine (1985), have opened up new possibilities for the formation and growth of social movements, the national context still remains critical in understanding the relations of power between state and non-state actors, as is emphasized by Osaghae and Mohanty in this volume.

Mushakoji (1993: xiii–xiv) refers to three dominant understandings of mobilization and social movements in the South that are useful to this discussion. The first is that social movements in the South were originally preoccupied with the struggle against colonization and were in effect struggling within their own ranks for access to state structures. Ongoing social movement activity is thus not necessarily part of the solution to the crisis of the state in these countries, but is in actual fact a manifestation of the crisis itself. The second view looks at social movements as new actors; these actors are not aiming at assuming power, '... but rather in creating free space from where a democratic society can emerge'. The third view sees social movements as '... preparing a future desirable society' that in its grassroots authenticity will move the current state of democratic 'window dressing' to one of true democratic development. Theorists such as Amin (1993: 97–8) and Kothari (2005: 122), respectively, have also discussed the need for and roles of 'revolutionary intelligentsia' or mediator activists who will enable the masses to organize themselves sufficiently to challenge the state.

While the chapters in this volume examine the role of social move-ments in claiming rights and ensuring 'real' or 'people's' democracy, the role of 'liberation movements' that have transmuted into political parties and the effects of this process on social organization should not be under-estimated. Osaghae's chapter examines the interplay between the state as the 'authentic representative of the people' and the kinds of resource inequalities that arise from the disjunctures between ethnic domination and class and political power. Tapscott's chapter, similarly, considers how a former liberation movement has dominated formal participatory structures and arrogated the right to decide on citizens' needs, while Piper and Nadvi demonstrate how political parties not only dominate local democratic structures, but also crowd out any attempts at popular participation. Cortez's detailed analysis of the Zapatista movement in Mexico also focuses on the ways in which social movements can give rise to parallel governance structures that directly confront the state's resource allocation biases.

The impact of mobilization strategies and social movements on democratization processes also raises the troublesome question of locating the 'sole and authentic' representatives of the people. The role of professionalized NGOs, which simply reproduce resource inequalities while at the same time speaking the language of development and democracy, is a critical issue, as is the question of who legitimately speaks for the masses. Amin and Kothari, among others, refer to the need for leaders or mediators to enable the masses to organize themselves. At the same time, Tapscott in this volume illustrates how knowledge of the media and the courts privileges middle-class movements in the South, while Alonso et al. emphasize the trade-offs with government that sometimes have to be made in order for issue-based movements such as the environmental movement in Brazil to become a 'visible' political force.

As Kothari (2005) and others have pointed out, political parties are fond of reminding society of their sole and authentic status, especially where this is as a result of previous liberation struggle credentials, or as a result of previous CSO- (civil society organization) or NGO-based activism. Mushakoji (1993) points out that where popular movements have gained access to political power, the ongoing struggles between themselves and other mass-based forms of political organization have often given rise to the very instability and lack of popular democracy they are ostensibly working to overcome. Osaghae's and Cortez's chapters in this volume underline this point in relation to oppressive policies advanced by ruling elites in the name of democracy and stability.

Who protests? The North American literature on the protest potential of the marginalized refers back to the Gamson (1990 [1975]) versus Piven and Cloward (1979) debate. Gamson's study, which examined which forms of social movement activity lead to 'success', defined as the provision of tangible benefits for movement members and political legitimacy, concluded that levels of organization are key to success. Piven and Cloward, on the other hand, argued that movements characterized by large numbers of the poor tend to be largely unorganized, as the poor do not have the resources to mobilize large-scale resistance, and that such organization is in any case not desirable since it leads to eventual demobilization owing to the high costs involved. Later texts (Norris and

Cable 1994; Jenkins and Wallace 1996) place a heavy stress on the protest potential of certain groups over others (for example, African-Americans; 'autonomous' women; secularist groups; and educated professionals) as well as the position of certain groups in broader socio-economic and political contexts, portrayed as the new 'class discussion'. Yet it is not clear how these discussions translate into recognizable patterns of activism (organized or unorganized) in contexts of both absolute as well as relative deprivation, even though the North American study of social movements tends to posit a reasonably high-level correlation between deprivation and protest potential. While the older literature on social movements places a strong emphasis on structural (socio-economic) factors, the literature on new social movements, as indicated, strongly emphasizes the importance of networks, the framing of collective grievances and movement coalitions.

The question of state and non-state political power structures and the relationship between rights and 'realized' rights in determining 'protest potential' is clearly at issue. Alonso et al. (this volume) trace the evolution of the environmental movement in Brazil to the opening of the political opportunity structures and the ability to frame collective issues, but it is clear that in this instance the role of educated groups was pivotal. In contrast, it is evident that the movement to claim compensation for asbestos-related illnesses in South Africa relied heavily on transnational linkages, knowledge and litigation processes to realize its claims, albeit, as intimated, in ways that were felt to be ultimately disempowering to some indigenous communities (see Simpson and Waldman, this volume). The Zapatista movement in Mexico and the Treatment Action Campaign (pressing for the rights of HIV/AIDS sufferers) in South Africa show, perhaps most clearly, the collective power of global networks and the ways in which issues of education and class may, in some cases, be superseded by other aspects of collective organization and action.

While a determination of the extent to which the link between formal organization and mass defiance constitutes a social movement remains conceptually vague, subsequent theoretical developments in the literature on social movements in the North have included a much more nuanced take on how collective action arises. In that respect, Klandermans and Oegema (1987: 520) state that '[h]owever successfully a movement mobilises consensus ... if it does not have access to recruitment networks, its mobilisation potential cannot be realised'. Such networks include civic organizations, but also, very importantly, religious, friendship and family networks. Again, what motivates collective action, effected either through professional SMOs or through more unorganized forms of mass action, remains debated. The importance of 'micro-mobilization contexts', including the differential role of formal and informal networks in participation, as well as the actual context of interpersonal relationships within specific networks, nevertheless, is recognized to be of significance in when and how people mobilize (McAdam et al. 1996; Guigni 1998).

Micro-mobilization contexts, together with the 'framing' of collective action, are often necessary preconditions for the successful negotiation of political opportunity structures, as Alonso et al. argue in this volume. Yet the chapters by Mohanty on social movements of the poor in India and Tapscott's discussion of the limits to mobilization in accessing state housing in South Africa show the importance of understanding the overlap between global and national political, historical and 'micro-mobilization' contexts. They also illustrate the necessity of analysing the role of the state and its structural element even in these contexts, as Tilly (1978, 2003) and others have continued to emphasize. It is the combination of these endogenous and exogenous factors in specific historical contexts and moments which helps to explain successful social movement formation and mobilization in the South.

As Mohanty's, Coelho and Favareto's, and Mahmud's chapters also underline, those who are not part of organized labour, or who do not have access to strong mediator support through NGOs or the like, are often unable to manage collective action in ways that challenge the status quo. As a consequence, we need to think through the linkages between more issue-based social movements and development and democratization processes to better understand why '[h]istory does not give a single example in which the urban movement, or the religious movement on its own, or the workers' movement without alliances succeeded in changing fundamentally the existing system of domination' (Comacho 1993: 54). While Comacho wrote in the context of Latin America, his point is applicable to the South in general, and, as will be seen in the discussion that follows, also to social mobilization in the North.

In summation, in considering the type of people who protest, the factors that trigger collective action and those who create movements, we can distil three key interrelated themes from the broad strands of Northern and Southern thought on mobilization and social movements. First, there are perspectives that emphasize the role of grievances, resource mobilization and political opportunity structures to both informal and more formal types of social movement action. Second, there are perspectives that emphasize the importance of the collective framing of issues and the forging of collective identities, networks, alliances and coalitions, both within states and in the global context, even where these may shift and change over time and historical and geographical context. These may be broad-based or issue-based, but they have at core a commitment to working towards socio-economic justice. Finally, to effectively understand the question of what triggers collective action in the South, we need to remember Amin's (1993) caution that social movements need to be contextualized historically in relation to broader global configurations of political power and capital accumulation.

The next section examines the linkages between the literature on social movements in the North and some of the debates surrounding the critical issue of who mobilizes in the South. The final section of the chapter turns to a discussion of the linkages between local and national social movements and the global political economy, and the ways in which social movements in the South are integrated into global social movements (GSMs).

The transformative potential of social movements in the South

Analysts in both the North and the South have argued that the material conditions of the very marginalized can act both as an incentive and a disincentive to mobilization. Notions of the transformative power of social activism and social movements are balanced by the acknowledgement of the limited resources and political power of the very marginalized (Castells 1997, 2003; Amin 1993; Kothari 1993, 2005). Social movements, nevertheless, do hold the potential to challenge the hegemony of states exercised through formal democratic institutions and practices. In that respect, while much of the focus in mainstream literature has been on the genesis and character of social movements, relatively little attention has been paid to their collective impact in shaping state–citizen relationships. While Marxists scholars have portrayed these multiple protests as the manifestation of ongoing class struggle, they do not necessarily represent a direct challenge to the legitimacy of the state. As Kothari (2005) has pointed out in the context of India, despite the poor treatment they have received from the state, most still turn to the state for services and resources. Thus, it is not always the political order which they wish to change, as much as their position in that order. In this context, social movements in the South should not be seen simply as anti-statist organizations in the making (although some undoubtedly are), but as new forms of citizen engagement with the state which have replaced other less successful political channels.

The legitimacy of protest, especially of the mass-action variety, or 'unconventional political action', as Dalton (2002) refers to it, has historically been viewed with some scepticism by influential theorists in the North such as Samuel Huntington (1991). In fact, given the tendency towards mass action and the resultant political and socio-economic turmoil, some analysts (again, the work of Huntington is an exemplar) have argued that growth and development may not be reconcilable with democracy in the South. For many years Huntington and others debated the relationship between the demands of social movements for greater availability and dispersion of public goods and the ability of the state, even in the North, to function effectively (Huntington 1984, 1991; Dalton 2002). The limits-to-public-goods argument cannot be dismissed out of hand, but it clearly has unsavoury implications and possibly repressive policy applications when applied to states in the South. Perhaps more importantly, far from being a deviation from the norm of democratic practice, social mobilization and protest have increasingly become an integral part of the political landscape in some states in the South and coexist with, and in some instances supplant, formal institutional channels for engagement with the state. In such contexts (evident in the case studies of India and South Africa in this volume), social movements have become the conventional vehicle for the attainment of democratic rights for ever-increasing numbers of citizens, and particularly for the poor. In this context, it must be noted, resource mobilization and political opportunity structures assume significance in the extent to which such movements are able to effect changes in the economic and political order.

The idea of mobilization that is aimed at transforming state–society relations framed by theorists such as Amin (1976, 1993), Mamdani (1996) and others rejects the type of 'bourgeois democracy' that serves elites inside and outside of the state, and which does not redress resource inequalities that are much more starkly unequal in the South than in the North. The language of political opportunity structure in this sense is potentially problematic as it implies distinct institutional options that movements may pursue, which may not always be present in states controlled by powerful political and economic elites. Thus, while resources and political opportunity structures clearly cannot be ignored, the struggles of communities through collective action in the South are also more likely to relate to issues of basic socio-economic entitlements which are no longer in question in more developed states.

The next section examines the linkages between notions of global citizenship in the context of the marginalization of certain groups in the South and local, national and global social movements.

Globalization, marginalization and social movements

In recent years there has been a growing interest in the notion of global citizenship (see Edwards 1999; Edwards and Gaventa 2001; Mayo 2005, among others) as a vehicle for forging a transnational solidarity that is capable of transcending the often undemocratic political formations of the South and the seemingly inexorable forces of global capital. As McIntyre-Mills asserts: 'The concept of global citizenship shifts rights and responsibilities from a national to an institutional context' (McIntyre-Mills 2000: 19). For some scholars, global citizenship is not just an important area of research on citizenship, it is of central importance to any theorizing on the topic. Thus, according to Mayo, '[t]he emergence of global citizenship action has been widely recognised as having been key to the discourse and practices of democratic politics and social change' (Mayo 2005: 1).[8]

While the move towards global mobilization remains an important field of study, however, its proponents tend frequently to overstate its importance in the broader scheme of 'everyday' resistance which makes up the bulk of social protest and mobilization (Laclau and Mouffe 1985; Appadurai 2002; Leach et al. 2005, 2007). Various chapters in this volume reaffirm the significance of global social movements (Alonso et al., Mehta et al., Cortez), but others also underscore the fact that there is nothing inevitable about the emergence of this form of social mobilization (Mahmud). They point out that even where the conditions lend themselves to the growth of global action, this may not occur owing to the specificity of the prevailing political, economic and cultural conditions.

The connections between national and global forms of activism, and what has become known as the local–global content of social mobilization, has been the focus of a great deal of research on the transformative potential of global networks. Multilevel case-study analyses that show the positive linkages between the local and the global have gained popularity, despite reservations from critics about combining very different levels of analysis (see, for example, Dahl 2003 and Habermas 2003 for a critique of the notion of democratic global institutions and global citizens respectively). There is also related debate about the extent to which GSMs bring about *change* in the global arena, although it is mostly agreed that GSMs do exercise some *influence* over multilateral institutions (Stavenhagen 1997; O'Brien et al. 2000; Murphy 2002). O'Brien et al. (2000: 12) define

GSMs (as distinct from global civil society, or international society) as being

[b]y definition not members of the elite in their societies. They are anti-systemic. That is they are working to forward priorities at odds with the existing organisation of the system. They rely on mass mobilisation because they do not directly control the levers of power such as the state. A global social movement is one which operates in a global as well as local, national and international space.

The ability of Northern-interest and social movement organizations to represent very different contexts and political, social and economic identities (see, for example, Held and McGrew 2003; Held et al. 2003), nevertheless, remains a real concern. Steady (2002: 79–94), for example, argues that global solidarity with the 'white feminist' movement has been of limited usefulness to African women's movement needs, particularly in terms of economic marginalization. There are, furthermore, numerous examples of these contradictions of representation, which characterize both 'old' (e.g. trade unions) and 'new' (e.g. women's rights, environment and HIV/AIDS activist) social movements (see also Held et al. 2003).

Who speaks for whom? Global social movements in the global political economy

Inherent in left-oriented perspectives on social action is the conviction that social movements, represented by organizations with the correct political orientation, can bring about transformation as they truly represent the poor. In a similar fashion, by conflating social movements with social movement organizations (or interest groups), some INGOs claim social movement status despite the lack of clear linkages to a collective global support base.

Those who support the normative project of global social movements underline the fact that the strength of GSMs is their 'global vision' and '... the way in which they might contribute to increasing democracy by creating a global civil society' (O'Brien et al. 2000: 22). Yet analysts such as Dahl (2003), Habermas (2003), Held and McGrew (2003), Karns and Mingst (2004) and others range from cautious to sceptical about the degree to which global social movements are truly able to be democratically representative of any transnational group, including the poor, as issues relating to identity and action may be superseded by elite agendas and a lack of accountability, among other things. This reality is evidenced in the case study of the Griqua community discussed by Simpson and

23

Waldman in this volume, which makes the point that, despite the solidarity shown towards their cause, their cultural identity was such that they remained deeply distrustful of and resentful towards those attempting to assist them.

As the chapters in this volume emphasize, it is in challenging global marginalization that the positive strength of global linkages is most evident, and it is in this realm that movements in the South have the most to gain from global social movement solidarity, knowledge and resources. Stavenhagen (1997: 33) points out, for example, that '... in the span of a few years, the international human rights movement has become a major actor in the multilateral field. Governments can no longer afford to violate the rights of their citizens with impunity, arguing undue interference in their internal affairs.' The relative success of the human rights movement, however, can be juxtaposed against the relative lack of influence of movements opposed to the globalization of capital or globalization more broadly stated. Yet Rucht (2003: 211–22) reminds us that global mobilizations against neoliberal capitalism, as witnessed in Seattle (and later Prague, Genoa and New York), have forged collective social movement solidarities but have achieved relatively few substantive gains.

Also pertinent here are the arguments made by, among others, Touraine (2001), Arrighi et al. (1989) and Amin (1993), who argue that globalization is in fact the globalization of capital or what Castells (2003) refers to as 'global informational capitalism' – that is, capitalism based on information, technology and capital flows. This changing global milieu is said to severely restrict the ability of less-informed and less-educated communities in national contexts to overcome their marginalization. Thus, as O'Brien et al. (2000: 15) point out, '[w]hile social movements may extol the virtues of global civil society, that space has been and is largely dominated by the extensive formal and informal contacts of transnational business and their allies ... any arrangement that limited the prerogatives of global business would encounter great resistance'. This view is reinforced by compelling arguments, made by Kothari (2005) and others, about the effects of markets and technological innovation on increasing economic inequalities in the South.

It is also clear that the internationalization of social movements and the opportunities for local and national movements to link and find additional support for normative causes relating, for example, to gender, the environment, health and even socio-economic exploitation are *far greater* than they were in the evolution of social movements in the

24

North American and western European contexts (see Held et al. 2003 and Kothari 2005 for a discussion of this). Underscoring this point, Waldman and Simpson discuss the challenges of a relationship established between local resistance organizations and broader forms of social movement representation, effected through transnational litigation, showing both the potential as well as the limitations of the local–global nexus. Cortez's chapter on the Zapatista movement also echoes the possibility of successful alliances between national and global social movements. In contrast, Mehta et al. and Mohanty stress the challenges of linking to global social movements where local forms of resistance and organization are relatively constrained.

In short, we re-emphasize that it is hardly possible to discuss the potential for democratic gains and losses on the part of social movements in the South without discussing the global political economy, and global social movements and their links with national and local movements. At the same time the role of the state in the South should not be underestimated, nor should the degree to which citizens are constrained by the repressive potential of even so-called democratic regimes in the South.

Social movements in the North and South: towards more synthetic understandings

Much of the research in this volume seeks to speak to mobilization that originates at the local or grassroots level, but it is recognized that much more needs to be done to achieve an understanding of broader trends and tendencies. Relating forms of mobilization and protest action (and, in some instances, their absence) at the local level to broader social movements helps to understand the ways in which certain issues give rise to collective action and others not, as well as which types of activism have more impact and are more readily taken up by new or existing national and global social movements. This book explores the potential for developing more synthetic analyses as well as contextual understandings of why and how social movements arise in relation to historical, geographical and global contexts. It also considers the role played by social movements in defining collective identities and agendas, while at the same time remaining mindful of the fact that not all mobilization and collective action, nor indeed even all social movement action, necessarily implies the development of democracy and citizenship either locally, nationally or globally.

As we have discussed, the analytical understandings of the factors giving rise to and shaping social movements in the South share some

25

similarities with their Northern counterparts, as well as a few critical differences. Many of what we have termed 'middle-range' theories of social movements, which aim to synthesize grievance, resource mobilization, political opportunity structures and framing approaches, assist our understanding of how movements arise and sustain themselves. There are, nevertheless, a number of significant differences in the form and content of social movements in the North and in the South which must be taken into account when applying Northern theory in Southern contexts.

The first of these differences relates to the fact that the global economic order not only shapes power relations between states but also, in the context of the South, within states. Thus, access to resources on the part of the poor in Southern states is constantly mediated by a range of both national and global factors, which, in turn, impact on the extent to which they are able to mobilize, and the extent to which they are able to extract concessions from the state.

The second discernible difference relates to the fact that mobilization and social movements in the South have become a key (in some instances, the most prominent) form of popular engagement with the state. To that extent, and in contrast to conditions which prevail in most Northern states, social mobilization and the social movements that emerge from them have become an important vehicle for the attainment of citizenship rights and, significantly, they have, in many instances, supplanted, or rendered irrelevant, extant political channels, the invited spaces for state–citizen engagement.

In this context, a third discernible difference is evident, namely that the bulk of the social mobilization described in this volume is oriented towards the attainment of socio-economic rights rather than more generalized human rights. The struggle for socio-economic rights, furthermore, has in many respects become the key dimension in the struggle to realize citizenship rights in the South. In that respect, it is significant that the case studies discussed in this volume all involve states that already have in place the institutions necessary for the development of substantive forms of democracy. In most instances, furthermore, formal channels for citizen–state engagement have been established. It is clear, nevertheless, that the poor and disempowered are, for the most part, unable to realize their rights through these invited spaces and have consistently striven to create their own forms of engagement with the state.

The case studies discussed, furthermore, explicitly challenge the notion that development, conceived predominantly in terms of economic growth, will facilitate the deepening of democracy in highly dualistic societies. As the case studies of South Africa, Nigeria and India illustrate, major infrastructural and extractive projects, undertaken in the name of the public good, can serve to adversely affect the rights and livelihood of the poor and disadvantaged. The mobilization of communities against these projects, consequently, represents not only resistance to adverse policies but also an assertion of their status and rights as citizens. Social movements, in this context, form part of a broader process of holding the state accountable for the welfare of all its citizens.

Notes

1 We would like to express our appreciation to Neil Stammers, John Gaventa and Eghosa Osaghae, who provided invaluable advice on this chapter.

2 Our categorization of states as being situated in the global 'North' or 'South' is unavoidably an analytically imprecise one. Since the end of the cold war, the global order has undergone enormous changes and former states of the Eastern bloc now coalesce uneasily in 'Northern' or Western alliances such as the European Union without the necessary structural economic strength of many of their partner states. In contradistinction, some states in the 'South', or which have allied themselves with the South, are becoming much stronger international economic, if not political, players, and here China, Brazil and India are of particular note. The distinction between North and South is retained here as a way of distinguishing between historical economic blocs.

3 The terms 'collective action', 'social mobilization', 'social movements' and 'social movement organizations' are sometimes used interchangeably in the literature. In this context we refer to social mobilization as a prerequisite of collective action. We distinguish between collective action and social movements in our exploration of why certain forms of collective action give rise to social movements while others do not (see the section in this chapter entitled *What makes a movement?*).

4 We are grateful to Neil Stammers for reminding us of this point.

5 See in particular Kabeer (2005).

6 The linkages between mobilization and democratic practices are to be further explored in a forthcoming Zed volume entitled *Mobilizing for Democracy*, edited by Coelho and von Lieres.

7 We term them 'middle-range' in the sense that they do not aspire to the status of meta-theory and they provide at least a partial framework for the analysis of social movements in the South.

8 This theme is explored at length by Gaventa and Tandon in a forthcoming volume in this series.

References

Alvarez, S., E. Dagnino and A. Escobar (eds) (1998) *Cultures of Politics/Politics of Cultures: Revisioning Latin American Social Movements*, Boulder, CO: Westview Press.

Amin, S. (1976) *Unequal Development*, New York: Monthly Review Press.

— (1993) 'Social movements at the

periphery', in P. Wignaraja (ed)., *New Social Movements in the South: Empowering the People*, New Delhi: Vistaar Publications.

Appadurai, A. (2002) 'Deep democracy: urban governmentality and the horizon of politics', *Public Culture*, 14: 21–47.

Arrighi, G., T. K. Hopkins and I. Wallerstein (1989) *Anti-systemic Movements*, London: Verso.

Ballard, R., A. Habib and I. Valodia (eds) (2006) *Voices of Protest: Social Movements in Post-Apartheid South Africa*, University of KwaZulu Natal Press.

Benford, R. and D. Snow (2000) 'Framing processes and social movements: an overview and assessment', *Annual Review of Sociology*, 26, August.

Bond, P. (2002) *Unsustainable South Africa: Environment, Development and Social Protest*, London: Merlin Press.

Castells, M. (1997) *The Power of Identity: The Information Age*, Oxford: Blackwell.

— (2003) 'Global informational capitalism', in D. Held and A. McGrew (eds), *The Global Transformations Reader*, Cambridge: Polity Press.

Comacho, D. (1993) 'Latin America: a society in motion', in P. Wignaraja (ed.), *New Social Movements in the South: Empowering the People*, New Delhi: Vistaar Publications.

Cornwall, A. (2004) 'New democratic spaces? The politics and dynamics of institutionalised participation', *IDS Bulletin*, 35(2).

Cornwall, A. and V. S. Coelho (eds) (2007) *Spaces for Change? Participation, Inclusion and Voice*, London: Zed Books.

Cox, R. (1987) *Production, Power and World Order, Social Forces and the Making of History*, New York: Columbia.

— (ed.) (1997) *The New Realism: Perspectives on Multilateralism and World Order*, Tokyo: United Nations University Press.

Dahl, R. A. (2003) 'Can international organisations be democratic? A sceptic's view', in D. Held and A. McGrew (eds), *The Global Transformations Reader*, Cambridge: Polity Press.

Dalton, R. J. (2002) *Citizen Politics: Public opinion and political parties in advanced industrial democracies*, 3rd edn, New York: Chatham House.

Della Porta, D. and M. Diani (1999) *Social Movements: An Introduction*, Oxford: Blackwell.

Diani, M. (1992) 'The concept of social movement', *Sociological Review*, 40: 1–25.

Eckersley, R. (1994) *Environmentalism and Political Theory*, London: UCl Press.

Edelman, M. (2001) 'Social movements: changing paradigms and forms of politics', *Annual Review of Anthropology*, 30, October.

Edwards, M. (1999) *Future Positive, International Co-operation in the 21st Century*, London: Earthscan.

Edwards, M. and J. Gaventa (eds) (2001) *Global Citizen Action*, Colorado/London: Lynne Rienner/Earthscan.

Epstein, S. (1996) *Impure Science: Aids, Activism and the Politics of Knowledge*, Berkeley: University of California Press.

Escobar, A. (1996) 'Imagining a post-development era', in J. Crush (ed.), *The Power of Development*, London: Routledge.

Freeman, J. (1999) *Waves of Protest:*

Social Movements since the Sixties, Lanham, MD: Rowman and Littlefield.

Gamson, W. (1982) *Encounters with Unjust Authority*, Homewood, IL: Dorsey Press.

— (1990 [1975]) *The Strategy of Social Protest*, Homewood, IL: Dorsey Press.

— (1992) 'The social psychology of collective action', in C. M. Mueller and A. D. Morris (eds), *Frontiers in Social Movement Theory*, New Haven, CT, and London: Yale University Press.

Gaventa, J. (1999) 'Crossing the great divide: building links between NGOs and community based organisations in North and South', in D. Lewis (ed.), *International Perspectives on the Third Sector*, London: Earthscan.

— (2000) 'Exploring, citizenship, participation and accountability', *IDS Bulletin*, 23, April.

Guigni, M. G. (1998) 'Was it worth the effort? The outcomes and consequences of Social Movements', *ARS*, 24.

Habermas, J. (2003) 'The postnational constellation', in D. Held and A. McGrew (eds), *The Global Transformations Reader*, Cambridge: Polity Press.

Hajer, M. (1995) *The Politics of Environmental Discourse*, Oxford: Clarendon.

Held, D. and A. McGrew (eds) (2003) *The Global Transformations Reader*, Cambridge: Polity Press.

Held, D., A. McGrew, D. Goldblatt and J. Perraton (2003) *Global Transformations*, Oxford: Polity Press.

Huntington, S. (1974) 'Postindustrial politics: how benign will it be?', *Comparative Politics*, 6.

— (1984) 'Will more countries become democratic?', *Political Science Quarterly*, 99.

— (1991) *The Third Wave*, Norman: University of Oklahoma Press.

Ibarra, P. (ed.) (2003) *Social Movements and Democracy*, New York: Palgrave Macmillan.

Jenkins C. (1983) 'Resource Mobilisation Theory and the study of social movements', *Annual Review of Sociology*, 9.

Jenkins, J. C. and M. Wallace (1996) 'The generalised action potential of protest movements: the new class, social trends, and political exclusion explanations', *Sociological Forum*, 11(2).

Kabeer, N. (ed.) (2005) *Inclusive Citizenship: Meanings and Expressions*, London: Zed Books.

Karns, M. P. and K. A. Mingst (2004) *International Organizations: The Politics and Processes of Global Governance*, London: Lynne Rienner.

Klandermans, B. (1984) 'Mobilization and participation: socialpsychological expansions of resource mobilization theory', *American Sociological Review*, 49(5).

— (1997) *The Social Sociology of Protest*, Oxford: Blackwell.

Klandermans, B. and D. Oegema (1987) 'Potentials, networks, motivations and barriers: steps towards participation in social movements', *American Sociological Review*, 52(4).

Kothari, R. (1993). 'Rethinking development and democracy', in P. Wignaraja (ed.) (1993) *New Social Movements in the South: Empowering the People*, New Delhi: Vistaar Publications.

— (2005) *Rethinking Democracy*, New Delhi: Orient Longman.

Laclau, E. and C. Mouffe (1985) *Hegemony and Socialist Strategy: Towards a radical democratic politics*, London: Verso.

Leach, M., I. Scoones and B. Wynne (eds) (2005) *Science and Citizens: Globalisation and the Challenge of Engagement*, London: Zed Books.

Leys, C. (1996) *The Rise and Fall of Development Theory*, Oxford: EAEP.

Lindberg, S. and A. Sverrison (eds) (1997) *Social Movements in Development*, London: Macmillan.

Luckham, R., A. Goetz and M. Kaldor (2000) 'Democratic institutions and politics in contexts of inequality, poverty and conflict', *IDS Working Paper* 104, Brighton: IDS.

Mamdani, M. (1996) *Citizen and the Subject: Contemporary Africa and the legacy of late colonialism*, Cape Town: David Phillip.

Mamdani, M., T. Mkandawire and E. Wamba-dia-Wamba (1993). 'Social movements and democracy in Africa', in P. Wignaraja (ed.) (1993), *New Social Movements in the South: Empowering the People*, New Delhi: Vistaar Publications.

Mayo, M. (2005) *Global Citizenship, Social Movements and the Challenge of Globalisation*, London: Zed Books.

McAdam, D. (1986) 'Recruitment to high risk activism: the case of Freedom Summer', *American Journal of Sociology*, 92(1).

McAdam, D., J. D. McCarthy and M. N. Zald (eds) (1996) *Comparative Perspectives on Social Movements: Political Opportunities, Mobilising Structures and Cultural Framings*, New York: Cambridge University Press.

McAdam, D., S. Tarrow and C. Tilly (2001) *Dynamics of Contention*, Cambridge: Cambridge University Press.

McCarthy, J. D. and M. N. Zald (1977) 'Resource mobilization and social movements: a partial theory', *American Journal of Sociology*, 82(6).

McIntyre-Mills, J. (2000) *Global Citizenship and Social Movements: Creating Transcultural Webs for the New Millennium*, Amsterdam: Hartwood Academic Publishers.

Melucci, A. (1995) 'The new social movements revisited: reflections on a sociological misunderstanding', in L. Malhue (ed.), *Social Movements and Social Classes: The future of collective action*, London: Sage.

— (1996) *Challenging Codes: Collective action in the information age*, Cambridge: Cambridge University Press.

Mhone, G. (2003) 'Democratisation, economic liberalisation and the quest for sustainable development in South Africa', in G. Mhone and O. Edigheji, *Governance in the New South Africa: The challenges of globalisation*, Cape Town: UCT Press.

Murphy, C. N. (ed.) (2002) *Egalitarian Politics in the Age of Globalisation*, London: Palgrave.

Mushakoji, K. (1993) 'Foreword', in P. Wignaraja (ed.), *New Social Movements in the South: Empowering the People*, New Delhi: Vistaar Publications.

Newell, P. and J. Wheeler (eds) (2006) *Rights, Resources and the Politics of Accountability*, London: Zed Books.

Norris, L and S. Cable (1994) 'The seeds of protest: from elite initiators to grassroots mobilisation',

Sociological Perspectives, 37: 24–268.

Nyamu-Musembi, C. (2005) 'Towards an actor oriented perspective on human rights', in N. Kabeer (ed.), *Inclusive Citizenship: Meanings and expressions*, London: Zed Books.

Oberschall, A. (1973) *Social Conflict and Social Movements*, Englewood Cliffs, NJ: Prentice-Hall.

O'Brien, R., A. M. Goetz, J. A. Scholte and M. Williams (2000) *Contesting Global Governance: Multilateral Economic Institutions and Global Social Movements*, Cambridge: Cambridge University Press.

Offe, C. (1985) 'New social movements: challenging the boundaries of institutional politics', *Social Research*, 52(4).

Oliver, P., J. Cadena-Roa and K. Strawn (2003) 'Emerging trends in the study of protest and social movements', in B. Dobratz, T. Buzzell and L. Waldner, *Political Sociology for the 21st Century*, vol. 12, Oxford: Elsevier.

Olsen, M. (1965) *The Logic of Collective Action: Public Goods and the Theory of Groups*, Cambridge, MA: Harvard University Press.

Oommen, T. K. (1997) 'Social movements in the Third World', in S. Lindberg and A. Sverrison (eds), *Social Movements in Development*, London: Macmillan.

Opp, K. (1988) 'Grievances and participation in social movements', *American Sociological Review*, 53(6).

Park, R. (1969 [1921]) 'Collective behavior', in R. Park and E. W. Burgess (eds), *Introduction to the Science of Sociology*, New York: Greenwood Press.

Piven, F. and R. Cloward (1979) *Poor People's Movements: Why they succeed and how they fail*, New York: Pantheon.

Robins, S. (2005) 'Rights passages from "near death" to "new life": AIDS activism and treatment testimonies in South Africa', IDS Working Paper 251, Brighton: IDS.

Rucht, D. (2003) 'Social movements challenging neo-liberal globalisation', in P. Ibarra (ed.), *Social Movements and Democracy*, New York: Palgrave Macmillan.

Smelser, N. (1962) *Theory of Collective Behavior*, New York: Free Press.

Snow, D. and R. Benford (1988) 'Ideology, frame resonance and participant mobilization', in B. Klandermans, K. Hanspeter and S. Tarrow (eds), *International Social Movement Research: From Structure to Action*, Greenwich: JAI Press.

— (1992) 'Master frames and cycles of protest', in C. M. Mueller and A. D. Morris (eds), *Frontiers in Social Movement Theory*, New Haven, CT, and London: Yale University Press.

Stammers, N. (2005) 'The emergence of human rights in the North: towards historical re-evaluation', in N. Kabeer (ed.), *Inclusive Citizenship: Meanings and Expressions*, London: Zed Books.

— (2009) *Human Rights and Social Movements*, London: Pluto Press,

Stavenhagen, R. (1997) 'People's movements, the anti-systemic challenge', in R. W. Cox (ed.), *The New Realism: Perspectives on Multilateralism and World Order*, Tokyo: United Nations University Press.

Steady, F. C. (2002) 'Engendering change through egalitarian movements: the African experience', in C. N. Murphy (ed.), *Egalitarian Politics in the Age of Globalisation*, London: Palgrave.

Stienstra, D. (1999) 'Of roots, leaves and trees: gender, social movements and global governance', in M. K. Meyer and E. Prugl (eds), *Gender Politics in Global Governance*, Boston, MA: Rowman and Littlefield.

Tarrow, S. (1989) *Democracy and Disorder: Protests and Politics in Italy 1965–75*, Oxford: Clarendon.

— (1994) *Power in Movement: Social Movements, Collective Action and Politics*, New York: Cambridge University Press.

Thompson, L. (2005) 'Managing mobilization? Participatory processes and dam building in South Africa, the Berg River project', IDS Working Paper 254, Brighton: IDS.

Tilly, C. (1975) *The Formation of National States in Western Europe*, Princeton, NJ: Princeton University Press.

— (1978) *From Mobilization to Revolution*, Reading, MA: Addison-Wesley.

— (2003) 'When do (and don't) social movements promote democratisation?', in P. Ibarra (ed.), *Social Movements and Democracy*, New York: Palgrave Macmillan.

Touraine, A. (1985) 'An introduction to the study of new social movements', *Social Research*, 52(4).

— (2001) *Beyond Neoliberalism*, Cambridge: Polity Press.

Wignaraja, P. (ed.) (1993) *New Social Movements in the South: Empowering the People*, New Delhi: Vistaar Publications.

ONE | Socio-economic rights and social movements

2 | Social movements and rights claims: the case of action groups in the Niger Delta

EGHOSA E. OSAGHAE

Several factors have made human rights one of the defining elements of post-cold-war globalization. They include the contradictions of globalization itself, arising from the cross-pressures of closure and openness, exclusion and inclusion, localism and globalism, sameness and difference, and equality and inequality, as well as democratization and liberalization, all of which have accentuated the contestations over state ownership, power relations and citizenship, and have led, in many cases, to protracted and violent conflicts and wars. These have mostly involved marginalized, previously excluded and oppressed groups – 'minorities at risk' (Gurr 1993), indigenous peoples, women's and youth groups, refugees, illegal immigrants, etc. – that have seized the momentum offered by global trends conducive to 'struggles from below' to seek redress of various forms that typically have to do with equal citizenship, equitable power relations and self-determination. The main weapons of struggle are human rights, whose perceived emancipatory and empowering attributes have drawn equity- and justice-seeking groups to them. The very notion that people have rights that entitle them to protection, equality, development and self-determination is enough reason to take the risks of struggling in mostly non-systemic ways.

The foregoing provides the context for analysing the proliferation of what have variously been characterized as 'new grassroots stirrings', 'new social movements' and 'action groups' (Melluci 1985; Cohen 1985; Wignaraja 1993; Haynes 1997). The history of social movements generally revolves around popular, bottom-up and grassroots struggles and resistance by groups under oppressive and unjust regimes as they seek redress and more equitable power configurations. According to a recent definition, social movements 'are usually understood to be collective challenges mounted by relatively marginal groups against powerful elites and dominant ideologies' (Medearis 2005: 54).

For fairly obvious reasons that have to do with long histories of external meddlesomeness (including colonialism and (neo)imperialism), bad governance, oppression, exclusion, poverty, conflict, war, scarcity of resources and, more recently, huge foreign debt and state decline or collapse, the bulk of these movements have been in the Third World and Africa (see Sall 2004). The increased global salience of the politics of difference, as well as of issues of citizenship, environmental justice, gender equity, youth empowerment, local political autonomy and resource control, has been a reinforcing factor in the evolving scenarios. The situation in the oil-rich Niger Delta region of Nigeria, which has witnessed an unparalleled prevalence of uprisings by aggrieved minority groups that has transformed the struggles from accommodation-seeking nationalism to self-determination nationalism (Osaghae 2001), represents one of the prototypical and paradigmatic cases of the evolving trends and patterns of new social movements in Africa.

In the case of the Niger Delta (and perhaps other similar African and Third World situations), where sub-national governmental units, specifically state and local governments, have also played leading roles in articulating the populist grievances and demands for equity and justice associated with social movements, and have even been involved in – 'hijacked' might be a better word – grassroots mass organization and struggles, it is necessary to further distinguish social movements as non-governmental organizations that are autonomous of the state and its agencies. Indeed, being by their nature against the status quo, social movements cannot ordinarily be aligned with the very system they seek to overthrow, of which sub-national governments that exert various forms of control over instruments of state coercion, including the police, are an integral part. Thus, following Osadolor (2004: 35), action groups in the Niger Delta may be regarded as

> resistance movements [which] emerged ... with an ideology based on the principle of self-determination as a driving force for ethnic autonomy. Such movements were the expressed actions taken by the various ethnic nationalities to make their formal declarations and issuance of Bills of Rights in demand for freedom, access to basic needs and resources, protection from environmental pollution, and equal participation in the polity.

In this chapter, I want to examine how the various claims to and demands for rights have enabled and shaped the range of equity- and justice-seeking social movements that have emerged in the Niger Delta; the key point, of course, being that claims to rights are fundamental to the logic and coherence of social movements.

The chapter is in three sections. The first sets the conceptual and analytical frame by elaborating on the rights–social movements nexus. This is followed by a discussion of the historical and conceptual location of the Niger Delta. The rest of the chapter interrogates the contexts of relative deprivation, rights denial and injustice within which social movements have emerged in the Niger Delta region. A major objective is to explain why the social movements have been largely ethnic and most recently generational, and to analyse the dynamics and outcomes of the rights struggles waged by the various social movements.

Setting the framework: rights and social movements

The coherence of social movements is highly dependent on the ability of members to forge common interests, goals and strategies. Human rights tend to be fundamental to these interests and strategies because, on the one hand, allegations and perceptions of discrimination, exclusion, oppression, injustice, domination and exploitation, which all arise from denials and violations of human rights, underlie the emergence of social movements. On the other hand, notwithstanding the character of the struggle waged by members of the movement, whether it be war, violent conflict, riots or protests and the like, the bottom line of social movements is the demand for rights which they believe can be most meaningfully enjoyed when extant (oppressive) social relations are transformed. This makes social movements essentially anti-status-quo (Cohen 1985). According to Touraine (1985: 749), social movements have actors

> involved in social conflict, whose goals and strategies have a social coherence and rationality of their own. [Their functions] cannot be understood within the logic of the existing institutional order, since their overriding function is precisely to challenge that logic and transform the social relations which it mirrors and reinforces.

Medearis (2005: 54) makes a similar point:

> And acting as they do, in societies characterized by significant inequalities of power, [social movements] face systematic barriers to democratic inclusion for themselves and their arguments. In addition to their weak social positions, they are almost always bearers of ideas that are uncongenial to prevalent institutions and practices. (See also Tarrow 1998)

In these struggles, human rights provide the necessary justificatory and organizing principles that give coherence to the movements. The conception of rights as existential and, more specifically, claims to (denied) rights are central to understanding the origins and activities of the action groups

37

of the Niger Delta (Ogbogbo 2003) that are the focus of this chapter. As defined by Jeff Haynes (1997: 3), 'action groups' are basically ordinary people's development and empowerment groups that represent 'a popular Third World response to growing poverty and lack of power'. Those lacking in power who find the groups most attractive include the poor, women, young people and ethnic and religious minorities.

To put the rights–social movements nexus in proper perspective, it is necessary to elaborate on the nature of rights, including their supposed liberatory powers, and the interface that makes them fundamental to social movements. The relevance of human rights for peace and conflict management in general has been the theme of a number of recent studies (e.g. Galtung 1996; Osaghae 1996; Mahajan 1998; Chandra 2000). One of the major points to have emerged so far is that the denial of rights, which itself is an instrument of inequality, injustice, discrimination, exclusion and domination, is a precipitant of conflicts. By the same token, the granting, recognition, enjoyment and protection of rights, to the extent that they can remove or minimize the basis of inequality, injustice, exclusion and domination, are necessary, though not sufficient, conditions for peace and conflict management. This is especially true for weak, oppressed and marginal groups, typically minorities, that demand political, civil, cultural, social and economic rights to protect the identity and other interests of the group and redress unjust and inequitable power relations. Rights are demanded, as it were, because they are believed to be potent emancipatory weapons within existing states.

The types of rights demanded, however, depend on the particular contexts of oppression or discrimination within which minorities have to struggle. In cases of assimilation by dominant groups, for example, the accent tends to be on rights that protect group identity. Where the problem is discrimination in employment, admission to schools and the like, redressive and equality-enhancing rights are favoured, while, at the extreme, separatist rights, including the right to self-determination and secession, are sought in cases of seemingly absolute structural domination, such as that of the Tamils in Sri Lanka.

Irrespective of the types of rights demanded, however, the 'logic' of rights struggles by oppressed groups is that the individual rights of members of the group are closely tied to and contingent upon the collective rights of the group as a whole. Fittingly, in the chapter of his book entitled 'Protection of human rights', Chandra (2000: 145) makes the argument that 'individual rights may be necessary but are not sufficient to manage ethnic conflicts. Group rights which regard ethnic groups as deserving of protection and justice in competition with others are also needed.' The point is that unless the right of the group to existence/survival, language, culture, self-determination, human dignity, development and equality with other groups, for instance, is established, the chances that members of the group will be able to enjoy individual rights are almost zero. Thus, by way of illustration, the humanity of slaves had to be asserted in order for ex-slaves to enjoy basic freedoms, just as the right of colonized peoples to self-determination gave individuals in the former colonies the right to enjoy 'fundamental' human rights.

Although the foregoing rights logic is plausible, especially from the point of view of groups that have suffered structural discrimination, deprivation and exclusion, it has nevertheless provoked a debate between hardcore liberals, for whom individual rights are fundamental and supreme, and who assume that individual liberty and equality are sufficient to nourish and protect diversity, and proponents of communitarian rights, who argue that group rights are necessary for dealing with problems of citizenship in multi-ethnic and multicultural societies. This is not the place to dwell at length on that debate, which, in any case, is only tangentially relevant to the concerns of this chapter; suffice it to note that the communitarian perspective is more popular in African and non-Western human rights discourses for at least two reasons. The first is the centrality of primary groups in social formations and political relations, which has been reinforced over the years by the ethnic profiling and group-arithmetic politics practised by state managers, which tie the access and opportunities available to citizens to the ethnic and religious groups they belong to. Second, the struggle in Africa has historically been more for collective rights than for individual rights. In the era of decolonization, which marked the beginning of the contemporary rights struggles, the emphasis was on the right of peoples and states to self-determination, while post-colonial struggles have basically been to protect, defend and further the interests of groups, depending on their positions in the unequal power and resource configuration. For fairly obvious reasons, oppressed, excluded and dominated groups have been most notable in the latter category.

In both instances, the rights of the individual are subsumed under collective rights.

> [O]n the one hand, the interest of the nation-state prevailed over individual liberty and, on the other, community practices received priority. On both counts, individual autonomy was restricted and the principle of

equal rights of citizenship fell by the wayside. In place of the individual, the community [ethnic or religious] was privileged. (Mahajan 1998: 163)[1]

This underlies the group basis of conflicts.

Since the issue of individual liberty and self-determination has been continuously sidelined ... political conflict has manifested itself in terms of contestations between two distinctive types of communities: religious/cultural community and political community or the nation-state. (ibid.: 163)

Thus, although struggles for equal citizenship ought to focus on the rights of the individual à la plebiscitarian citizenship, which maintains a direct relationship between the individual and the state, they instead involve group struggles à la functional citizenship, in which relations between individuals and the state are intermediated by the primary groups to which they belong. (See Osaghae 1994 for a discussion of these elements of citizenship.) The obvious danger here lies in the fact that the rights of the individual then tend to be taken for granted. From the point of view of social movements that sensitize and mobilize people to demand rights, such a possibility would amount to a failure, as is argued in the concluding part of this chapter.

The preponderance of social movements in the civil society landscape of many African states and their roles as key agents of political transformation can be explained by the conjunction of a number of factors. These include gross inequalities among competing groups and the resultant hierarchical citizenship, blocked access to the power and resources to which group members are ordinarily entitled, an accent on group interests and group rights, and the chronic failure of the state to respond to demands for redress by aggrieved groups except by unleashing its coercive powers on those making the demands.

These factors have been conducive to the building of communities of interest by social movements. In building, articulating and mobilizing constituencies of interests, social movements have embraced human rights as key organizing principles. It is for this reason that the struggle for rights is crucial to their very definition and existence. But the connection between social movements and rights is not a given and cannot be assumed, not least because rights in and of themselves are necessary but not sufficient factors for the existence of social movements. We need to know the historical context of the struggles, the social basis of the movements, how the particular constituency of interests is mobilized, why certain rights and not others are demanded and the prospects for success of the rights struggle, which also requires some analysis of the nature of the state and its engagement with social movements. These parameters provide the framework within which the rights struggles by the minority movements in Nigeria's oil-rich Niger Delta are analysed in this paper.

The Niger Delta in perspective

The Niger Delta comprises the coastal lowlands and waters – marshland, creeks, tributaries and lagoons – of the southernmost ends of Nigeria that drain the Niger river into the Atlantic at the Bight of Biafra (Ibeanu 2000). At its core are Bayelsa, Rivers, Delta, Akwa Ibom and Cross River states, which are the littoral states of the South-South geopolitical zone of the country, and the riverine parts of Ondo state, which are home to over forty minority ethnic groups, including the Ijaw, Urhobo, Itsekiri, Efik, Ibibio, Ogoni, Ilaje, Kalabari and Ikwerre.

Perhaps the single most important factor in the definition and development (or non-development) of the region is its tortuous (political) geography. Historically, the difficult terrain of waters and swamps, which keeps most communities in the area isolated and accessible only by boat, and which has been cited as the major obstacle to the development of the region, has been its main defining element.[2] This is to the extent that environmental problems, suffering and the attendant underdevelopment (for which inhabitants of the area hold the colonial and post-colonial states responsible) have served as unifying factors for the region's minority groups in their various struggles for development, equity and justice in the Nigerian state. The struggles, as we shall see in the next section, have passed through several phases.

Today crude oil, whose exploitation has multiplied the environmental and developmental problems of the various communities, has become the most critical factor in the definition of the Niger Delta. The tendency is now to regard the oil-bearing states, which mostly belong to the South-South (minorities) geopolitical zone, including Edo, as constituting the Niger Delta. But while the centrality of oil to the creation of new communities of interest and to Niger Delta relations with the Nigerian state cannot be denied, the historical Niger Delta of the Calabar-Ogoja-Rivers and present-day Delta state axis remains the hub of what has emerged as distinctive Niger Delta politics. It is as such that the core Niger Delta continues to be distinguished by 'Deltans' from the wider geopolitical region, whether of ethnic minorities (South-South) or of oil-bearing areas. This is the sense in which 'Niger Delta' is used in this chapter.

The geopolitics of the Niger Delta, specifically its difficult terrain and

41

ethnic minority composition, has also been the principal factor in the underdevelopment of the region, relative to most other parts of southern Nigeria. Thus, although the area had what should have been something of a head start in being one of the earliest parts of the country to have contacts with Europeans and the forces of Westernization, the terrain constituted a major obstacle to development. The Willink Minorities Commission, which was appointed by the colonial government to enquire into the fears of minorities and the means of allaying them, acknowledged this fact and recommended the establishment of a special board, the Niger Delta Development Board, to address the peculiar problems of the region. Strikingly, after several years of neglect and lack of seriousness, the federal government returned to the Willink route in the 1990s to establish special development agencies for the region, most notably the Oil Mineral Producing Area Development Commission (OMPADEC) and the Niger Delta Development Commission (NDDC).

Although the 'difficult terrain' argument has some validity, aggrieved Niger Delta communities regard it as a ruse. Pointing out that the region does not, in fact, have the most difficult terrain in the country – Lagos, the former federal capital, with its modern and well-developed infrastructure, has equally difficult terrain and is situated mainly on land reclaimed from the sea, and many arid and desert parts of the country have been transformed for modern habitation – they attribute underdevelopment to the deliberate policies of discrimination, deprivation and criminal neglect that minority groups in general have suffered in the country. What is more, the finances for the development of other parts of the country, including most notably Abuja, the new federal capital, have come largely from oil wealth. Spokespersons of the communities insist that at the very least, part of the wealth should be used to develop the Niger Delta, from which it is derived, as some form of compensation for the environmental degradation and hazards. They also demand a reasonable (some say 'negotiated') share of the rents and royalties paid by the multinational corporations to the federal government.

But, instead of such benefits, the communities have suffered want, poverty and neglect in the midst of plenty. Unemployment rates are high, as jobs in the lucrative oil sector, including junior and unskilled posts, are given to expatriates and Nigerians from other parts of the country. The decimation of fishing and farming, the main occupations of the rural dwellers, through spillages, pollution, gas flaring and other hazards, has made the situation much worse. Roads, potable water and electricity supply, healthcare facilities and public school facilities are poorly developed, while areas occupied by the multinationals and their privileged employees boast First World facilities.

So Niger Delta leaders hold the state and its successive managers, rather than difficult terrain, responsible for the region's underdevelopment. Indeed, a recent account of Ijaw underdevelopment traces the discrimination, neglect and injustice suffered by the region back to the fifteenth century and, since then, colonialism. According to Prince Preboye (2005), the plight of the Iduwini (or Izon) people, who constitute the core of the region, began with the loss of their privileged status as middlemen in the coastal trade in slaves and legitimate goods, which initially involved the Portuguese. The British, who took over the trade, seemed determined to punish the Iduwini, who were believed to have prevented earlier entry by the British out of preference for the Portuguese.

Although this argument is highly conjectural, Preboye explains the subsequent actions of the British traders and colonial authorities, such as discrimination in favour of the Itsekiri people in employment and residential allocations, the long delay in establishing schools in the area, which denied the peoples of the area one of the benefits of early contact with Westernization, and the relocation of the headquarters of the oil rivers from Forcados to Burutu, as calculated to punish the Iduwini. At several points, the author sees an interesting continuity between the 'wickedness' of the colonialists and that of the Nigerian inheritors of the post-colonial state, and even suggests that on balance the colonialists were more benevolent to the Delta than Nigerian leaders have proved to be! For example, the only head of state ever to visit Ofougbene, the ancestral home of the Iduwini, was Sir Bernard Henry Bourdillon, the British colonial governor of Nigeria, who visited in September 1939. No post-colonial head of state has visited that part of the Delta.

Preboye's account suggests that, contrary to popular notions linking the grievances of Niger Delta communities with the political economy of oil, the region has a long history of perceived neglect, deprivation and injustice.[3] This long history, according to Preboye, explains the continuous emancipatory struggles in the area, which include the anti-colonial movements, the seven-day revolution led by Isaac Adaka Boro and the Niger Delta revolutionaries, and the violent uprisings of the 1990s. But such interpretation risks the danger of imposing contemporary categories on past realities. To begin with, there was no Niger Delta community in the past; indeed, some would say there is still no such community. Neither were there Ijaw, Ogoni, Urhobo or Kalabari ethnic groups as we know them today. Second, Niger Delta politics has been shaped within

43

the context of the Nigerian state, and it would be misleading to analyse the region's past outside of that. Indeed, the beginnings of Niger Delta politics lie in the agitation for separate states by regional minorities in the early 1950s, and subsequent dynamics have been greatly influenced by the cycles of minority politics in the country since then. The emergence of a strong Niger Delta protest identity in the 1990s is a latter-day development produced by the complex dynamics of oil politics, prolonged military authoritarian rule, democratization, structural adjustment, liberalization and globalization, as analysed below. All this is not, however, to discountenance the point about entrenched disaffection and perceptions of discrimination, injustice, deprivation and exploitation, which are germane to the history of rights struggles in the Niger Delta.

Rights struggles and the emergence of social movements

Images of the Niger Delta today conjure up not only a deprived, neglected and oppressed geopolitical region of ethnic minorities, but also a community of interests which has evolved around issues of oil politics and the determination of groups in the area to optimize the political and material benefits derivable from the resource, around environmental problems and around the struggle for environmental justice, minority rights and other empowering and emancipatory rights. Social movements in the region have generally taken their cue from, and been organized around, disaffections and grievances over these issues and the kinds of rights demanded to redress them.

On this basis, there have been at least four distinct phases of rights struggles. First was the pre-colonial phase of resistance to colonial subjugation, which involved individual ethnic groups (the Niger Delta 'community' not having evolved at this time). The most notable of these pre-colonial struggles involved the Ijaw and Itsekiri, the two most powerful trading groups, whose leaders (Jaja of Opobo and Nana respectively) sought to protect their economic interests and privileges. Second was the era of the nationalist struggles, in which progressives from the region such as Ernest Ikoli and Udo Udoma teamed up with nationalists from other parts of Nigeria to demand independence for the country.

The sharpening of regional, ethnic and religious cleavages and nationalisms, especially on the part of the three dominant ethnic groups (Hausa/Fulani, Igbo and Yoruba), which occurred simultaneously with the independence movement, polarized the struggle and produced, in its wake, minority sub-nationalism. This basically took the form of dissenting or opposition politics in the regions and agitation from the regions for separate states, both directed against the dominant majorities that had transformed the regions into internal colonies. The minorities alleged discrimination, exclusion, oppression, exploitation and forced cultural assimilation on the part of the dominant ethnic groups in the regions and argued that only political autonomy through the creation of separate states could solve the problem.

In the Niger Delta, minorities organized the United National Independence Party, the Niger Delta Congress and other political associations that opposed the Igbo and its political front, the National Council of Nigeria and the Cameroons (which later became the National Council of Nigerian Citizens), to pursue these interests in the former Eastern Region. The major state demanded was the Calabar-Ogoja-Rivers state, though there were also demands for separate Calabar, Ogoja and Rivers states. To the disappointment of minorities all over the country, the Willink Commission failed to recommend the creation of separate states. It recommended instead that the solution to the problems of the minorities lay in the introduction of appropriate political and constitutional mechanisms, including the establishment of a joint federal-regional development board for the Niger Delta, a bill of rights and centralization of the police force (Willink et al. 1958; Osaghae 1998).

The third phase of rights struggles in the Niger Delta covered the post-Willink and post-independence period up until 1967, which saw the intensification of demands for separate states (or a separate state). The federal and Eastern regional governments remained opposed to the creation of a minorities' state for the Niger Delta minorities, but the growing importance of oil in the region's and federation's economy was bound to change the complexion and tempo of demands, not least because of the environmental degradation and other hazards associated with exploration.

Matters came to a head sooner than expected with the twelve-day revolution led by Isaac Adaka Boro, Sam Onwunaru and Nottingham Dick in February 1966, a few weeks after the first military government in the country came to power. Cataloguing 'the problems of marginalization, criminal neglect of the people, degradation of our environment, denial of our right to self-determination' (Onwunaru 2004: 14), the revolutionaries declared an independent Niger Delta People's Republic. (See Boro 1982 for a detailed account of and reasons for the revolution.) Although the secessionist bid failed and its leaders were promptly arrested and jailed, it marked a turning point in the history of rights struggles in the Niger Delta region in several important ways.

It signified the beginning of a more sharply focused and narrowly defined Niger Delta political identity and consciousness that increasingly centred on the present Rivers–Bayelsa–Delta states axis. The humiliation, discrimination and oppression suffered at the hands of the Igbo during the civil war that soon ensued further helped this process of identity construction and consolidation. In one case, the Ikwerre of Rivers, who had all along been regarded as an Igbo subgroup, were forced to redefine themselves as non-Igbo. Second, the twelve-day revolution marked the beginning of a generational shift in the rights struggles, as politicized, frustrated and impatient youths took over the scene from the older elite, whom they sometimes accused of 'selling out' to the oppressors. Third, the revolution showed clearly that it was dangerous to ignore the situation in the Niger Delta or continue to take it for granted, especially in the light of the growing importance of crude oil during and after the civil war. In this regard, the military government proved to be responsive, as it created a separate Rivers state for Niger Delta minorities in the 1967 states creation exercise – and it is likely that a Calabar-Ogoja-Rivers state, the more historically enduring state demanded, would have been created if the revolution had not occurred.

The fourth and final phase of the rights struggles in the Niger Delta, which is the main focus of this chapter, covers the period after more states were created in the region until the present. From two (Rivers and Cross River) in 1967, the number increased to four (Bayelsa, Rivers, Akwa Ibom and Cross River) in 1995, with a fifth state, Delta, carved out of the former Bendel state making the fifth core Delta state. This phase witnessed the emergence and proliferation of social movements that were mostly built on ethnic identities and organized by youths.

The backdrop to the struggles in this phase was the failure of separate or 'own' states – and local governments – to solve the problems of minorities, as it had long been envisaged they would. This certainly disproved the notion that the creation of more states would solve the problem of minorities in the country (Osaghae 1986). It undoubtedly had much to do with the erosion of the fiscal and jurisdictional powers and weakened governance capacities of state governments relative to those wielded by the former regions under military rule at the time, although the poor performance of state governments that received allocations from the federal government and still had responsibility for many areas of development was also a major factor.

With regard to fiscal powers in particular, which saw state governments becoming appendages of a central government that controlled all the major sources of revenue, Niger Delta spokespersons continually lamented the phenomenal reduction in the proportion of the Federation Account allocated on the basis of derivation, which fell from 50 per cent in the period of regional governments to a mere 1.5 per cent in the 1990s. This was seen as a deliberate design on the part of successive federal military governments, dominated as they were by elements from the major ethnic groups, to prevent the Niger Delta minorities from enjoying the benefits of the oil resource in the way regions had when their agricultural commodities were the country's main revenue earners. Even after the Niger Delta states managed to secure an increase in the derivation quota of allocation to 13 per cent in 1999, the federal authorities came up with an onshore–offshore dichotomy bill, which sought to restrict derivable revenue to onshore oil, contrary to the convention established by Section 140(6) of the 1963 constitution that, for the purposes of the derivation provision in that constitution, 'the continental shelf of a [state] shall be deemed to be part of that [state]'. Although the Supreme Court abrogated the dichotomy, it nevertheless restricted the littoral states' portion of the continental shelf to 24 seaward miles.

In a subsequent act, the federal government modified this to read '200 metre isobath' – that is, a line joining all points off the coast of Nigeria (from Lagos to the boundary with Cameroon) where the sea is 200 metres deep. The injustice and deprivation inherent in the new act are best captured in the following 'exposé' by Sagay (2005):

The implication of this new Act is that the derivation principle only applies to those areas between this 200 metre depth line and the Nigerian coast or low water mark. Any part of the Nigerian Continental Shelf, deeper than 200 metres, is outside the derivation zone and proceeds of resources in this area of the sea will go straight to the Federation account. Coastal States derive nothing from this vast area. The area concerned could be as narrow as 5 miles in the Lagos and Western coastal areas, reaching a maximum belt of about 40 miles in the Akwa Ibom area in the East. This is a far cry from the 200 miles of the continental shelf of the Niger Delta States as stipulated in the founding constitutions of Nigeria and Article 76 of the 1982 Convention on the Law of the Sea. By far the most disturbing consequence of the coastal States' limitation to a 200 metre depth belt for derivation purposes, is that all the major offshore oil and gas finds are now in the deep off-shore zone between 1,000 and 2,500 metres as against the 200 metre limitation for coastal states. There are currently about sixty deep sea blocks available for allocation

47

to oil companies. Moreover, some gigantic oil and gas fields have been discovered in the deep sea bed since 1996. These include Bonga 1996; Bosi 1996/7; Abo 1997; Agbami 1998; Erha 1999; Akpo 1999 and Boriga-SW 2001. Many others are in the process of discovery or test drilling. Available information indicates that at the end of 2003, one hundred and ten (110) wells had been drilled in the deep off-shore; the shallowest, Okpok-1, being 1,260 metres deep and the deepest, Aje-1, had a depth of 5,800 metres. It was drilled by Yinka Folawiyo and Co. These drilling operations have resulted in 4 billion barrels of recoverable oil reserves whilst gas reserves are estimated at 25 trillion cubic feet. The Nigerian coastal States off whose shores these tremendous findings are being made will not enjoy any derivative rights in these deep sea areas, since derivation is limited to 200 metres.

The absolute control over oil resources exercised by the federal government, which was given legal backing by such legislation as the Petroleum Act of 1969 and 1971, the Offshore Revenue Act of 1971, the Petroleum Control Act of 1967, the Exclusive Economic Zone Act of 1978 and the Land Use Act of 1978, was another grievance. These laws excluded the communities from participation in the agreements with the multinational oil companies, thereby denying them any share in the royalties paid by the companies or an opportunity to negotiate different terms and conditions of oil exploration and production, including employment and other social benefits for members of the communities, environmental impact assessments and compensation for environmental degradation and other hazards.

For a long time, the unfavourable response by oil majors (Shell, Chevron, Mobil) to petitions from the Delta communities for compensation for gas flaring, pollution and other hazards, employment, the provision of basic infrastructure and community development was to insist that their agreements were with the federal authorities, whose responsibility it was to develop the areas.

It was the abysmal failure of state governments – and the federal government, of which they were appendages – to deliver the political, social and economic benefits that had been expected to come the way of the Niger Delta from oil, and to offer protection against the environmental hazards as well as the excesses and high-handedness of the oil multinationals, which finally forced the aggrieved communities to take up arms to fight for themselves. Adding salt to the wound, 'their leaderships and agitation were treated with disdain, denied access and ignored,

the movements operated as clandestine and underground organiza-
tions and militia groups. Notable examples were the Ijaw, Itsekiri and
Urhobo militia groups in Warri; the Niger Delta People's Volunteer Force,
an Ijaw militia group led by Alhaji Muhajid Asari Dokubo; the Egbesu
Boys, another Ijaw militia group; and the various 'secret cults' in Rivers,
Bayelsa and Cross River states.

The clandestine and militia groups were mainly distinguished by their
violent, terrorist and criminal strategies of 'resistance', which included
illegal bunkering, piracy on the high seas, the abduction and kidnapping
of oil workers, the blockage or closure of oil wells and other sabotage
activities. They were also the major actors in confrontations and violent conflicts with state military, police and security forces, as well as in
communal clashes involving rival communities. Early in 2005, Dokubo's
threat to blow up oil installations attracted world attention because of
the effect it had on escalating crude oil prices, and this forced the federal
government, under pressure from the USA and other powerful interests,
to negotiate a 'ceasefire'. These extremist movements, whose activities
sometimes posed a serious threat to the democratization process, represented the 'perverse manifestation of civil society' (Ikelegbe 2001a).

The result of the ethnicization of the rights struggle and the violent
strategies adopted by some of the movements, not surprisingly, is that
deep cleavages and conflicts – so-called 'communal clashes' – occur
among the movements and the groups they represent. Many of the conflicts have arisen around the 'ownership' of oil-bearing territories, which
is crucial for negotiating revenue and other benefits with the government
and the oil companies. The perennial conflicts among the Ijaw, Itsekiri
and Urhobo in Warri, as well as those between the Ogoni and Andoni,
are good examples. These conflicts demonstrably had the overall effect
of weakening efforts at forging a pan-Niger Delta community of interests,
especially because they offered the state, oil multinationals and other
'enemies' of the region a pretext to pursue divide-and-rule strategies that
kept the people apart for a long time.

This is not, however, to discountenance the attempts that have been
made by various civil society groups, politicians and state governments
to forge Niger Delta and South-South alliances on the basis of the
common problems of environmental justice, resource control and self-
determination.[5] Three types of environmental and civil rights groups
have been identified in the region: environmental and civil rights groups
based in the Niger Delta, such as Environmental Rights Action, the Niger
Delta Human and Environmental Rescue Organization, the Oil Watch

compromised by inducements while negotiations either failed or agreements if any were broken' (Ikelegbe 2001b: 441). The name chosen by
the prototypical social movement of the period, the Movement for the
Survival of Ogoni People (MOSOP), was most instructive because, as Ken
Saro-Wiwa (1992), founder of the movement, argued, what the Ogonis
and indeed other Niger Delta communities faced was 'genocide'. (See
also Osaghae 1995.)

To be sure, localized resistance, protest and rights-seeking initiatives
involving the obstruction of access routes, petition-writing, delegations
to state governments and oil majors by traditional leaders, and demands
for social amenities by community-based organizations had flourished
at various points, especially from the time of the twelve-day revolution,
but they finally erupted in a rash from the late 1980s, when material and
physical conditions in the region reached their worst levels yet. Not only
did pollution and gas flaring persist, destroying marine and farming life,
but the people reeled under massive unemployment, run-down infrastructure, health problems[4] and other burdens. All this was happening at
a time when many other parts of the country, especially Abuja, the new
federal capital, were being extensively developed with oil wealth, when
northern-dominated military governments were using oil to build a new
class of client billionaires and when the enclaves of the oil majors in
Port Harcourt, Warri, Eket and other places were revelling in First World
affluence. Acute feelings of relative deprivation, neglect, marginalization
and injustice inevitably developed throughout the Niger Delta, and 'the
grievances, anger, frustration and disillusionment that emerged led to
an upsurge in agitation and protests' (Ikelegbe 2001b: 440).

A combination of other internal and external events and developments
facilitated the Niger Delta uprising, or help explain it. Internally, economic
recession; massive declines in state capacity to provide public goods, which
led to the development of parallel state structures; the havoc wreaked by
structural adjustment and its poverty-aggravating consequences; the frustrations of an almost endless military-to-civil-rule transition programme,
including the annulment of the 12 June 1993 presidential election and
the resultant diminution of state legitimacy; and the opportunities for
redress-seeking provided by the rise of a vocal pro-democracy human
rights movement and other civil society constituents were the major factors. (See Obi 2002 for a detailed analysis.) Other factors were the weakness or underdevelopment and lack of integrity of legal constitutional
institutions and frameworks, which narrowed the options for seeking
redress to extralegal and unconventional methods, and the repressive

character of the state, which made military action, reprisal attacks and state terrorism typical responses to anti-state mobilization, rather than negotiation, constitutional reform or other peaceful strategies.

With regard to the latter, the execution of Ken Saro-Wiwa and eight other Ogoni leaders, the destruction of Odi and Umuchem, and the regime of state terror in Warri, Kaiama, Uzere, Iko, Ubeji and other flashpoints are notable examples. The oil companies were not left out of this because, as Ibeanu (2000) points out, on many occasions they invited the police, army and navy to quell disturbances on installations without recourse to the government. They were also accused of buying arms and supplying them to security agencies and instigating 'third force' activities to weaken resistance movements. These acts only served to increase the militancy of the Niger Delta movements and justify the violent strategies adopted by some of them out of the conviction that force was the only language capable of attracting the government's attention – and that of the oil multinationals (Osaghae 2003).

Indeed, it was the destabilizing consequences of the regime of ungovernability in the Niger Delta caused by the protests and resistance movements, especially for the country's oil-dependent economy, which forced the federal government in particular to introduce the palliatives that have brought some succour to the communities and have been counted as among the concrete achievements of the costly struggles. The palliatives include the establishment of special bodies (OMPADEC and later NDDC) to address developmental problems in the Niger Delta, the increase in the percentage of revenue allocation based on derivation from 1.5 per cent to 3 per cent in 1992 and 13 per cent in 1999, and the changing attitudes of the oil companies to issues of community development and the employment and well-being of peoples in the oil-bearing areas. On the other hand, the absence of political parties and legislatures, as well as the suppression of civil society – in short, the absence of democracy under the military – was also a major precipitant of the recourse to self-preservation nationalism.

This being the case, the situation of the rights struggle was bound to change, however gradually, after the country returned to democracy in 1999. The return of party politics, elections, legislatures, constitutional rule and other structures of democracy, as well as the accent on rights and the expansion of political space for interest articulation and aggregation, have increased the options for engagement between aggrieved groups and the state. For instance, litigation, peace dialogues and interventions by South-South branches of the major political parties, politicians and

state governments, as well as by the national and state ... been on the increase since 1999. Also, more and more ... organizations in the Niger Delta have become attracted t... in the search for constitutional solutions through reform ... (ERA 2000).

Externally, the multiplier effect of the global democratic re... swept through eastern Europe, Latin America, Asia and Africa ... This was especially because that revolution, in its unfoldin ... around issues of human rights, equity and justice, including t... minority and indigenous peoples to self-determination, envi... protection and justice. The United Nations, the European Union... France, Britain, major transnational non-governmental organizat... other influential members of the international community becar... sympathetic to and supportive of the plight of marginalized and e... groups and their struggles for rights of equity and self-determi... including independent statehood.

The Niger Delta proved to be a major beneficiary of internat... sympathy and support, partly because of the international dimen... represented by Shell and other oil multinationals and partly beca... the Niger Delta struggles quickly became paradigmatic for the advoc... of minority and environmental rights and justice. The sledgehamm... response to the Ogoni uprising by the Nigerian military governmen... which resulted in the execution of Ken Saro-Wiwa and eight othe... MOSOP leaders, brought the Niger Delta question full world attention... and support. The momentum of international interest was sustained by... the repressive regime imposed by the federal government in the Niger... Delta, as well as the direct and mostly negative effects of the crisis on... the volatile oil market.

The nature of social movements

Having analysed the historical context within which contemporary social movements emerged in the Niger Delta, we next examine the form and character of the movements. The point to begin with is that although Niger Delta movements are usually referred to in a manner that suggests a community of interests, the core movements were built around ethnic identities and have pursued mostly parochial interests. The more notable ethnic movements include MOSOP, the Ijaw National Congress, the Egbema National Congress, the Movement for Reparation to Ogbia, the Movement for the Survival of Itsekiri Ethnic Nationality and the Movement for the Survival of the Izon Ethnic Nationality. Some

Group and the Ijaw Council for Human Rights; national civil rights and pro-democracy organizations that have been active in the Niger Delta, notably the Civil Liberties Organization, the Campaign for Democracy and the Constitutional Rights Project; and international civil society groups, including Human Rights Watch, Project Underground and Amnesty International. While these various groups have played crucial roles as rights advocates and monitors, and have established linkages and networks with the grassroots movements in the Niger Delta, they fall outside the scope of the social movements focused on in this paper because they generally lack the grassroots presence and mobilization that are central to the definition of those movements. At best, they may be regarded as among the enablers and reinforcers of the rights struggles that produced social movements beginning in the 1980s. As for the highly instrumentalist and opportunistic alliances and initiatives by state governments and politicians in the South-South geopolitical zone, all that needs be said is that they also fall outside the purview of social movements, which are basically non-governmental, bottom-up and anti-status-quo in orientation.

The main explanation for the ethnicization of new social movements lies in the fact that, in the final analysis, it was ethnic communities rather than, say, states or local governments which bore the brunt of the sometimes callous and insensitive activities of the oil majors, environmentally induced and aggravated immiseration, marginalization, neglect and injustice. And, for some unexplained reason, the traditional ethnic and home-town associations such as the Urhobo Progress Union and Isoko Development Union, which would normally be in the forefront of seeking redress, did not become actively involved in the oil agitations. This left the stage open for aggrieved and frustrated youths, whose ascendancy represented a generational vote of no confidence in the older brigade represented by traditional rulers and an elite including leaders of the old ethnic unions, who were believed to be compromised. A similar slant can be given to the periodic intervention of women's groups, which generally occurred spontaneously. In one instance, women in Bayelsa state forced the closure of an oil well to protest at the failure of the oil companies to employ their husbands and children. Some of the more active and influential youth organizations were the National Youth Council of Ogoni People (NYCOP), the Ijaw Youth Council (IYC), the Urhobo Youth Movement, the Egi Youth Federation, the Ikwerre Youth Movement and the Bayelsa Youth Federation. Some, like NYCOP and the IYC, had strategic affiliations with the umbrella movements – in these cases, MOSOP and INC respectively. As rightly noted by Ikelegbe (2001b: 443), the youth

53

organizations 'have been more mobilizational in their approach, raised awareness and provided a grassroots base for the Niger Delta agitation'. The NYCOP, for example, provided 'foot soldiers' for MOSOP's uprising under Saro-Wiwa (Osaghae 1995).

The other distinctive characteristic of the new social movements, which also strengthened their ethnic coloration and gave some of them an aura of mystery, was the recourse to traditional forms of solidarity and organization, including juju, oaths of secrecy and togetherness, rituals, and reward and punishment. This form of retribalization, which involves 'a reinvention and utilization of "traditional" cultural practice and the growing definition of local identity through ethnic discourse', and has been found to be common with emergent youth-generational ethnicity in Nigeria (Nolte 2004: 61), was widespread in the Niger Delta. One of the most notable examples was the Egbesu Boys, whose members subscribed to Egbesu, the supreme juju of the Ijaws, and were believed to possess supernatural powers. The connection with tradition and rituals proved to be one of the successful strategies for recruiting members and mobilizing support in the communities. It created bonds of solidarity and made it much easier for most ordinary people in both urban and rural areas to identify with the cause of the struggles.

Advocacy and sensitization campaigns through the declaration of bills of rights, the exposure of atrocities by oil multinationals and the state, night vigils, rallies and periodic meetings, and the encouragement of acts of defiance and civil disobedience (as in the campaigns by MOSOP for Ogonis to boycott the 1993 elections) were some of the other strategies employed by the movements. A major component of the sensitization campaign was the promise of material upliftment and a better life for all as the ultimate prize of the struggles. (In the case of the Ogoni, huge sums of 'compensation money' were said to be promised to all at the end of the day!) Most of these activities went on underground, however, because of the suffocating presence of state security. This was the case from the late 1980s, except of course when dramatic and sensational events such as abduction, kidnapping, the seizure of oil wells and open confrontation with state forces elicited their own dynamics of sensitization and mobilization.

To sum up, the new social movements in the Niger Delta that arose at the height of frustrations over the inability of the state to protect the communities from the ravages of environmental degradation, increased immiseration and the high-handedness of the oil multinationals, or to provide the expected political, social and economic benefits, were mostly ethnic-based and led by youths whose takeover amounted to a form of generational revolution. The movements mobilized support on the basis of mixed strategies of retribalization, sensitization and advocacy. But the most common justification for the existence of the social movements, and the basis of their coherence, is the struggle for rights. So what exactly was this about? What forms did the struggle take, and what rights were demanded?

The rights framework and the future

The emergence of new social movements in the Niger Delta reinforces the thesis that struggles for human rights are fundamental to the evolution and coherence of such movements. Simply stated, situations of structural inequality, injustice, marginalization and exclusion are conducive to the emergence of social movements, which then seek to employ the instrument of rights in the struggle to right wrongs and injustices. The extent to which this can be done becomes a function of the appropriateness of the rights demanded, and not so much of the blood and costs of the struggles. In this concluding section, we shall discuss the rights framework of the Niger Delta struggles and attempt a prognosis of what the outcomes are likely to be.

The framework for the post-1980s rights struggles in the Niger Delta was largely shaped by the Ogoni Bill of Rights, which MOSOP presented to the then federal military government in 1990. The bill touches on virtually every aspect of what has come to be known as the Niger Delta question and summarizes the rights demanded in three major categories. The first comprises what I have described elsewhere as *survival, equity* and *self-determination* rights: rights to culture, language, religion and political autonomy to participate as a distinct and separate unit within the Nigerian federation (Osaghae 2004). Second, the bill demands the right to a fair share of economic resources derived from Ogoniland. This was the precursor to the key demand in all subsequent charters and bills for the right to control resources in the Delta region. Resource control has also sometimes been closely tied (almost as a back-up option) to an increase in the proportion of federal revenue allocated on the basis of derivation. The third category consists of demands for the protection of the oil-producing environment from further degradation, as well as lump-sum compensation from the oil companies for pollution, gas flaring, the decimation of fishing and farming activities, and other hazards and suffering over the years.

The Ogoni Bill of Rights opened the floodgates to bills, declarations and charters by several other groups, along basically similar lines. Most notable among these were the Kaiama Declaration of the Ijaw People, the Aklaba Declaration of the Egi People, the Oron Bill of Rights and the Urhobo Economic Summit Resolutions. Even the alliances initiated by state governments, political parties and politicians were on the same lines. Thus, for example, the South-South People's Assembly (SSPA) adopted the Calabar Declaration in November 2004 as the 'unassailable roadmap to the fundamental quest of our people for freedom, justice, equity and economic emancipation'. The youth wing of the SSPA did the same in its fifteen-point charter of demands entitled 'This is our stand'.

To be sure, the rights framework bears the imprint of the perceptions of deprivation, neglect, poverty, underdevelopment, injustice and marginalization that provided the antecedents to the rise of the new social movements. As summarized by Ogbogbo (2003: 84), the human rights factors crystallized around three basic issues: the ownership and control of the resources within the Niger Delta region; environmental degradation arising from oil exploration and exploitation; and the reactions of the government and the oil multinationals to the protests and agitation of the host communities.

But the question is: are the rights demanded appropriate and capable of redressing the rights deficits and chronic developmental problems of the Niger Delta – such that the struggles could really be deemed to have been successful? Let us begin with the conception of freedom, which is essentially collectivist and says little or nothing about the freedom of the individual. To the extent that the crisis in the Niger Delta is as much a crisis of governance as it is of politics, the need to guarantee the basic civil and political rights of individuals to enable them to participate in the political process cannot be overemphasized. Indeed, one of the outcomes of successful mobilization by social movements, as the experience of South Africa shows very well, is the acute politicization of the community. How can those who lead social 'revolutions' hope to renegotiate citizenship without individual rights? Related to this is the fact that the bills, declarations and charters are rather silent on the social and economic rights that are necessary for the empowerment of ordinary citizens. In particular, there is no clear effort to address poverty, which is by far the most formidable obstacle to democracy and development. Assuming the oil majors change their orientation and begin to address local issues of development, how would equity and justice be assured at the individual level? The social movements would have failed if the rights revolution that is expected to follow the struggles does not address these questions.

The other point relates to the fact that the rights demanded are highly political and basically federalist in nature. This is true of political and fiscal autonomy, which includes the demand for resource control. The realization that this demand cannot be met without a fundamental re-structuring of the country's highly centralized federal system has led, logically, to demands for true federalism.

Two problems arise here. One is that the social movements and other claimants have failed to see – or have chosen to overlook – the complicity of state (and local) governments in the Niger Delta crisis. State governments are as guilty as the federal government and oil majors of the under-development of the Niger Delta, and the question of their responsibility has to be made an integral part of the clamour for true federalism. The second problem, which involves a much more difficult bargain, is that an emphasis on true federalism and resource control would most likely give prominence to formal sector and government representatives. What would then become of the social movements? They would either get co-opted, which is already beginning to happen, or they would have to articulate a different agenda for continued struggle.

Notes

1 In relation to non-discrimination, for instance, it has been pointed out that 'the principle of non-discrimination itself contains a group reference. Even the assertion that no one must be disadvantaged on account of his/her social identity draws attention to collective community identities and group membership' (Mahajan 1998: 156).

2 Ibeanu (2000: 4) describes the Niger Delta as 'an easily disequilibrated environment' that suffers from 'a serious scarcity of arable land and fresh water', among other things.

3 Some corroboration of the alleged discrimination is found in the accounts of a German explorer who visited the Niger Delta in the 1880s and found, among other things, that Kru men from Accra had preferential employment and were paid higher salaries than the indigenes in Brass and Akassa. (See Staudinger 1990.)

4 In April 2005 a front-line NGO in the Niger Delta, Environmental Rights Action (ERA), raised the alarm about the high levels of carcinogens in the region and the attendant high risks of skin, lung, breast and abdominal cancer. ERA referred to findings by the Faculty of Pharmacy at the University of Lagos and reported in the *Nigerian Quarterly Journal of Medicine* (2004), which showed that the toxic materials discharged by oil companies into the Niger Delta waters were the main sources of the carcinogens. See Vanguard (2005).

5 As documented by Ikelegbe (2001b: 441–2), major alliances that were formed in the 1990s included the following: the Conference of Traditional Rulers of Oil Producing States, the Organization for the Restoration of Actual Rights of Oil Communities, the Concerned Youths of Oil Producing States, the National

Association of Oil Mineral Producing Communities, the Ethnic Minority Rights Organization of Nigeria, the Niger Delta Peoples Movement for Self-Determination and Environmental Protection, the Movement for the Protection and Survival of Oil, the Mineral and Natural Gas Producing Communities of Nigeria, the Association of Minority Oil States, the Delta Oil Producing Communities Association, the Nigerian Society for the Protection of the Environment, the Niger Delta Peace Project Committee, the Niger Delta Peace and Development Forum, the Pan-Niger Delta Revolutionary Militia and the Committee on Vital Environmental Resources. Others are the Chicoco Movement, Niger Delta Women for Justice, Niger Delta Professionals and the Union of Niger Delta. Since 1999, associations such as the South-South Forum, the South-South People's Conference and the South-South People's Assembly, which entail much looser, strategic conceptions of the Niger Delta and are mostly initiatives of state governments, political parties and politicians, have also emerged.

References

Boro, I. J. A. (1982) *The Twelve-Day Revolution*, Benin City: Idodo Umeh Publishers.

Chandra, A. (2000) *Human Rights and Conflict Resolution*, Delhi: Rajat Publications.

Cohen, J. (1985) 'Strategy or identity: new theoretical paradigms and contemporary social movements', *Social Research*, 52(4).

ERA (2000) *The Emperor Has No Clothes: Report of the Conference on the Peoples of the Niger Delta and the 1999 Constitution, Port Har-*court, 2–4 November 1999, Benin City: ERA/Friends of the Earth.

Galtung, J. (1996) *Peace by Peaceful Means: Peace and Conflict, Development and Civilization*, London: Sage.

Gurr, T. R. (1993) *Minorities at Risk*, Washington, DC: Institute of Peace.

Haynes, J. (1997) *Democracy and Civil Society in the Third World: Politics and New Political Movements*, Cambridge: Polity Press.

Ibeanu, O. (2000) 'Oiling the friction: environmental conflict management in the Niger Delta', *Environmental Change and Security Project Report*, 6.

Ikelegbe, A. (2001a) 'The perverse manifestation of civil society: evidence from Nigeria', *Journal of Modern African Studies*, 39(1).

— (2001b) 'Civil society, oil and conflict in the Niger Delta region of Nigeria: ramifications of civil society for a regional resource struggle', *Journal of Modern African Studies*, 39(3).

Mahajan, G. (1998) *Identities and Rights: Aspects of Liberal Democracy in India*, Delhi: Oxford University Press.

Medearis, J. (2005) 'Social movements and deliberative democratic theory', *British Journal of Political Science*, 53(1).

Melucci, A. (1985) 'The symbolic challenge of contemporary movements', *Social Research*, 52(4).

Nolte, I. (2004) 'Identity and violence: the politics of youth in Ijebu-Remo, Nigeria', *Journal of Modern African Studies*, 42(1).

Obi, C. I. (2002) 'Ethnic minority agitation and the specter of national disintegration', in T. Falola (ed.), *Nigeria in the Twentieth Century*,

Durham, NC: Carolina Academic Press.

Ogbogbo, C. B. N. (2003) 'Human rights issues and the Niger Delta crisis', *Ibadan Law Journal*, 2(1).

Onwunaru, S. (2004) Interview in *The Punch*, Lagos, 5 April.

Osadolor, O. B. (2004) *The Niger Delta Question: Background to Constitutional Reform*, Programme on Ethnic and Federal Studies, University of Ibadan.

Osaghae, E. E. (1986) 'Do ethnic minorities still exist in Nigeria?', *Journal of Commonwealth and Comparative Politics*, 24(2).

— (1994) 'Introduction: between the individual and the state in Africa: the imperative of development', in E. Osaghae (ed.), *Between State and Civil Society in Africa*, Dakar: CODESRIA Books.

— (1995) 'The Ogoni uprising: oil politics, minority agitation, and the future of the Nigerian state', *African Affairs*, 94.

— (1996) 'Human rights and ethnic conflict management: the case of Nigeria', *Journal of Peace Research*, 33(2).

— (1998) 'Managing multiple minority problems in a divided society: the Nigerian experience', *Journal of Modern African Studies*, 36(1).

— (2001) 'From accommodation to self-determination: minority nationalism and the restructuring of the Nigerian state', *Nationalism and Ethnic Politics*, 7(1).

— (2003) 'Explaining the changing patterns of ethnic politics in Nigeria', *Nationalism and Ethnic Politics*, 9(3).

— (2004) 'Human rights and transition societies in western Africa', in S. Horowitz and A. Schnabel (eds), *Human Rights and Societies in Transition: Causes, Consequences, Responses*, Tokyo: United Nations University Press.

— (2005) 'Ethnicity and civil society in Africa', *Politeia*, 24(1).

Preboye, I. C. (2005) *The Core Delta: Iduwini Clan, Otounkuku 'The Lost Tribe'*, Ibadan: Rural Development Nigeria Ltd.

Sagay, I. (2005) 'Needs of the South-South in a federal set-up: why the South-South is aggrieved', *Vanguard*, Lagos, 23 April.

Sall, E. (2004) 'Social movements in the renegotiation of the basis for citizenship in West Africa', *Current Sociology*, 52(4).

Saro-Wiwa, K. (1992) *Genocide in Nigeria: The Ogoni Tragedy*, London: Saros International Pulishers.

Staudinger, P. (1990) *In the Heart of the Hausa States*, vol. 1, trans. J. E. Moody, Africa Series no. 56, Ohio: Ohio University Center for International Studies Monographs in International Studies.

Tarrow, S. (1998) *Power in Movement: Social Movements and Contentious Politics*, Cambridge: Cambridge University Press.

Touraine, A. (1985) 'An introduction to the study of New Social Movements', *Social Research*, 52(4).

Vanguard (2005) 'ERA urges government to declare Niger Delta a disaster zone', Lagos, 20 April.

Wignaraja, P. (ed.) (1993) *New Social Movements in the South*, London: Zed Books.

Willink, H., G. Hadow, P. Mason and J. B. Shearer (1958) *Report of the Commission Appointed to Enquire into the Fears of Minorities and the Means of Allaying Them*, London: HMSO.

3 | Why do garment workers in Bangladesh fail to mobilize?

SIMEEN MAHMUD

The failure of garment workers in Bangladesh to mobilize for their rights as workers and citizens in spite of the intense publicity generated by international campaigns, as well as the unusual visibility of the country's large female workforce, remains poorly understood.[1]

The 'resource mobilization' theory of social movement is premised on the existence of the rational 'active citizen' who would overcome the dilemma of participation and be motivated to become involved in collective struggle from self-interest if there were 'selective incentives' (rewards) and a collectivity of social relations and social life with a strong organizational base (Oberschall 1973; Olsen 1965). On the other hand, the 'political process' approach to analysing collective action explains mobilization primarily in relation to the external political and institutional context (the state), so that movements vary in their strategy, structure and outcomes under different political contexts (Tilly 1978; Tarrow 1998). Explanations of collective struggles and mobilizations have also been posed in terms of how the collective action is 'framed' or, in other words, how participants are convinced that their cause is just and important (Tarrow 1998).

While the above frameworks may provide an entry point for exploring mobilization or its absence in countries of the South such as Bangladesh, they cannot capture the entirety of the dynamics behind the political behaviour of citizens in these contexts, for instance the unwillingness of garment workers in Bangladesh to organize and mobilize in order to challenge the structure and the power base.

In Bangladesh research and policy attention on workers' rights and labour relations in the private sector and the informal economy have been scarce; most of the attention has been on labour relations in the formal economy and on public sector workers (Mondal 2002; Khan 2001). The development of informal labour relations within a formal production process is unique to export garment manufacturing and presents barriers to workers' mobilization and other accountability processes that are usually relied upon to safeguard labour rights in the formal sector. This uniqueness of the labour contract reduces the relevance of much of the existing theory on social mobilization in explaining the inability of garment workers to mobilize.

This chapter seeks to address the empirical question posed in the title from the perspective of garment workers themselves and other actors in the process. The analysis draws upon in-depth interviews with twenty garment workers and interviews with officials of the Department of Labour, officers of the Bangladesh Garment Manufacturers and Exporters Association (BGMEA) and staff of non-governmental organizations (NGOs) (the Bangladesh Legal Aid and Services Trust and Ain o Salish Kendra) that provide rights awareness and legal aid to garment workers, employers and factory managers. There were visits to garment factories in Dhaka and in the export processing zone (EPZ). The chapter also relies upon information collected from a survey of garment workers in 2002 in Dhaka and media reports, especially regarding worker struggles and mobilization, because the workers involved could not be found. (Many had returned to their village homes or had to move out to other areas and other jobs.)

The chapter is arranged as follows. The first section elaborates the institutional context for mobilization. The next section discusses the unique labour contract in export garment manufacturing. The two sections following discuss the role of workers' associations in garment workers' struggles for rights and describe the different types of protests that have evolved over time. The section after that assesses their cost for garment workers. In the final section the chapter tries to draw some conclusions.

The institutional context and political opportunity structures

Labour legislation in Bangladesh harks back to British times and much of it is obsolete and outdated.[2] After partition in 1947 some of these laws were adapted and twenty-five new laws were passed. Since independence from Pakistan in 1971, thirteen more labour laws have been promulgated (Mondal 2002). In manufacturing and industry, labour relations are currently governed by the Factories Act of 1965 and the Factories Rules of 1979, both of which are designed to protect labour and provide for safe and hygienic workplace conditions in fairly large factory situations. In other words, existing labour legislation and provisions primarily protect skilled and semi-skilled adult male workers who are represented by unions and collective bargaining associations, which in Bangladesh means the so-called privileged working class: mainly the urban, male workforce employed by the public sector and a tiny formal private sector found in financial services and larger-scale manufacturing. Labour legislation in Bangladesh not only excludes the majority of workers in Bangladesh; it also fails to protect those it does formally include.

Existing labour legislation is therefore inadequate to meet the requirements and challenges of a liberalizing economy that aspires to compete in a globalizing world using flexible and almost unregulated labour relations. In addition, since existing labour legislation assumes a predominantly male workforce, it is often at a loss to deal with the specific needs and concerns of the overwhelmingly female and unskilled workforce employed in garment manufacturing. This is even more critical in the export garment sector, where a highly flexible and fragmented production process exposes workers to new vulnerabilities in a new economic order that can limit even the autonomy of state action within national boundaries.

The blind eye of the state The Bangladesh government, both constitutionally and as signatory to various international conventions, is committed to protecting the rights of workers and ensuring non-exploitative and decent workplace conditions for all workers, whether in the formal or informal sector. Workers in Bangladesh, however, ranging from those in agriculture and in low-productivity cottage industries to those in non-traded service activities in the non-formal sectors, and even to garment factory workers, are exposed to exploitation and the violation of rights and remain unprotected by formal accountability processes. In this general context workers' rights in the export garment manufacturing sector have received relatively more attention internationally because the outsourcing of production processes has brought workers in the poorer countries of the South into direct competition with workers in the richer Northern countries and made the rights and standards that prevail in Southern countries of direct consequence to workers and consumers in the North (Mahmud and Kabeer 2007).

Although theoretically all workers in Bangladesh are supposed to be protected under existing labour legislation (in terms of the constitution), only a negligible fraction actually enjoy the protection of the state. For example, while the constitution of Bangladesh guarantees that the state will 'emancipate the toiling masses ... from all sorts of exploitation', the proportion of total workers protected by the existing legal framework is less than 3 per cent (Mondal 2002: 121). Although this legal framework provides for the fundamental right of all workers to freedom of association and collective bargaining, in reality the state is not able to ensure this right even for all its own employees in the public sector.[3] In fact, the protection of workers' rights in the private sector, including those of garment workers, is left to the assumed goodwill and good intentions of employers and to market forces. It is only the international gaze upon garment workers and the fact that their labour is directly instrumental in earning three-quarters of the country's foreign exchange earnings which have compelled the government to pay some attention to their plight. Other informal and private sector workers have not been that fortunate.

The peculiarity of the garment industry in Bangladesh means that the implementation of the existing labour code has had to be balanced between, on the one hand, allowing flexibility in the labour contract and mode of production for the sake of efficiency and competition (in global markets) and, on the other, ensuring adequate protection to workers. The government has not acted responsibly, however, and has not only neglected to protect the rights of workers, but has even exposed workers to new vulnerabilities by its failure to review and revise labour policies and practices in a timely fashion, while at the same time it has liberalized the economy and opened it up to foreign investment and for participation in global markets.[4] No adequate safeguards were instituted to protect labour employed in these new and flexible modes of production in a liberalized economy.

Only after the early 1990s did the government realize that many of the existing laws had lost currency and needed to be reviewed, although there were some that could still deliver if properly implemented. A new unified labour code drafted in 1994 emphasized the promotion of mutual trust and cooperation between workers and employers, covering both formal and informal sector workers, including garment factory workers. The process of drafting the new code was the responsibility of a high-powered government-appointed commission. The draft code was submitted to the government for approval in 1994, but is still pending cabinet approval to be placed before parliament for passing into law.

The bureaucratic inertia confronting the new labour code belied the official position that the government was under pressure to comply with ratified International Labour Organization standards and core conventions and was embarrassed by its inability to get employers to abide by labour legislation. The delay in approval indicated a lack of intent on the part of the state to put pressure upon garment factory owners to comply with national labour laws. The common perception is that state institutions and agencies, including the legal system and law enforcers, are biased towards protecting the rights of capital rather than the rights of labour.

Socio-economic context Perspectives on the rights of workers and acceptable labour standards are quite different in labour-surplus Bangladesh from those of Northern developed countries. This is because the vast majority of the workforce in Bangladesh are employed in agriculture, services and cottage industries: the informal or so-called 'unorganized' sectors, which are unrepresented by labour unions and remain outside the purview of formal processes of mobilization. Norms and practices with respect to labour relations and workplace conditions derive primarily from, and are bounded by, the reality of employer–worker relationships prevalent in informal casual employment (no written contract, no weekly holiday, no fringe benefits, etc.). Such norms and practices are openly followed by employers and unquestioningly accepted by workers as legitimate in the private manufacturing industry, including garment manufacturing. These practices – even those in direct contravention of international labour standards, such as the practice of employing children – are seen by employers and society at large as quite legitimate and are tacitly overlooked by weak state monitoring mechanisms. They are hardly likely to be challenged by workers, who are in any case generally not aware that they are entitled to rights and, even when they are, do not have the organizational capacity or bargaining power, what could be called social opportunity structures, to challenge employers.[5]

Standards set by national labour legislation, of which many employers may not be aware, seem unnecessary within the socio-economic reality of Bangladesh. Employers feel even less obliged, unless absolutely compelled, to comply with unfamiliar, sometimes unreasonable standards and regulations prescribed from outside that seem inappropriate and even irrelevant to the contemporary socio-economic context of Bangladesh.

It was this institutional context which saw the emergence of the export garment industry, with a new entrepreneurial class and a new workforce, engaged in new forms of production and under a flexible labour contract. To this we turn in the following section.

Garment manufacturing and the labour contract

The history of the garment manufacturing export industry in Bangladesh is quite remarkable. A traditional custom-made garment industry, working out of tailoring shops to service the domestic market, has existed in Bangladesh for a long time.[6] The breakthrough came when, in 1978, Noorul Quader of Desh Garments signed a five-year agreement with Daewoo Corporation of South Korea on technical and marketing cooperation for the production and export of apparel. Daewoo gave virtually free training to 130 Desh supervisors and managers at its state-of-the-art Pusan garment plant, the biggest in the world at the time. In return Daewoo would get 8 per cent marketing commission on all exports by Desh during the contract period. Desh's modern factory in Chittagong, the largest in Asia outside Korea at the time, went into operation in 1980, employing 600 workers in six production lines, with a capacity of 5 million pieces per year and a $1.3 million investment.

What happened after Desh was 'a story of leaks, unintended consequences, and increasing returns' (Easterly 2002: 147). The benefits of Daewoo's initial investment (in imparting knowledge and training) spread well beyond what Daewoo had intended or anyone had expected. The Desh workers and managers took with them what they had learnt about 'making shirts, selling shirts abroad, using special bonded warehouse systems, and using back-to-back import letters of credit' and started their own garment factories. Before the establishment of the Desh factory the return on an investment in a Bangladesh garment factory had been low. Once the industry got rolling, with leaked knowledge, the returns became high.

The number of plants rapidly multiplied, and the establishment of the BGMEA in 1982, to promote and protect the ready-made garment sector, was an indication that the sector had assumed the proportions of a full-fledged industry in just five years since its inception in 1977.[7] The number of factories rose from around fifty in the early 1980s to over three thousand in 1999, and employment reached 1.8 million workers, of whom 1.5 million were women. A direct consequence of the extremely rapid expansion of the sector[8] was that firms were not all equally proficient in bargaining with buyers and customer relations, with significant implications for the nature of the labour contract. In 1993, three-quarters of the firms were subcontracting out to smaller firms while more than half were subcontracting in, bound by tight production and delivery schedules.[9]

Evolution of the entrepreneur class The rapidly growing industry attracted a new type of entrepreneur – modern, smart, well educated, well travelled and able to deal with complicated banking requirements – different from the traders and merchants who had traditionally dominated the business class in Bangladesh. From the beginning the intention of garment producers – whether the pioneering East Asian firms trying to find ways around the MFA[10] in the late 1970s or the new generation of young Bangladeshi entrepreneurs who began as local suppliers for those firms, but eventually set up their own production factories in the mid-1980s – was to produce low-cost garments for the North American and European markets by employing labour as cheaply as possible. Garments were produced entirely from imported raw materials,[11] with the only local value addition coming from labour. There were no links with any local markets – only rejected items found their way into the domestic ready-made garment markets – nor were there any attempts to establish backward linkages in textiles or to develop indigenous raw materials sectors.

In other words, the sole purpose was to tap into the abundantly available low-skilled, low-cost workforce and take advantage of informal labour recruitment and workplace policies. The intention never was to develop garment manufacturing into a sustainable industry that had social obligations to its workforce. Thus employers felt no responsibility to look after the welfare of the workforce; in fact, such concerns did not feature at all in the factory owners' list of priorities. Their primary worry was that 'at the formative phase of their manufacturing businesses they could not be distracted by unreasonable workers' demands and unnecessary disruptions' (Khan 2001: 169). Unfortunately this attitude was quite entrenched and has largely persisted to the present.[12] Concepts of just and non-personal employer–worker relationships, and of giving workers a fair deal instead of exploiting them to extract the greatest surplus, are absent. Instead there is a sort of carry-over of the traditional clientelistic and paternalistic practices observed in the rest of the economy.

Employers are seen as willing to look after workers' basic survival needs so long as they remain loyal and subservient and do not disturb the production process, a perception shared by workers themselves, as aptly expressed by Jahanara, a female garment worker leader:

> The true character of the owners must be looked at here: whether they are real industrialists. Many of these people enter the industry in the hope of becoming millionaires overnight by taking bank loans and making quick money. ... They have not developed industrialist personalities. ... One cannot imagine how much abuse and mismanagement goes on in these factories. ... A true industrialist will talk to his workers to solve any problem. But they try to solve problems by hiring goons. The workers are always kept under pressure.

Evolution of the workforce Currently the export garment industry employs 1.8 million workers, of whom 1.5 million (83 per cent) are women. Within a span of a few years, the entrance of this predominantly female workforce into an otherwise male-dominated labour market dramatically changed the character of the urban manufacturing labour force.[13] Not only that, it 'feminized' the face of metropolitan Dhaka. The workforce consists primarily of young unmarried women from rural areas with a few years of schooling, who are not only first-time factory workers but workers in their first paid job. This is in stark contrast to the male predominance in the general workforce, where there are three male workers for every female worker (Labour Force Survey 2006–07).

In the social hierarchy, female garment workers are at the bottom of the ladder because of patriarchy and social norms that accord value and power on the basis of gender and age. Besides, before joining a factory these young women generally have almost no idea of factory work and the rules and regulations of factory employment, nor do they have any awareness of their legal rights as factory workers. This situation has remained more or less the same since the beginning.

As the sector becomes more competitive locally and internationally, however, employers increasingly demand a higher education level, so workers' level of education is rising, although this is also partly explained by the aggregate improvement in the school enrolment of girls in general. This increase in the level of workers' education may be contributing to a reduction in male–female wage differences and to the clear decline in sexual harassment faced by female workers in the work place (Mahmud and Ahmed 2005). It could also be linked to a change in the character of the workforce, with female workers being less likely to put up with some of the more extreme forms of abuse, such as physical violence on the shop floor and verbal abuse by management. The rise in education levels is also bringing about an increase in workers' knowledge of labour rights and provisions: garment workers in the EPZ factories who had more years of schooling than Dhaka garment workers were more likely to have heard of labour laws (Kabeer and Mahmud 2004: 102).

The increase in the education level of workers, however, has not been able to change their attitude and agency with respect to becoming organized and unionized; garment workers are still by and large reluctant to join trade and labour unions. They have a perception of themselves as workers who have to fend for themselves, as the following comments reveal. Rahima, a female machine operator, said, 'I was ill for a week and couldn't go to work for two days. When I returned I had no job. I didn't get any help from anyone.' Yakub, a male machine operator and leader who had taken part in a protest in Pallabi, said, 'It is not possible to say who played what role, but it is true that there is nobody to speak in favour of the workers, all are in favour of the owner – the government, police, musclemen. The [workers'] federations also do not do anything at all.'

Since female workers see factory work as temporary work, that workforce also takes on an 'unprofessional' character.[14] Many have no long-term professional ambitions and do not regard garment work as a sustainable employment option for their future; they expect to work only until they get married or have a baby or leave because of the toll on their health. The majority of workers who leave garment factory work after some years will rejoin the labour force some time later, but usually self-employed, if they have managed some savings, or in domestic service, but rarely to return to their factory jobs. One survey found that over 90 per cent of workers had started out in garment factory work only in the immediately preceding five years, so there are hardly any long-term workers in the industry (ibid.).

Workers are confused and often do not understand the rules and regulations of factory work which employers strictly enforce to discipline workers – rules that are in contrast to the general casual nature of hiring and firing, and of fixing salary. Workers feel that they are being treated unfairly when such formal and unfamiliar rules are applied to them, confirming their perception of themselves as informal workers rather than formal factory workers who have to follow rules of appointment. Rahima was confused about why her salary was cut even when she had not been absent. 'If one is late for three days in a month, even for a minute, one day's salary is deducted.'

The lack of professionalism among workers is compounded by the 'unprofessional' conduct of managers, who openly prefer pretty young workers and are more likely to promote them instead of more experienced older workers who need to be paid higher salaries. The types of punishment meted out for minor offences also confirm this attitude. Female garment worker leaders and one male quality supervisor had the following comments.

Jahanara:

> The age of garment workers has not changed; it's the same as it was ten years ago. When they get older they are made to leave, and expert workers are thrown out to make space for new workers. ... It's easy to get a job in a garment factory. ... Another problem is that the manager or in-charge

Three

is more attentive to the pretty girls. Had I been prettier and taller I could have moved past the supervisor level.

Ahad, a male cutting supervisor and garment worker leader (relating an incident in his factory):

> A female worker was taking away a box of thread, so the guard caught her and cut her hair. Instead of cutting her hair in this way it would have been fair if the management would have terminated her from the job or given any other punishment. She may encounter lots of difficulty for this while walking in the streets. Imagine what her husband or other relatives might think about her.

Unequal employer–worker relationship In the conventional employer–worker model 'there are two sides engaged in economic activity – workers and employers – whose interests are different yet reconcilable' (Jenkins et al. 2002: 35). The two sides themselves resolve their differences, with the state performing a supervisory and monitoring role because individual workers lack power vis-à-vis employers. The main tool for conflict resolution is negotiation and collective bargaining, where workers' power comes from organization.

Workers and employers are locked into an interdependent relationship, but without being able to rely fully upon one another's good intentions. The interdependence arises because a temporary, unskilled and almost seasonal workforce has to be employed in the formal, highly time-bound, risky and financially complex activity of manufacturing products for export. As a result, both sides tend to make unilateral decisions and use non-negotiable threats rather than reconciliation to resolve differences and disputes. Employers use constant threats of firing, laying off or withholding salaries and overtime payment to impose highly oppressive, even demeaning rules (such as not taking too long in the toilet or submitting to body searches when leaving the factory) – rules aimed at maintaining a smoothly running production process and keeping costs as low as possible with night work, long hours and no weekly holiday.

Workers, on the other hand, move from one factory to another when they find themselves caught up by rules they cannot adhere to – such as when they overstay leave or are late for work too frequently – or even for slightly higher wages, and may even use the threat of leaving to strike a better deal with management. The easy entry and exit and highly informal and very personalized recruitment policy contribute to this situation, with both sides taking advantage of it.

The MD of a medium-sized factory in the middle of Dhaka city, when asked why workers do not like to work under rules and change factories frequently, commented:

> Actually they [the workers] don't like to work under any rules. They work for some days, if they need to go home they leave without any notice and come back to join another factory. ... It's like a habit. They are young and a bit independent; they have no family members to control them.

The extreme informality of the employer–worker relationship has been justified on the grounds that flexible labour and informal employment conditions are necessary given the fragmented production process. At the same time, however, a well-controlled and well-behaved workforce is essential to meet shipment deadlines, so employers are 'inflexible' about shop-floor discipline and strictly implement rules to manage workers.

From the outset most ready-made garment factory owners tried their best to keep the factory units as informalized as possible because that would provide them with greater flexibility in terms of labour management, unit production and working hours without significant social obligation to their workforce. Any kind of unionization, including in-house unions, was also perceived as undesirable (Khan 2001: 169).

Even the workplace itself has an informal appearance very unlike a modern manufacturing unit, since the factories are generally not purpose built. In the majority of cases the 'factory' is a converted residential or office building, lacking the facilities required for workplace safety and hygiene and the very basic amenities for a healthy work environment prescribed under the factory rules. Even today there are numerous factories located in the middle of residential areas, housed in small multi-storey buildings with an entrance opening directly on to a busy road, a narrow staircase, inadequate toilets, no place to eat lunch, and extremely crowded machine rooms, as evident in a remark from Rahima: 'There are no facilities to eat here or keep one's children. We eat where we work, sometimes we would eat on the stairs, sometimes on the roof.'

Missing 'cultures of accountability' Employers do not feel strongly compelled to refrain from violating workers' rights or to comply with basic legislation. This is not only because of state negligence and weak supervisory structures and processes, but also because of the lack of a 'culture of accountability' that permeates society. The implicit assumption by government that the protection of workers' rights in the private sector can be left to the 'goodwill' and 'good intentions' of employers has no basis. On the contrary, employers see workers almost as bonded labour, locked in a totally dependent relationship, to whom they are not answerable; their only obligation is to provide their minimum needs for survival. The mindset arising from the long-entrenched patron–client relations governing nearly all social and economic relationships in rural areas, where most informal private sector workers and all garment workers originate, and in urban slum areas, where they all live, has not entirely disappeared, despite the fact that Bangladesh has entered the global market and is rapidly modernizing.[15] Employers and management believe that 'happy' workers are an indication that workers' welfare is ensured; there is no need for any trade unions in the factory if workers are satisfied with the terms and conditions. As the MD of a textile factory in the EPZ said, 'Workers are very happy here; they are well looked after so there is no migration. Workers are not interested in joining unions.'

Codes of conduct imposed by foreign buyers are seen only as necessary conditions that must be met in order to stay in business, rather than as the fulfilment of employers' obligations to provide workers with a fair deal and exploitation-free working conditions. The MD of a large compliant factory in Dhaka city said, 'In the beginning it was beyond the imagination of factory owners to provide such facilities for the workers. But now owners believe that without compliance it is not possible to stay in this highly competitive business. So there is no alternative.'

Some of the comments from factory managers indicate that employers see workers as 'undisciplined' (not wanting to abide by rules and regulations) and as 'unprofessional' (leaving as soon as they get a higher wage in another factory); hence they do not need to be treated as a workforce with rights and having a claim to formal workplace conditions. An illustration of this perception can be found in the comment of an MD and partner of a medium-sized factory in Dhaka city, who said, 'I know of factories where workers are given all kinds of facilities, but even then workers leave if they get slightly higher pay. Some workers have a habit of changing.'

The hand of factory owners is strengthened by the fact that poor unskilled women, who make up the majority of the workforce, have in any case few alternatives and even fewer better employment opportunities.[16] Employers prefer female workers not only because they are cheaper and abundantly available, but also because they are more vulnerable, docile and manageable than male workers. They accept without protest the flexible terms of employment (being prepared to work extra hours when needed and easier to lay off when not) and are also thought less likely

71

to be organized or susceptible to 'anti-management propaganda from outside' (Khan 2001). Besides, women workers have more at stake if they lose their jobs. Maya summarizes the most common reason for female workers to accept these working conditions: 'Because I work here now we can live and eat regularly and take care of our children. If I can't work what will we eat and where will we live?'

Next we turn to the framing of the collective struggle and why it has bypassed garment workers in Bangladesh.

Workers' associations: framing the collective struggle

Garment workers have been left largely unorganized and unrepresented by trade and labour unions. There are about fourteen federations of garment workers' unions in the country, but many of them exist in name only and are not registered with the Directorate of Labour (ibid.). This is seen as evidence both of corrupt practices by officials of the Registrar of Trade Unions and the Inspector of Factories and Establishments and of the non-functionality of most federations. Even the ones that are functional operate largely as mediators in disputes and are not very strong in mobilizing workers. Although the negative attitude of the employers towards unionism is partly responsible, the non-functionality of workers' unions contributes to the fact that most of the garment factories in Bangladesh are not unionized (ibid.).

Some workers' organizations, however, have tried to bypass and manoeuvre around factory owners' aversion to unionization in order to motivate workers to organize. One such union is BIGUF, the Bangladesh Independent Garment Workers Union Federation. Four female garment workers who worked together and were frustrated with the work of other federations, having had very negative experiences with them, founded this union in 1994. With the help of an international agency, they started their work with a general convention.

Jahanara:

> It is very difficult to organize garment workers as trade unions are not allowed. If the owner finds out that a worker is involved in an organization then s/he is fired. At first we tried to form unions in a few factories. Most workers gave us support, but that did not work. ... So next we quickly started organizing workers through local committees in areas where there were many factories, we talked to them about their rights. So now if any worker is fired she herself will contact one of our workers in the area and come to our office. Then we help them to solve the problem.

... If workers are not paid their salaries for many months we ask workers to strike and ask for their pay within a fixed date. We bargain with the owners only if a strike has been called and if police and the goons are threatening the workers. ... Sometimes we show the owner that we are forming workers' welfare committee in order to help the workers.

There are a few federations (Garment Workers Unity Forum, Bangladesh Garment Workers Unity Council and National Garment Workers Federation) that are involved with the BGMEA arbitration cell and in a limited way in organizing workers outside factory premises. Khan (ibid.) found that ever since various restrictions against their activities were imposed, the existing active federations have succeeded in providing legal and advisory support to the workers at times of crisis. The workers usually seek their help in times of unlawful dismissals, disputes with management or lay-offs. In some cases federations even extend financial help to the workers. The federations also educate the workers regarding their rights through workshops and group discussions. As a result, the workers are, over time, becoming more aware regarding their rights and they are increasingly participating in unions.

The negative attitudes of the employers towards unionism make it very difficult for the federations to form their units in various factories and to maintain regular contacts after the formation of unit unions. Thus the federations have limited support or contact with the respective unit levels. Federation members have to meet the members of the units during lunch break or on holidays. They always fear action by management against such activities.

On the other hand, traditional trade unions suffer from a lack of credibility in mobilizing garment workers. In many cases the political parties use them: the union leaders work with the political leaders for their self-interest and ignore the broad issues of workers' rights, and this ultimately destroys the unity among the workers. Workers have no faith in trade union leaders and do not seem to trust them, as leaders have often let them down and even sided with management on occasion, thus undermining workers' movements. Workers also complain that TU leaders only come to their support when there is a movement or agitation, but not at other times or to deal with more routine matters.

Factory owners and management justify their negative attitude by arguing that unionization creates special problems in garment manufacturing because of the highly labour-intensive production process, in which a single item can depend upon the labour of as many as 150 workers.

73

Some of the bigger factories, however, are beginning to allow the formation of workers' welfare associations under pressure from buyers. These associations are often organized by NGOs rather than trade unions and usually with the active involvement of management, possibly to deter any outside influence from trade unions.

The MD of a medium-sized factory in Dhaka city:

> There is a workers' welfare association in the EPZ. It is not necessary outside the EPZ. Rather it creates more problems because many workers are not interested in working. Here devotion to the job is needed and workers come from various places; 150 workers are required to produce a [pair of] pant[s], so a lot of motivation is essential. The union in the EPZ is only at the pressure of the US government.

Very recently, workers' associations have been allowed in a limited manner in the country's EPZs owing to pressure by the US government and strong lobbying from the American trade union body AFL-CIO (American Federation of Labor and Congress of Industrial Organizations). Workers' membership of associations in factories outside the EPZ, however, remains negligible. A recent survey found that only 1 per cent of female workers reported having a workers' union in their factory, and the situation has not improved visibly since the early days of the industry (Kabeer and Mahmud 2004). Thus the struggles and mobilizations of garment workers that have taken place so far have been virtually without support, and often as a last resort, with little room for negotiation.

Workers' mobilizations and struggles: horizontal participation

In the mid-1980s, when the garment industry began to expand and factories started to crop up almost daily in the two main cities of Dhaka and Chittagong, large numbers of new workers were attracted from rural areas to join garment factories in the cities. Garment factory work was unlike any work on offer previously. Workers joining the industry had no first-hand or even second-hand experience of factory employment or any comprehension of what it entailed. At the time, workers' knowledge of labour rights and legal provisions was non-existent. Although awareness has increased with greater experience, knowledge is still very limited, even after two decades, especially among female workers. In a 2001 survey of female garment workers in Dhaka, the majority (82 per cent) had no knowledge of existing labour law in the country, and this is reflected in the following comments.

Asma, a female garment worker leader:

74

In 1984 [when knowledge of the minimum wage was negligible] several NGOs got together and brought out a leaflet on workers' rights and minimum wage. But now [even after so many years] at this stage 30 per cent of female workers still don't know the minimum wage.

Ahad:

In my present factory most of the workers here are women, they know little as they come from the village and have little education. Considering this I tell them that you have this and that right and must agitate for those rights.

The proportion of female wage workers in other sectors of the urban economy who had ever heard of labour laws was a mere 3 per cent, however, indicating that garment workers were more likely to have heard of labour laws than the rest of the informal female workforce (ibid.). Indeed, workers who have been in a factory job for a few years have been able to gain information about labour laws and provisions, sometimes from other workers and sometimes from NGO activists.

Hashi, a machine operator, said, 'I know some rules and regulations of garment factories. I live with workers from different factories. When we chat I can find out various information, like maternity leave should be for three months, we are meant to work eight-hour days.' Maya learnt about benefits with time. 'I didn't know about women's special benefits then as I was new. But now I know that we are entitled to three months' maternity leave with salary. We also get annual leave and increment.'

The elastic supply of labour for the garment industry has created a sense of vulnerability among workers. Consequently they are afraid of doing anything that jeopardizes their jobs, and organizing to improve their bargaining position vis-à-vis employers is the last thing on the minds of most workers. As Asma said, 'Workers are afraid to form organizations because the owners throw them out immediately.' Jahanara elaborated, 'The big sweater factories do not allow trade unions to form. Workers can be fired any time. The owners consider it an audacity if they even ask for their salaries. There's no accounting for the number of workers fired every day.'

How has the capacity to mobilize evolved over time? Various types of workers' struggles and mobilizations have been gathering momentum since the early 1990s. Protests are generally mobilized around the issue of wages and overtime, and rarely around workplace conditions, since,

75

as the workers themselves say, getting paid their wages on time is the biggest problem for garment workers. Consequently workers have not protested to the extent expected around issues of workplace safety, despite the fact that factory fires have almost become routine and have claimed many lives.

In addition, only the most extreme struggles and protests that have spilt out into the streets have been visible. Over time these visible mobilizations have increased in frequency and in their level of violence. The more silent and less visible mobilizations also taking place on the shop floors must be much more significant in terms of number of workers and frequency. In all cases workers use such outbursts and protests only as a last resort, having put up with unfair and exploitative treatment for a long time before deciding to take action, because the costs of such action can be quite high.

With maturity and experience has come some development in workers' negotiating skills. This maturity also arises from the changing perception of garment work as necessary for the family's survival and well-being. More value is accorded to garment work than before, both by workers themselves and by others. There is an increasing realization among workers of the need to mobilize and organize in order to protect their jobs, protest against unfair treatment and hold employers to account.

Maya:

I'll go and say [to the production manager] 'give me leave or I'll quit my job'. Then he will give me leave. But those who are new and can't speak up don't get leave. ... It has been written down in the books that basic salary should be 930 [taka; Tk], but in reality people get only Tk600. They add rent and conveyance and show it as Tk930. None of the [other] rules are followed. ... We have not protested this, or talked to anyone. It won't work if I do this [protest] alone, everyone has to do it.

Jahanara:

Earlier it used to be much more difficult to make the workers understand about different issues. They would ask many questions. But now they understand the importance of organizations; when a worker loses their job but eventually gets it by filing a case through the labour court they stand to gain much. ... Now they understand about the ILO convention and the law, and ask for information.

Yakub, however, holds that, 'If all the workers work together against injustices and deprivations that take place here then the owner is bound to fulfil our demands. But I don't see a person who can unite the workers.'

What different kinds of struggles have there been? The current employer–worker situation is precarious and unstable, relying as it does upon an unfair balance of power; hence it is liable to degenerate into labour unrest and industrial disputes. In fact, industrial and labour management relations began to worsen in the early 1990s, and the dismal factory situation became apparent when the frequency of assaults on management, *gheraos* (a South Asian form of protest action) and strikes, demonstrations, work stoppages, protests and lay-offs increased. This was evident from reports in various newspapers, which appeared to be the only champions of the workers at that time (Khan 2001: 171).

Visible struggles In situations of extreme and prolonged violation of rights primarily related to the delay or non-payment of wages and overtime dues, protests spill on to the streets. Such visible struggles are usually led by male workers who have been factory workers for some time and have larger salary arrears, and hence a greater stake in the protest. Protests are usually planned for some time in secrecy, as managers fire anyone they suspect of creating a disturbance. It often requires very drastic action by the owners or management, such as beating up a worker or closing the entrance gate, to spark off an outburst that unites all the workers and moves off the factory floor.

Yakub explains what provoked a street protest in Pallabi:

The movement had begun for many reasons; however, payment of arrears was the main reason. Some of the older workers were not getting their salaries for several months. Basically, they were the front-runners in this movement. All these issues used to be discussed with us secretly. But we were unable to understand much since we were newcomers. ... The discussion among the workers was going on that no one would join the duty tomorrow. ... The next day, although all were waiting outside the gate, none were allowed to join their duty. At that time the clamour began when all the workers tried to enter together by breaking the factory gate. The owner informed police and when police started beating the workers many were injured. All the workers came down to the street, even those who were unaware. Basically at that time all the workers became united.

Trade union leaders are usually not directly involved in this process, but may provide guidance to workers' leaders from outside. They are not present when the planning is done or even when the protest begins, but may join the workers later in the street processions. As Yakub said, 'The workers stayed in the street the whole day. Later the labour leaders joined them and they all brought out processions. The leaders had a meeting with the owners.'

Trade union leaders also have a role in the negotiations with management to strike deals that will bring the workers back to work. The story of one male machine operator suggests that usually these deals fall short and fail to deliver what was negotiated.

When Jalil, a male machine operator, asked the manager when he would pay their overtime bills, which had not been paid for the preceding two months, the manager, instead of answering, picked a quarrel, asking Jalil why his fingers were dirty. He struck Jalil on the head with a light tube and then beat him with a stick. Hearing Jalil's cry and finding him bleeding, around fifty workers, including women, stormed into the manager's office, beat him with light tubes and ransacked the room. The workers rushed out of the building, hitting the security guards and shoving them aside, and blocked the main road, yelling slogans against the manager and demanding their dues, until police dispersed them after a couple of hours. The factory management later fixed dates for settling the workers' dues in phases. A few days earlier, around nine hundred employees had taken part in a strike demanding their overdue pay, and on that occasion the manager had persuaded them to terminate the strike on the assurance that what they were due would be paid on 4 September, the day before this incident (Daily Star 2004a).

Spontaneous protests on the factory premises and shop floor There are less visible and less confrontational struggles on the shop floor, in which some workers get together more or less spontaneously to lodge a protest with the factory management. In most cases these are also led by experienced male workers, who are seen as physically stronger and able to use force if necessary. Women workers may not lead, but do join in the agitation.

Siraj, a male quality controller:

> The wages in Narayanganj [a town neighbouring Dhaka] factories were always lower, but we still used to work there because they paid us on time. We went straight to the GM [general manager] and asked for a raise, but he said if we don't improve the quality of our work then our salaries would go down … there was one among us who then mobilized

us to agitate; later nineteen of us joined. He had no links with politics, nor did we have any connections with anyone outside. ... We started the agitation ourselves and our only intention was to raise our rates and salaries. ... The owner used his [security] force to threaten and scare us, but because we stuck together they could not do anything to us. After everyone stopped working the news spread and the workers' union leaders came to assess the situation. They told us they would help if we wanted. Then the authorities accepted all our demands and an agreement was made on the ninth day and the union leader signed the agreement on our behalf. Even after all this we were supposed to get attendance bonus, but don't.

Maya:

When I first joined I was told I would not have night duty, but afterwards I had to do night duty. When I first started night duty I would get Tk50 daily, later that became Tk40. We were not paid regularly for the night work. The manager tried to pacify us by saying we would get our night duty payment today or tomorrow, but the boys didn't listen. The manager then went to the MD for the night bill but the MD called him unfit, at which the manager came back and told the boys off. The boys then came to the second floor with the knitting instruments and brought out the 'finishing' girls, and went and beat up the MD. As a result we got our attendance fees.

Individual protests Finally, individual action by workers is also increasingly being used to protest unfair treatment, bargain for higher wages or demand late wages and overtime payments. The individual protests usually have less impact than shop-floor protests. Older and more experienced workers who have more self-confidence and have learnt some negotiating skills are generally the ones who resort to individual action. With luck, workers can use the threat of leaving to strike individual deals with factory management. Such action, however, may be quite costly for a worker, since it is quite easy for management to fire one worker without too much of a disturbing effect on other workers. Hence only the most desperate workers or those who know they can easily find another job choose this option. Often, when conditions become too oppressive or there is no scope for bargaining, a worker simply leaves the job, either for good or to join another factory, as a sort of silent protest.

Ahad:

The authorities used to oppress the workers sometimes, therefore we used to protest. In one such situation ... I protested to the GM. After listening the GM called me and scolded me a lot. He told me, 'You provoke the workers, as a result our production has been wasted, and workers do not work, so the owner has asked that you do not join your duties.' I told him in that case they would have to give me a termination letter mentioning the reason for termination. He said I should come at the end of the month to collect my dues.

Yet frequent migration contributes to the difficulty of forming organizations or associations among workers. Migration, in the perception of both employers and workers, indicates a lack of permanence in the job. Frequent migration is also seen by employers as an 'unprofessional' attitude on the part of workers, which hampers any long-term training or skills upgrading or other kind of investment in increasing workers' welfare and improving workplace conditions.

The 'cost' of protest

The cost–benefit of such workers' struggles is difficult to assess. Garment worker leaders believe that workers' demands have been met, in part, as a result of their actions. Some factories now allow a weekly holiday and pay the minimum wage, grant limited maternity leave (though not the full three months) and so on. It is not clear, however, to what extent workers' movements have played a role in this, and to what extent it has been in response to the imposition of buyers' codes of conduct.

Ordinary workers, however, feel that not much has been achieved. They believe that things are just the same as before, since employers promise to meet workers' demands when a movement is active, but seldom keep their promise. In fact, after any protest or movement owners become stricter, if anything. After a strike by 900 workers at a factory in 2004 for the payment of overtime arrears, the manager promised them payment the following week. Instead of keeping his promise, however, the manager beat up a worker who had demanded his overtime payment (Daily Star 2004a).

Yakub:

At that time [of the movement] the owner told us that the factory will remain closed on Friday, but nothing happened. Many of those who were in the movement have lost their jobs. Therefore, we have to work in silence. We did not gain anything as such from that movement. Rather it became stricter now than it was before. There is no opportunity to argue. If you like to work then carry on; otherwise you are no more required.

Workers who participate in movements and agitation may have their salaries cut or may even be sacked. The costs are particularly high when there is violence and confrontation with police, and workers are punished by having criminal cases filed against them. As Jahanara reported, 'There's a factory in Mirpur that has filed a case against thirteen of its workers, four of them have been arrested. Their crime: they went to ask for their salaries.'

The *Daily Star* (2004b) reported a similar incident in Chittagong in October 2004.

> Seventy-two garment workers – all women – yesterday got bail in the police assault case filed in connection with Thursday's workers–police clash at Lagoon Garments Ltd in the port city's Bahodderhat area. The Court ... sent to jail custody 13 of their male colleagues arrested with them on Thursday. The clash took place as the workers agitated over three months' arrear wages. ... The clash left 30 people including 10 cops injured and two army vehicles damaged. ... A sub-inspector at Panchlaish Police Station filed a case accusing the workers of assaulting police. ... Meanwhile, Garments Mazdoor [workers'] Union yesterday condemned harassment, assault and arrest of the garments workers.

The sustainability of mobilization is undermined by the 'divide and rule' strategy of employers, which is very effective. Employers strongly suppress any agitation or movement for fear that this may spread and disrupt production. They do this by a variety of methods: sacking the more vocal workers, buying out leaders, placing their own agents among the workers to identify the 'troublemakers', hiring goons and *mastans* (gangsters) to beat up workers, and so on.

Besides, struggles are generally very hard to sustain because of the high costs workers have to pay and the negligible benefits they gain in return. The large surplus of female labour and the temporary nature of employment mean that workers have little personal interest in or incentive for joining trade unions. Asma:

> The workers don't even get time to form an organization. They have to work late every day and many don't even get weekly holiday. Only those who lose their jobs keep in touch with us [garment workers' federation]. As soon as we get them a job they stop coming because of lack of time.

The other barrier to workers' mobilization is the lack of unity among organizers and trade unions, which are highly politicized and oblige members to toe a particular political line.

81

Asma:

Garment factory owners have one organization, BGMEA. Organizations like ours [the National Garment Workers Federation] are thirty-six in number, but there is no solidarity. Because of this there are no powerful movements taking place. Even some of the leaders take bribes from owners.

On the other hand, trade unions claim that workers do not really understand the true nature of trade unions and their role in protecting workers' rights. One trade union leader, Wajid Ali Khan of the Bangladesh Trade Union Centre, lamented the fact as follows:

> It is very difficult to organize garment workers as trade unions are not [tolerated]. If the owner finds out that a worker is involved they are fired. When we first tried to form unions in a few factories most workers gave us support. But once the owner finds out the situation reaches almost bloodshedding levels. First they try to buy off the workers. When that doesn't work they resort to violence. Unions can't be forced, they won't survive. When workers start losing their jobs they begin to misunderstand the essence of a trade union.

Conclusions

As the workers' stories have demonstrated, there are formidable barriers preventing the mobilization of Bangladesh garment workers to claim their rights and challenge the power of employers to make unilateral decisions regarding the labour contract and workplace conditions. These barriers span the cultural, social and economic spheres of the lives of the working poor of Bangladesh, and do not fit neatly into existing theoretical prescriptions.

While the 'indivisibility' of rights, according to which each right is essential to the realization of the others (as opposed to the 'hierarchy' of rights), is clearly evident, it is equally evident that the realization of certain rights may have to be prioritized rather than all rights being simultaneously pursued (Kabeer 2005b: 16). Thus, in mobilizing garment workers, economic and social rights (the right to fair wages, decent workplace conditions, paid leave and maternity leave, the right to personal security, the right to education and information, and so on) may have to precede more 'fundamental' political rights, such as the right to association and the right to collective bargaining, in order to transform workers from 'commodities' into citizens.

The difficulty of the 'crystallization of a collective conscience' in the South has been recognized (Oommen 2004: 216) and is clearly evident in this case. Creating the collective conscience and building among garment workers the solidarity that is essential for collective action and struggle of any kind are constrained by their narrowly defined community, which is restricted to their immediate circle of family, kin and neighbours. The extremely resilient social structures operating in the Bangladeshi society and economy (clientelist attitudes and the absence of a culture of accountability) have reproduced themselves in the factory, preventing the emergence of horizontal solidarities that could be used for mobilization. This lack of what might be termed social opportunity structures inhibits effective mobilization and the formation of strong social movements.

The problem of the poverty of garment workers is not simply a lack of material resources, which makes them highly risk-averse, but a lack of voice, agency and organization as embedded in hierarchical social and economic relationships. In this situation, there has not been a purposive construction and nurturing of social relations that reflect horizontal alliances to replace the need for patron–client types of alliances and to confront non-accountable institutions. A critical need remains, in situations like this, for external catalysts to overcome this lack of the aspiration, agency and organization necessary to forge solidarity for collective action and struggle (Kabeer 2005a). Unfortunately, the process of transition to 'democracy' in Bangladesh, a process spanning one and a half decades, has failed to touch unorganized workers, including garment workers, in their struggle for recognition as workers and citizens of a 'democratic' state.

Notes

1 The Bangladesh export garment industry employs over two million workers, of whom three-quarters are women, representing a rapid 'feminization' of the urban labour force within a span of a few years. The proportion of women in the manufacturing workforce rose from around 4 per cent in 1974 to 55 per cent by 1984/85, while urban female labour force participation generally rose from around 12 per cent from the mid-1980s to 26 per cent by the late 1990s (Kabeer and Mahmud 2004).

2 Bangladesh has fifty-one labour laws, of which thirteen originated in British India.

3 Trade union membership accounts for less than 3 per cent of the workforce and only a third of regular formal employees (Mondal 2002: 128).

4 In order to attract foreign investment and allow entrepreneurs to compete in global product markets, the government facilitated capital and investment by adopting and introducing several innovative

83

policy tools (bonded warehouses, back-to-back letters of credit, tax concessions, etc.).

5 The relatively successful, though still debated, elimination of child labour from the garment sector came about only through persistent pressure from the United States government, leading to a memorandum of understanding between employers and NGOs. Child labour continues to be used in other sectors, however.

6 The most common clothing worn by Bangladeshis, the lungi and the sari, do not need stitching.

7 The BGMEA was established in 1977 to protect the interests of a very large number of diverse and heterogeneous garment producers and exporters vis-à-vis the government and financial agencies as well as foreign buyers.

8 During the 1990s the ready-made garment sector grew at the compound rate of 15 per cent per year, which is exceptional by any standards for any industry worldwide (Bhattacharya and Rahman 2000: 2–3). From relatively low levels (about $1 million) in the late 1970s, ready-made garment and apparel exports from Bangladesh grew to over $4 million in 1999.

9 Larger firms send their own supervisors and managers to monitor quality in the smaller firms to which they subcontract.

10 The USA, Canada and several western European countries used the MFA in an attempt to protect their domestic garment industries from the onslaught of cheap imports of garments from the developing countries, mainly in East Asia.

11 This has changed over time and currently about 80 per cent of

accessories (trims and labels) are produced locally.

12 Exceptions are some big factories such as Bantai and Voyager that provide many facilities but still no right of association, according to interviews with a female garment worker leader and with the managing director (MD) of a large compliant factory.

13 The percentage of working women in manufacturing rose from around 4 per cent in 1974 to 55 per cent in 1984/85, while urban female labour force participation rates rose from around 12 per cent in 1883/84 to 26 per cent in 1999/2000 (Kabeer and Mahmud 2004).

14 Two-thirds of garment workers in Dhaka reported themselves as temporary workers (Kabeer and Mahmud 2004).

15 Bangladesh is becoming increasingly urbanized, with growing use of the Internet and mobile phones and stronger links with the rest of the world.

16 Women have a higher propensity than men to be employed in informal and unorganized economic activity (85 per cent for the female labour force compared to 75 per cent for the entire labour force).

References

Amin, A. M. and A. Hussain (2004) 'Another garment factory tragedy: could it have been averted?', *Star Weekend Magazine*, 21 May, www.thedailystar.net/magazine/2004/05/03/coverstory.htm, accessed 12 February 2009.

Bhattacharya, D. and M. Rahman (2000) 'Bangladesh's apparel sector: growth trends and the post-MFA challenges', *Proceedings of a National Seminar on Growth of*

Garment Industry in Bangladesh: Economic and Social Dimensions, Dhaka: BIDS and Oxfam Bangladesh.

Daily Star (2004a) 'Twenty injured as garment workers go on rampage over dues', 5 September, www.thedailystar.net/2004/09/05/d40905011010.htm, accessed 12 February 2009.

— (2004b) 'Woman arrestees get bail, male colleagues sent to jail', 30 October, www.thedailystar.net/2004/10/30/d41030012221.htm, accessed 12 February 2009.

Easterly, W. (2002) *The Elusive Quest for Growth: Economists' Adventures and Misadventures in the Tropics*, Cambridge, MA, and London: MIT Press.

Jenkins, R., R. Pearson and G. Seyfang (2002) *Corporate Responsibility and Labour Rights: Codes of Conduct in the Global Economy*, London and Sterling, VA: Earthscan.

Kabeer, N. (2005a) 'Growing citizenship from the grassroots: Nijera Kori and social mobilization in Bangladesh', in N. Kabeer (ed.), *Inclusive Citizenship*, London and New York: Zed Books.

— (2005b) 'The search for inclusive citizenship: meanings and expressions in an interconnected world', in N. Kabeer (ed.), *Inclusive Citizenship*, London and New York: Zed Books.

Kabeer, N. and S. Mahmud (2004) 'Globalization, gender and poverty: Bangladeshi women workers in export and local markets', *Journal of International Development*, 16(1): 93–109.

Khan, S. I. (2001) 'Gender issues and the readymade garment industry of Bangladesh: the trade union context', in R. Sobhan and N.

Khundker (eds), *Globalization and Gender: Changing Patterns of Women's Employment in Bangladesh*, Dhaka: University Press Ltd.

Labour Force Survey (2006–07) Government publication, 2007.

Mahmud, S. (2003) 'Is Bangladesh experiencing a feminization of the labour force?', *Bangladesh Development Studies*, XXIX(1/2).

Mahmud, S. and N. Ahmed (2005) 'Accountability for workers' rights in the export garment sector in Bangladesh', Draft, Dhaka: Bangladesh Institute of Development Studies (BIDS).

Mahmud, S. and N. Kabeer (2007) 'Compliance versus accountability: struggles for dignity and daily bread in the Bangladesh garment industry', in P. Newell and J. Wheeler (eds), *Rights, Resources and the Politics of Accountability*, London and New York: Zed Books.

Mondal, A. H. (2002) 'Globalisation, industrial relations and labour policies: the need for renewed agenda', in M. Muqtada, A. Singh and M. A. Rashid (eds), *Bangladesh: Economic and Social Challenges of Globalisation*, Study prepared for the ILO, Geneva, Dhaka: University Press Ltd.

Oberschall, A. (1973) *Social Conflict and Social Movements*, Englewood Cliffs, NJ: Prentice-Hall.

Olsen, M. (1965) *The Logic of Collective Action: Public Goods and the Theory of Groups*, Cambridge, MA: Harvard University Press.

Oommen, T. K. (2004) 'Social movements in the Third World: some specificities', in *Nation, Civil Society and Social Movements: Essays in Political Sociology*, New Delhi and London: Sage Publications.

Tarrow, S. (1998) *Power in Movement:*

Social Movements, Collective Action and Politics, Cambridge: Cambridge University Press.

Tilly, C. (1978) *From Mobilization to Revolution*, Reading, MA: Addison-Wesley.

Wood, G. (2000) 'Prisoners and escapees: improving the institutional responsibility square in Bangladesh', *Public Administration and Development*, 20(3): 221–37.

4 | Mobilization through litigation: claiming health rights on asbestos issues in South Africa

NARDIA SIMPSON AND LINDA WALDMAN

Citizens seeking to claim their rights, demand redress for grievances or increase pressure for political change may, in many instances, turn to litigation to do so (see Felstiner et al. 1980; Hershkoff and Hollander 2000; Houtzager 2005). Indeed, civil rights movements have historically used the courts as a means to claim their rights as citizens. Recently, however, the legal landscape has been marked by the rise of transnational litigation against corporations and states, as citizens of developing countries have begun to use foreign courts, particularly in the United States and the United Kingdom, to redress wrongs that occurred in their home country. These class actions, undertaken by large numbers of citizens, rather than individuals, are generally underpinned by collective social activism in their home countries and thus operate in a unique transnational and legal context. Because of the focus on legal activism, these movements straddle global and national contexts in peculiar ways. They are integrated into – and draw upon – global social movements as stimulants for their activism while simultaneously the legal paradigms ground their actions in particular national contexts. This chapter examines one of the first examples of social mobilization and transnational litigation which was labelled as a legal success. In exploring the role of litigation and identity in transnational mobilization, it examines how mobilization – or the lack thereof – contributes to citizen empowerment in specific local contexts. Contrary to much of the literature which sees global mobilization networks as critical to citizen empowerment, and which has emphasized transnational civil society (Edelman 2001; Laclau and Mouffe 1985; Touraine 1988), this chapter argues that the effects of transnational litigation in conjunction with mobilization can be misinterpreted and uneven. Most critically, however, the chapter shows how processes of social mobilization and transnational litigation are reinterpreted according to local contexts and identities. Using the example of asbestos litigation and Griqua social identity, the chapter argues that the relationship between litigation and mobilization is more problematic than often assumed, and does not always result in citizen empowerment. As demonstrated in this chapter, even when the litigation is successful, some claimants interpret the case as a bitter defeat. We seek to explore why South Africans in two neighbouring towns experienced the case so differently. We do this by examining the construction of an international legal case in conjunction with the particular local sociocultural experiences and identities of the towns' residents.

In July 2003 a British company, Cape plc, which was formerly engaged in asbestos mining and milling operations, agreed to transfer £10.5 million to the Hendrik Afrika Trust, which was established to provide compensation for the 7,500-plus claimants in South Africa who suffer from asbestos-related diseases (ARDs). A further £10.5 million was to be paid into the fund over ten years. The creation of this trust was the culmination of an out-of-court settlement that occurred on 22 December 2001. Reaching the settlement had taken more than four years. However, after Cape defaulted from this payment, citing plummeting share values and financial instability, a final settlement of £7.5 million was paid and distributed among the claimants. In the small rural town of Prieska, in the Northern Cape, the settlement was part of a process that began in the 1980s when a local group of activists commenced a campaign for improved access to asbestos compensation. (See L. Waldman 2007 for a detailed analysis of this legal campaign.) The settlement and Cape plc's payment are often considered to be a legal success story. For many people within South Africa, this story of international litigation, local mobilization, activist networks and asbestos pollution is, without doubt, a David and Goliath story in which poor, disempowered people took on a powerful, international company and won. As Ward argues, the litigation is also a legal breakthrough as it is the first example of a foreign direct liability case in which personal injury actions were brought by South Africans against parent companies of English multinationals in the English High Court (Ward 2002). Along with other product liability cases around the world (Jasanoff 1995; Newell 2001), this has come to be seen by some as a means of ensuring that corporations are held accountable and as a way to deliver compensation to injured workers.

Throughout the litigation, non-governmental organizations (NGOs), academics and lawyers assumed that, although small by British standards, this compensation would greatly benefit impoverished communities. In fact, the poverty of the affected communities was identified as a key argument for pursuing international litigation against toxic abuses in South Africa, coupled with the lack of legal expertise or financial aid and the powerful incentives not to address corporate irresponsibility in the claimants' home country (McCulloch 2002; Meeran 2003). As such, the settlement can be viewed as a significant victory. As demonstrated below, however, some claimants see this case as a bitter defeat. In attempting to explain the diverse interpretations of the same litigation and the resultant tensions, this chapter draws on the literature of social movements, political mobilization, ethnic identity and millenarian movements, relating these to everyday economic and cultural experiences in the Northern Cape. It examines the protest against asbestos pollution, and the subsequent legal claims and compensation, from the perspective of the people of Griquatown and Prieska. The chapter argues that neither assumptions about the instrumental benefits of litigation nor theories of social movements alone can adequately explain people's emic interpretations of international litigation and political mobilization. Rather, it is the linkages between these literatures, informed by an understanding of local ethnic identity, which provide a framework for understanding social behaviour and evaluating the 'success' of transnational litigation.

Litigation and social movements

The securing of compensation via the legal process can play an important role not only in a context where a large number of people have been injured, placing strain on public resources, but also in individual circumstances when health services are a minimal public right or non-basic care is prohibitively expensive. In addition, access to legal services that can help secure financial resources to assist injured workers and their families has particular significance for poor populations where shocks in relation to the earning capacity of household members are very difficult to insure against.

Litigation is not, however, only about compensation and the satisfaction of material needs; litigation can also be considered beneficial if it generates publicity and mobilization around a particular cause. As Marcia Greenberger, former co-president of the National Women's Law Center (USA), explains, 'a concrete case could provide a way of highlighting the importance of a legal principle in the context of a real set of facts and actual people affected by the outcome. A case could serve to rally press and public attention to the legal principle at stake' (cited in Hershkoff and Hollander 2000: 96). Furthermore, the use of litigation can provide previously marginalized groups with a sense of legitimacy and protect members from public interference. As Joshi (2005) explains in relation to legal mobilization around the 'right to work' in India, a practical expectation of the litigation strategy was to cast a spotlight on the activities of

89

the local administration in order to protect NGO workers from arbitrary, vindictive action by state officials interested in suppressing the movement. These auxiliary legal aspects, which develop through association with legal processes, suggest that, even when a lawsuit fails in court, the legal process can legitimize the role of 'extra-community' actors, thereby endowing groups and social movements with additional forms of political capital (Hershkoff and Hollander 2000: 97).

There exists, however, an inevitable tension between litigation (and law generally) and social movements that seek to use the law to further collective causes because, in order for litigation to become an effective mobilizing tool, a social grievance must be transformed into or constructed as a legal dispute (Felstiner et al. 1980). Personal experiences of pain, injustice, sadness and loss of identity need to be recast into collective experiences and into recognizable legal claims such as for negligence and breach of contract; yet at the same time parties to a case must be named individually and be personally affected by a particular allegedly unlawful act, and a legal remedy such as compensation must be sought. There is no space within a legal dispute to appeal to sentiments of social justice unless such sentiments are first translated into legal propositions and second able to be coupled with a legal remedy. Thus, through its narrow focus, litigation can paradoxically secure beneficial outcomes for interested parties, yet at the same time this focus can drastically limit possibilities for militant action, as alternative expressions of discontent may prejudice the case.

A second tension exists in the relationship between social movements and ethnic identity. Ethnic identities are frequently Janus-faced in that notions of an idealized future and concerned attempts to secure resources for this future are made through assertions of a primordial, bounded and unchanging identity (Vail 1989). This contrasts with social movement theories of identity, which, as Touraine (1988) and Melucci (1996) suggest, tend to surface as a result of a crisis of modernity. They argue that these new social movements (NSMs) concentrate on symbolic, informational and cultural struggles, emphasizing the importance of rights to specificity and difference and thus rejecting primordial understandings of identity. The examination of NSMs should therefore include an exploration of how movements influence identity struggles during the course of the NSM and, in turn, shape the processes through which people construct meaning and interpret cultural attributes (Castells, in Edelman 2001: 298). While NSM literature has pointed to the fluid, multiple associations that people may have and has argued that involvement in NSMs is, of itself, identity-forming, it has not adequately addressed the manner in which these new social identities may interact with, or be shaped by, other enduring identities. While it is generally recognized that some ethnic identities do not have the same transformative potential as social movements, there is little understanding of how ethnic identities might mould the possibilities for social mobilization.[1] Some social movement theorists have, however, posited a distinction between 'everyday' and 'organized' resistance (Laclau and Mouffe 1985; Edelman 2001). This distinction allows for the recognition that everyday processes are often influenced by 'extra-community' actors who influence the political trajectories of local residents and, in so doing, shape the discursive content of the movement. Such everyday movement practices are comprised of people who have multiple subject positions, combining friendly relations with those of antipathy and resistance. Rather than being driven by a single principle of identity, everyday movement practices thus emphasize 'multiple social positions' (Edelman 2001).

In addressing the question 'Why do people mobilize in social movements?' the literature recognizes that actors may have 'multiple social positions', but it does not attempt to assess the relative weight of different positions or to indicate which may be more – or less – flexible in relation to social transformation and the creation of new identification. Although ethnic identities are widely interpreted in terms of fluidity and in terms of the people being able to negotiate the degree to which they wish to be identified according to certain ethnic (and often primordial) principles (Hamilton 1999; L. Waldman 2006), there is also widespread recognition that ethnic identity contains a strong element of boundary-making: i.e. that it is on the edges of ethnic collectivities, in relation to outsiders and in threatening contexts, that ethnic negotiation and reinforcement often take place (Barth 1969). It is here that actors take recourse in emphasizing fixed, primordial, unchanging and enduring aspects of their identity. In contrast, the literature on social movements recognizes the fluidity of identities, but does not seek to examine how identities associated with mobilization are made and reinforced in relation to context or when identities might be presented as rigid and unchanging. Rather, it is the shifting nature of these identities which are seen to shape social movements. The tension between social movements and ethnic identity is further compounded when social movements use a 'legal frame' to shape the content of the movement. This is because, as argued above, a legal frame determines the available identities and range of trajectories that the movement can pursue.

Since the mid-1990s mobilization around asbestos issues in South Africa has been articulated as a legal dispute. Working together with international lawyers, activists defined their movement as fitting within the legal framework. This also meant that ARDs, previously thought to be 'natural' (discussed in more detail below), had to be named as medical disorders by key actors. This disorder was blamed on the asbestos companies and subsequently the claim was for monetary compensation and/or environmental rehabilitation. In this way the demand that an injury or pollution be legally addressed became an integral part of the social demands of the movement (see Felstiner et al. 1980).

The process of transforming people's experience of injury into a legally articulated dispute (see ibid.) and international litigation campaign took the form of 'organized resistance' to one asbestos company. It brought together grassroots asbestos activists from all over South Africa, and saw the creation of networks that crossed national boundaries: a range of NGOs from both South Africa and the UK collaborated in the campaign while activists established coalitions with journalists and drew widely on support from the media. Using scientific evidence as a means of validating their claim (see Epstein 1996), the organizers developed relationships with medical professionals that could be drawn upon to support their work. A network of groups, organizations and individuals thus shared a unified vision that attempted to challenge existing patterns of power relations via an instrumental use of law. These alliances and the specific goal – of forcing one asbestos company to acknowledge and pay for its past abuses – fitted into and expanded an international social movement based on contemporary mobilization strategies that fought for justice for South African asbestos victims (see Scott 1991).

Context and identity: Prieska and Griquatown

During this campaign, certain towns became identified as places of mobilization. In the Northern Cape, the rural town of Prieska was particularly prominent. In the heyday of asbestos mining, a mill for crushing asbestos had been located in the centre of the town. This heightened the likelihood of people contracting a range of diseases with differing degrees of severity, as ARDs can affect anyone exposed to microscopic asbestos fibres.[2] As many of the town's residents suffer from ARDs, the UK-based lawyers[3] opened an office in the town and employed a number of people from the grassroots organization Concerned People Against Asbestos (CPAA) to work in the office and assist people with their claims (discussed in more detail below). Victims from the town were also featured prominently in the media and some individuals were selected to travel to London and give testimony in the High Court. By the late 1990s people from all over the Northern Cape were journeying to Prieska, despite the difficulties and high personal costs incurred, in order to have their medical conditions confirmed at the Prieska hospital (which had the necessary X-ray equipment to assist in diagnosis).

Prieska's geographical location in the heart of the asbestos deposits, coupled with the growth of the CPAA as a social movement[4] seeking to address issues of injustice, has contributed to its current positioning at the centre of a movement to challenge the legacy of asbestos mining. In addition, in order to facilitate the development of the legal case across vast geographic spaces, the lawyers provided the necessary funds to establish an office in Prieska. This meant that, equipped with a telephone, photostat machine, computer and email access, the CPAA – and through it Prieska's residents – came to be 'networked' into the international environmental justice movements (see Castells 1997). They were in constant communication with the lawyers through email and fax, and this enabled all Prieska's residents to follow the legal debates, assess the various trade-offs in terms of what evidence to put forward to the courts and, in so doing, to be part of the legal process. These experiences provided the context that enabled the CPAA to develop and maintain an identity that brought together local people's personal and everyday experiences with international campaigns and global anti-asbestos ambitions (see Laclau and Mouffe 1985).

Residents in the neighbouring town of Griquatown did not see themselves as having participated in an international movement aimed at challenging power relations and changing their 'way of life' (Touraine 1988). Despite the successful legal resolution of the case, most Griquatown claimants were bitterly disappointed. Their disappointment stemmed, in part, from the low settlements they received, in part from their failure to understand the legal processes (despite frequent discussion of these in community meetings and formal letters explaining various legal arrangements and decisions in their home languages). It also stemmed from their lack of familiarity with CPAA community workers, who went to great lengths to repeatedly explain to Prieska residents what was happening, and from their 'distance' (both in terms of physical, geographical distance and in terms of a lack of electronic 'connectedness' through phone, fax and email) from the CPAA and its debates over legal possibilities and strategies (L. Waldman 2007). Far from empowering them, and instead of their developing into a social movement, the experience can be seen to have perpetuated the marginalization of Griquatown's residents within

South Africa. Examining the relationships between the social expression of injustice and the construction of an 'appropriate' legal remedy, coupled with an understanding of Griqua identity and local conditions, explains why people in Prieska experienced this case in positive ways, which contrasted with the experiences of their Griquatown neighbours.

Residents in Griquatown and other Northern Cape towns were exposed to asbestos and affected by ARDs not because of mines or mills located in or near their towns, but because families had migrated to these mines throughout the 1950s, 1960s and 1970s in search of work. These residents were not able to participate in the campaign against asbestos in the same way as Prieska's population. Those in neighbouring Griquatown had to journey to Prieska in order to be diagnosed with ARDs or to check whether their condition had worsened. Although Griquatown was only 100 kilometres away from Prieska, the journey was a difficult undertaking on bad dirt roads. No public transport serviced these two towns and very few people in Griquatown owned cars. In addition, most residents could not afford to hire private taxis to transport them to Prieska. As a result, many Griquatown people joined the asbestos campaign and litigation as claimants, but knew very little about the organization of the campaign, the nature of the legal processes or what was happening. They waited instead for the campaigners – and in particular for the UK-based lawyers – to come to them and to inform them. When the lawyers did come to Griquatown, the community-based meetings focused primarily on the broad parameters of the legal case, whereas most Griquatown residents wanted explanations about their individual diagnosis (many of which were reviewed and revised during the case) and their accompanying claims (discussed in more detail below).

Most Griquatown residents classify themselves as either 'coloured' or 'Griqua' or both, depending on the context.[5] Within Griqua identity, Christianity is a primary influence and a marker of social status (Elbourne and Ross 1997: 40). These ideas about Christianity, Griqua identity and social status are entwined in the notions of *boorlings* and *inkommers*. *Inkommers* are newcomers to Griquatown (literally 'in-comers') and are coloured elites who have taken teaching or other government posts in the town. *Boorlings*, or people born in Griquatown, are, by contrast, 'nothing people'. Over the years their identity has been changed, shifted and manipulated. During apartheid Griqua people were seen by the National Party government as coloured: as people who were defined by what they were not.[6] Their Griqua heritage was largely dismissed by the Griquatown Council and by the central government. The powerful extended families and prominent historical leaders (see Ross 1974, 1976) remained only in people's memories as the process of proletarianization led to increasing impoverishment (see L. Waldman 2006). With *inkommers* occupying positions of status and formal leadership, the *boorlings* were reduced to defining themselves in terms of place: of where they were from (or of origin). Place, then, provided an incontestable category whereby people were either born in Griquatown (or the surrounding area) and were therefore *boorlings* or they were not.

The relationship between Griqua and coloured identity is best understood in terms of 'shifting allegiances', fluidity (Martin 1998; McEachern 1998; Hamilton 1999) and ambiguity. To be Griqua is to be both proud and poor. It is to hark back to a past legacy of supreme respectability (see Ross 1999) and to be an unemployed, proletarianized worker. As such, Griqua identity is something both affirmed and undermined. On the one hand Griqua identity is considered to be lower than that of coloured people and it contains negative associations. It stands in contrast to the apartheid ideology – internalized by many residents – that high status is associated with white society (Nurse 1975; Sonn 1996). The wealthiest coloured people tend therefore to have successfully adopted white standards: they are educated and have long smooth hair and pale skins. These people dismiss their Griqua and Khoi ancestry while poorer members of Griquatown refuse to abandon their Griqua identity. For them, identifying as Griqua provides a means of garnering esteem (see Ross 1976: 137). It means that pride and admiration stem from sources other than apartheid-dictated signs of whiteness or post-apartheid criteria of economic and educational success. Griqua historical associations with Christianity continue to provide respect and status (see Ross 1996) while forming important cultural markers. Griqua identity thus has a paradoxical status: it has remained an important reference point for people who consider themselves to be Griqua, yet there has been a widespread tendency for any Griqua people to be seen as primitive (L. Waldman 2006).

In Griquatown, the overlapping ethnic, religious and class identities – as expressed in the *boorling/inkommer* divide – come to assume primary importance. In Prieska, by contrast, there have been and continue to be many other forms of identification that people adopt. Prieska, like Griquatown, is comprised primarily of people who identify themselves as Griqua and/or coloured (many of whom are related to people in Griquatown). As the population of Prieska is more diverse, however, with greater Xhosa influence, the *boorling/inkommer* categories of identification are more diluted. As Prieska is also a far bigger town, with many more economic

95

opportunities than Griquatown, it has more people passing through it. While both Prieska and Griquatown suffer from unemployment and rely heavily on state pensions, Prieska offers more employment opportunities than Griquatown. Positioned on the banks of the Orange river and with abundant irrigated land, Prieska has an economy that includes intensive agricultural production of high-value crops (such as pistachio, olive and pecans), while sheep farming and game ranching occur on non-irrigated farms. Industrial development includes leather tanning, a cotton mill, furniture manufacture, the manufacture of cattle food pellets and a semi-precious stone industry. Griquatown, however, has only sheep farming and game ranching (both of which employ very few workers) as primary economic activities and a small semi-precious stone industry.

As Prieska is located on the main railway line from Namibia to Cape Town, it is easier for people to travel to and from the town, and many Prieska residents studied at the universities of Cape Town and the Western Cape or other tertiary institutions. This allowed young people to bring back and disseminate 'radical ideas'. During the apartheid era, many of Prieska's schoolchildren were involved in the struggle against apartheid. They were politically affiliated to banned organizations and to trade unions. During the 1980s, teenagers and young adults were involved in violent clashes with the police. They were arrested, detained without trial, interrogated, abused and assaulted. They fought against the state and had no faith in South Africa's legal system. As one Prieska resident testified to the Truth and Reconciliation Commission in 1996, as youngsters they believed that 'you should struggle and shouldn't become part of the system' (Case CT/04422/UPI 2–3 October 1996). These struggles were framed in terms of entitlement and demands for full citizenship. As a result, after the 1994 democratic elections, Prieska's 'radical' teenagers from the 1980s were recognized as African National Congress (ANC) leaders, as comrades and as appropriate persons to take over the newly constituted formal leadership positions in the Northern Cape. In Griquatown there was no evidence of political activity in the 1980s and, in stark contrast with Prieska, the majority of the residents continued to support the apartheid-based National Party even in the 1994 democratic elections. Griquatown's exposure to the ANC was primarily in the late 1990s and was, largely, a negative experience of fraud and corruption. In Griquatown, throughout the 1980s and 1990s, politics was framed within the apartheid racial structure and focused on local class struggles expressed through the idioms of *boorlings*, *inkommers* and Christianity. In particular, the *boorlings* felt that *inkommers* occupied all the good jobs and that this left them with few opportunities for manoeuvre. Because of this, one woman commented, *boorlings* had no option but to clasp their hands and wait. Such a passive stance is a reflection of Griqua/Christian values, which assert that God, not human beings, will pass judgment. Sinners will, in time, do penance for their actions and those who have been sinned against will receive retribution, if not in this life then in the next. The implication inherent in these convictions is that immediate political action is of little consequence and that 'true' compensation depends not on the mobilization effected by politicians, but on the moral values and belief system of individuals.

Collectively these identity issues affect Griquatown residents' attitudes towards asbestos mobilization and litigation. The Christian emphasis on divine justice reinforces other Christian values that emphasize individual responsibility and economic progress and, in so doing, militate against widespread collective mobilization. The Griqua categorization of residents as *boorlings* operates more ambiguously: on the one hand it hinders widespread social identification with outsiders (who, as 'extra-community' actors, play significant roles in social mobilization) and encourages residents to draw on personal, familial resources. On the other hand, it creates a sense of collective Griqua injustice (vis-à-vis *inkommers*), which could provide seeds of a mobilizing force. In order for these seeds to sprout, it is however necessary for asbestos litigation to be framed in Griqua (and possibly Christian) terms rather than as corporate responsibility, justice and an international victory. As demonstrated in the following sections, the lawyers and other asbestos campaigners – who were not from Griquatown and therefore not *boorlings* – were assimilated into the 'indigenous' Griquatown category of elite *inkommers* – a categorization that made it extremely difficult for Griqua *boorlings* to trust them and to believe in the campaign.

Class-based notions of *boorlings* and *inkommers*, coupled with Griqua ideas of divine retribution and the association of 'extra-community' actors with *inkommers*, challenge the construction of collective NSM identities framed in terms of legal plaintiffs *entitled* to compensation. This in turn has implications for how those in Griquatown became involved in – and in turn viewed – the 'justice' provided by the transnational litigation against Cape plc.

Legal compensation and dissatisfaction

In Griquatown, as a result of the incongruence between the identity of 'claimant' as constructed by the litigation-centred social movement and the 'passive recipient' constructed in Griqua identity, people saw the Cape plc court case primarily as a means of making money rather than as a means to claim entitlements. Residents commented that they had been promised huge sums of money; that they had been told of people winning cases involving unbelievable amounts. They had been waiting for this money for years. In the summer of 2003, the people of Griquatown were informed at a community meeting that the case had finally been settled and that their payment of compensation was imminent. In many respects such a meeting should have been a success, yet the mood before the meeting was angry. People believed that it would be another extension. They were tired of waiting for their money. All the claimants in Griquatown had previously been informed of how much they would receive and this was substantially less than they had initially been led to believe. The reduced payments stemmed from the depreciation of the South African rand against the British pound during the trial and from the need to use British legal categorizations of injury, which classified some forms of ARD as benign and were therefore not as lenient as those used by South Africa (see below). This information angered the claimants, who commented at the time of the meeting:

> They [the lawyers] got so much, but they are only paying out R8,000 [approximately £800] to some people. They make false declarations, they lied to the people.
>
> I am very unhappy, he [one of the lawyers] said that 80 per cent had pleural plaque and only 20 per cent get real money. Now I'm getting only R8,000.

People in Griquatown experienced this court case as an entrenchment of their oppression, rather than as an example of injured workers successfully holding a corporation accountable for its abusive and exploitative work practices. As is clear from the above quotes, their relationship with their lawyers was fraught with tension. In the long days of waiting for a settlement, they saw themselves as having been cheated by the lawyers. In an indication of the desperation and violation people experienced, one woman commented that 'he [one of the lawyers] come to enrich himself by gambling with sick people's lungs'.

In both Griquatown and Prieska, people had believed ARDs to be natural.[7] They were familiar with the disease because they had been exposed to asbestos fibres during their childhood – often being breastfed while their mothers cobbed asbestos fibre or playing on the asbestos dumps – and they had therefore seen many of their own family members die of a disease which they called *mynstof* or 'mine dust'. As Braun and Kisting (2006) explain, however, ARDs have been understood primarily as a medical condition. Such an interpretation focuses on disease causality and on the physiological action of the fibres and obscures the associations between workplace organization, occupational health legislation and disease. While residents clearly linked the disease to the asbestos mines, it was a disease about which they believed nothing could be done. In a medical sense, this is correct. Once one has been exposed to asbestos and has contracted ARD, there is no medical cure. In a political and economic sense, however, something could have been done but never was. Indeed, McCulloch (2002) documented the manner in which senior members of the apartheid state aligned themselves with the mining companies and, in so doing, supported the perpetuation of asbestos mining abuses. It was the grassroots realization that people were not being adequately compensated for their role in asbestos mining which caused the CPAA to be established in Prieska. The people of Prieska were thus able to recognize the wider impacts of the Cape plc litigation and to view their actions as part of a broad collective fighting for social justice. For many of the people of Griquatown, however, it was only when the CPAA and the lawyers first visited the town that they became aware of other possibilities and began to see ARD as a disease that could have been avoided. This reconceptualization of *mynstof* was a necessary antecedent step to the legal dispute in that it transformed an unperceived injurious experience into a perceived injurious experience (see Felstiner et al. 1980).

The naming of the injury, through the involvement of 'extra-community actors', did lead residents to reconsider their earlier understandings of ARDs and implicitly question established notions of justice (see Benford and Snow 2000). It did not, however, generate new cognitive interpretations of power relations in Griquatown and was not socially transformative. The town residents did not see this litigation as a means of challenging the actions of the mining companies, of enforcing rights or of increasing pressure for political change. Nonetheless, the case of Cape plc and the act of engaging in transnational litigation did not take place in neutral, culturally void contexts. As these poor, remote Northern Cape residents had never engaged as worthy claimants in a legal battle for social justice, they interpreted their case in terms of everyday contexts in which ethnic identity became far more salient than other possible social identities. The reasons for this centred on the way in which the social movement brought together grievances (as perceived injurious experiences), the lack of resources and, ultimately, the manner in which these processes were informed by other ethnic and cultural experiences, especially the history of asbestos payments in the area, cultural understandings of money and the way Griqua people conceptualized asbestos compensation. Griquatown is a context where it is impossible to secure good, well-paying jobs and impossible to save money. Most families survive through the receipt of old-age or disability pensions and, in this context of extreme poverty, individuals struggle to control any personal material property or money. On pension payment days people who receive pensions are overwhelmed by requests for food or loans (which will never be repaid). Underlying this communal reciprocity is the *boorling* ideology, which stresses that *boorlings* (and many *inkommers*) are interrelated and that Griquatown is one extended family. Ideas of kinship, place and belonging were therefore powerful and important resources, which meant that although individuals battled to control private resources, they were nestled within an extended family which, despite the widespread poverty, would always care for its members.

As a result, asbestos payments come to assume immense cultural importance. The South African government-run Medical Bureau for Occupational Diseases (MBOD) had compensated formally employed mineworkers for ARDs since 1956 (McCulloch 2002). The MBOD categorized ARD into two stages, based on the degree of damage to one's lungs, which it termed first- and second-degree damage, and it compensated people in lump-sum payments. Ouma Mol, for example, has been paid R11,000 (£1,100) and R6,000 (£600) for asbestosis. Because compensation was tied to length of employment in the mine and wages during employment, it was possible to receive far more than this example. Other people received payments ranging between R9,000 and R19,000 (£900 and £1,900) during the years 1989 to 1996. Because the MBOD saw ARD as progressing in a linear fashion from benign to malignant, most workers expected to receive a first lump-sum compensation payment after a diagnosis of first-degree asbestosis or pleural plaque (it used these terms somewhat interchangeably, which caused problems for the Cape plc case), with an additional payment for 'second-degree' infection, which could be mesothelioma or lung cancer but could also comprise asbestos infection plus additional damage to the lungs, either from pulmonary tuberculosis (Myers 1981: 241) or smoking. Everyone understood these payments to refer to the increased severity of *mynstof*.

The Cape plc court case did not use the South African categories of first- and second-degree asbestosis as a basis for litigation. Instead people were compensated according to UK legal categories, which included mesothelioma (R63,000 or £6,300), interstitial asbestosis (R40,000 or £4,000), pleural effusion (R27,000 or £2,700) and pleural plaque (R8,100 or £810). This meant that the bulk of the claimants (80 per cent) received R8,100 (£810). Some people who believed that they were seriously debilitated through *mynstof*, and who had received the MBOD's second payment as 'proof' of their asbestos-related illness, were now categorized as having pleural plaque and they received the minimum R8,100. The various people involved in this case thus utilized different framings of the disease, drawing on various – and sometimes conflicting – forms of evidence. The MBOD's scientific disease categorization differed from the manner in which lawyers construed the harm caused by ARDs for British courts. In contrast, Griqua people framed their understanding of the disease in terms of their personal experiences and in terms of the South African categorization of asbestos disease. They understood asbestos payments to be a very important source of income and many people were genuinely disappointed to discover that they were not suffering from *mynstof*.

Ironically perhaps, there is also a degree of status associated with the receipt of *myngelde* (literally, 'mine moneys'). Asbestosis sufferers are considered to be rich, albeit briefly, and hence valuable to their families. Stories about *mynstof* and the associated large sums of money circulated throughout Griquatown. For example, when Joseph Bankies died from *mynstof*, his descendants received R34,000 in compensation. In recounting what happened with the money, people explained that three gravestones costing R10,000 each were erected, Joseph's daughter got R10,000, each of the six grandchildren received R4,000 and with the remaining money, two more gravestones were purchased. According to the story, R84,000 and not R34,000 was used and distributed. This apocryphal story demonstrates the significance of asbestos compensation in a context where this is the only means of accumulating large sums of money.

Not all stories are concerned with the considerable wealth to be gained from asbestos diseases, however, and the following story documents the loss of vast sums of money. Oom Dirk was taken ill shortly before he received his contribution from the Cape plc case. During this time he often referred to his *mynstof* money. He, like many others in Griquatown, had often wondered how the money would be delivered. In discussions, people spoke about hiring a delivery truck to fetch the money because they believed it was too much to fit into a car. As Oom Dirk became increasingly ill, he began to believe that he had received his money. He related the following tale. The money was delivered to the Griquatown bank in two helicopters because there was too much money to fit into a delivery van. The bank manager called Oom Dirk and told him he would be the first to collect his money. Oom Dirk described how politely the bank manager spoke to him and how, when he left the bank, his pockets were bulging with money. Then, on exiting the bank, he met his wife and he gave her the money to go shopping in Kimberley. She returned with nothing but a hat. In the final days before his death, Oom Dirk frequently called his wife and asked her what she had done with all his money.

What are we to make of these accounts? In the first story, far more money is spent than is actually available, and in the second, pockets bulging with notes end up buying a hat. The ideas contained in these stories are like those described in millenarian movements in Melanesia, where 'cargo' in the form of immense social wealth is delivered by the gods or ancestors (Worsley 1957). Although millenarian movements – or in this case millenarian-like stories – are often thought to be bizarre, they generally make sense in terms of trying to explain people's everyday experiences (Burridge 1969).[8] The two stories reiterate the themes of life in Griqua-town: the ambiguity associated with their identity, which carries with it both positive and negative connotations; the role of extended kinship relations and how, within an extended family of Griqua *boorlings*, money is a communal resource; and the importance of ethnic identities, which emphasize the role of Griqua *boorlings* in contrast to 'extra-community' actors (such as *inkommers* or lawyers) who assist Griquatown residents when they feel like it but who have no obligation to do so.

The stories thus emphasize the significance of family, of descent and of place. In the first story, asbestos payments were being used to erect gravestones, to cement the relations between this large extended family of *boorlings* and the people from whom they were descended and drew their identity. The second story tells of emptiness, of how the place in which people have cemented their identity is barren and, even when presented with a helicopter full of money, is unable to develop or use this money in ways that preserve or increase its value. Rather the money is eaten, shared and lost.[9]

In Griquatown, cultural interpretations of money – and in particular of asbestos money – which, as seen in these two stories, focused on quantity and availability, were the criteria by which the people judged this case. Not being involved in the process, the people of Griquatown did not follow the legal debates. They did not see the court case as a means of enforcing corporate social responsibility. The complex economic and political relations that hid the culpability of the mining organizations and which the social movement activists sought to challenge were reinterpreted in terms of other, more local and, to many non-Griqua, more inexplicable ideas of power that sought to explain unattached money. Transnational litigation was a means to secure asbestos money – which was money that dropped from the sky in unbelievable quantities and which was completely unrelated to work, pensions and other sources of income, but nonetheless still to be circulated within the *boorling* community and used according to local cultural criteria. Although social movements emphasize the ability of actors to develop multiple shifting identities, this case shows how ethnic identity and cultural ways of classifying money, insiders, outsiders and experiences limited the social movement's transformative potential.

Although dissatisfactions with lawyers' actions and judges' decisions are not unusual in the world of asbestos litigation (Walker and LaMontagne 2004), they are seldom cast in terms as emotive and negative as these. Many claimants in the neighbouring town of Prieska did not share these views. They saw the court case as a victory, or perhaps a pyrrhic victory. In contrast to the Griquatown meeting described above, the same meeting in Prieska was attended by the mayor of the town, who welcomed the lawyers; the podium had been decorated with fresh flowers and the atmosphere was one of celebration and pride. Prieska's claimants may have been disappointed that they did not receive more money, but they did not see themselves as having been cheated. Indeed, as reflected in the town treasurer's closing comments at the final community meeting, these residents understood how their efforts and the struggle had empowered them to begin to take control over their own destiny.

> This is the last meeting. It is like reaching the end of a book. ABSA is the final chapter.[10] We may not see him [Richard Meeran, the human rights lawyer who took on the case for Leigh Day Solicitors in London] again. On behalf of the community, the government, the role players in the office, the National Union of Mineworkers, and everyone who took part in London to complete this whole case. Meeran says the compensation is too little, but we are grateful for what we will receive. Many, many thanks. You have been away from the UK for many months, away from family. At the end of the day, it has been worth the effort. The next chapter is ABSA which must invest in Prieska and start bursaries for our children.

Conclusion

The sentiments expressed in Griquatown were not widespread among the 7,500 claimants dispersed throughout South Africa and may have been specific to Griquatown. Such tension results from the fact that Griquatown residents' relationship with their lawyers was never imagined along the legal lines of 'claimants' and 'representatives' in the context of a social justice movement. Rather, the foundation of their relationship lay in the monetary benefit that such a relationship might bring and was mediated by the CPAA movement, which was based in Prieska. A partnership based on financial gain is not an anomaly to the law, however, it is within a context of a social movement of diverse peoples and identities which voices concerns in the language of justice, power and social change. In Griquatown, this perspective reinforces conventional ethnic categorizations and understandings of the world, and in so doing challenges the formation of new solidarities and identities.

A fundamental premise of transnational litigation is the universal applicability of the legal approach as a means of resolving conflict. This chapter shows, however, that using transnational litigation as a forum for seeking collective justice is not just about establishing a legal framework. It is also necessary to be aware of how the 'neutral' language of law is inserted into local cultural understandings of people's experiences and claims. In this case of Cape plc and the 7,500 asbestos claimants who benefited from the case, the tensions between legal framings, social movements' collective framings of justice and Griqua ethnic identities remained unresolved and ultimately resulted in the marginalization of Griquatown claimants, who experienced the legal victory as a bitter injustice.

In examining how transnational asbestos activism has contributed to citizens' empowerment, the chapter demonstrates the ways in which social mobilization processes are constructed, bringing together ideas of global solidarity, social and economic justice and local experiences of money, asbestos politics and identity. Earlier in this book, Thompson and Tapscott argued that the same structural and institutionalized resource bases of movements could not be assumed in the North and in the South, and asked whether the intersections between grievance and resource might look different from a Southern perspective. This chapter examines how social mobilization, resources and identity came together in Griquatown and Prieska to shape people's experiences of citizenship. It demonstrates that other ethnic identities, although fluid in their own right, may assume paramount significance and therefore rigidity in contexts of social mobilization. In so doing, it suggests that global interconnections and experiences of social mobilization are not automatically empowering. Instead of feeling successful and emboldened by international solidarity with human rights lawyers and other global actors, people in Griquatown felt cheated. International values, interpretations of processes, and determinations of successful mobilizations do not, ultimately, always hold true in Southern contexts.

Notes

1 See, however, Hvalkof's (2002) examination of the social movement connected with the Ashéninka's campaign to secure legal rights to territory in the Montane area of Peru. He shows that the movement was positively affected by people's conceptualization of their indigenous identity and hence their willingness to operate at both international and local levels of mobilization. Also see Warren's edited volume on pan-Mayan activists, which demonstrates how the revitalization of ethnic identifiers (including Indian languages, cultural calendrical and numerical systems and spiritualities) formed the basis of a social movement (Warren 1998).

2 Mossman and Gee (1989) categorize four types of benign pleural disorders, namely pleural effusion or fluid on the lungs, pleural plaques, pleural fibrosis and rounded atelectasis. Most people suffering from these benign pleural disorders do not experience pain or dyspnoea but do experience shortness of breath and some discomfort. Three forms of disease, which have more serious and debilitating consequences, have also been linked to asbestos. Asbestosis and lung cancer are primarily occupational hazards as contracting these diseases is linked to rates of exposure to asbestos. Mesothelioma (a malignant cancer) is unrelated to dosage and trivial exposure can lead to cancer of the abdominal cavity or lung lining. Exposure, followed by

an extended latency period (of up to forty years) before diagnosis, heightens the danger of this disease. The disease is always fatal and people afflicted with full-blown mesothelioma face a painful, imminent death.

3 Leigh Day Solicitors and John Pickering and Partners, Solicitors, both based in the UK and funded by British legal aid, orchestrated the Cape plc court case in conjunction with the Concerned People Against Asbestos (CPAA) and other South African victims. Both these law companies focused on environmental and abuse claims, with Leigh Day specializing in the human and environmental issues in a world of multinational organizations and global responsibility, while John Pickering specializes in victims of industrial disease.

4 The CPAA was a Prieska-based organization that initially campaigned against the South African government, seeking primarily to provide town residents with easier access to compensation for occupational exposure to asbestos. In this sense, it was an 'everyday movement practice' that contained within it limited possibilities for transforming power relations or for changing people's understanding of asbestos disease and its causes. As the case developed, however, the CPAA became more exposed to – and more sophisticated in its dealings with – the media and with various government and other actors (see

L. Waldman 2007). In particular, international networks enabled the CPAA activists to link up with transnational advocacy networks comprising a wide range of people from other social movements, media, unions, NGOs, intergovernmental and governmental organizations (Keck and Sikkink 1998). As the CPAA began to develop the idea of holding someone accountable for the 'gross human rights abuses' committed by the asbestos industry, it explored the possibility of challenging the whole system of occupational disease compensation in South Africa. It became clear, however, that suing the South African government was not a feasible option: the current ANC-led government represented a stark departure from the former apartheid government, under whose jurisdiction the mines had operated. In addition, the mines had closed a decade before the ANC-led government was democratically elected and the state had no vested interest in the mines. The government was financially incapable of addressing the multidimensional question of asbestos exposure, which it saw as one of many apartheid abuses of human life. It had, in addition to publicly expressing its support for this transnational case, undertaken all environmental rehabilitation of asbestos mines. In the Northern Cape this was estimated to cost in the region of R44 million (Kazan-Allen n.d.).

5 At the end of the twentieth century, the Griqua comprised a diverse category of people who were historically seen as the 'mixed-race' descendants of indigenous Khoi (nomadic pastoralists), autochthonous San (nomadic

hunter-gatherers), escaped slaves, Boer frontiersmen, Africans (predominantly Tswana) and European settlers (Ross 1976: 1). The name Griqua – which refers to the indigenous Khoi resident in the Cape Colony in the seventeenth century (called ≠Karixurikwa, Chariguriqua or /Karihur) – was adopted in 1813 when the London Missionary Society persuaded the heterogeneous collectivity at Klaarwater (Griquatown) – then called 'Bastaards' (literally, 'bastards') – to change their pejorative name (Halford 1949; Nurse 1975; Ross 1976). During the apartheid years (1948–94), the Griqua were subsumed under the government's broader racial category of 'coloured', which included the diverse conglomerates that resulted from people's interactions during the colonial era and other categories of people, such as Malays, not easily identified as either black or white. Griqua identity is thus a complex, heterogeneous identity combining many different traditions and overlain by, and entwined with, apartheid planning and structure for almost fifty years (Halford 1949; Ross 1976; Legassick 1979; Morris 1982; President's Commission 1983; P. L. Waldman 1989; Schoeman 1996; Martin 1998).

6 According to the President's Commission investigating the needs and demands of the Griqua, 'a Griqua is a coloured and a coloured is a Griqua on the grounds of the definition that "a coloured is neither white nor Black nor Asiatic", and thus all the other coloureds must be classified in this class' (President's Commission 1983: 76).

7 Bergland has identified this to be a feature of toxic waste contamination. She comments: 'Since,

in most circumstances, the source of danger is imperceptible to the senses, awareness of a danger is dependent on "being informed", and being recognized as a problem means it must be constituted in discourse' (2001: 322).

8 Millenarian movements tend to arise in situations where there is no apparent correlation between skills, hard work and honesty – the values taught by society in general – and who gets regular employment and good jobs, and makes money.

9 In this context, the Cape plc compensation payments were received as 'bitter cargo', a notion which resonates with Shipton's work on Luo economic transactions in Kenya. Shipton points out (1989: 55) that transactions which undermine Luo family and ancestral relations and landholding and which are linked to foreigners are interpreted as 'bitter transactions'. In labelling such transactions 'bitter' and in transferring this label to the people who perform such transactions, the Luo constrain individual opportunities and decision-making, forcing people to act according to culturally prescribed values and for the 'good' of the community.

10 The Amalgamated Banks of South Africa (ABSA) won the contract to distribute the money to the 7,500 claimants.

References

Barth, F. (1969) *Ethnic Groups and Boundaries*, London: George Allen and Unwin.

Benford, R. D. and D. A. Snow (2000) 'Framing processes and social movements: an overview and assessment', *Annual Review of Sociology*, 26: 611–39.

Bergland, E. (2001) 'Self-defeating environmentalism? Models and questions from an ethnography of toxic waste protest', *Critique of Anthropology*, 21(3): 317–36.

Braun, L. and S. Kisting (2006) 'Asbetos-related disease in South Africa: the social production of an invisible epidemic', *American Journal of Public Health*, 96(8): 2–12.

Burridge, K. (1969) *New Heaven, New Earth*, New York: Schocken.

Castells, M. (1997) *The Information Age – Economy, Society and Culture*, vol. 2: *The Power of Identity*, Oxford: Blackwell.

Edelman, M. (2001) 'Social movements: changing paradigms and forms of politics', *Annual Review of Anthropology*, 30: 285–317.

Elbourne, E. and R. Ross (1997) 'Early Khoisan ues of mission Christianity', in H. Bredenkamp and R. Ross (eds), *Missions and Christianity in South African History*, Johannesburg: Witwatersrand University Press.

Epstein, S. (1996) *Impure Science, Aids, Activism, and the Politics of Knowledge*, Berkeley: University of California Press.

Felstiner, W. L. F., R. L. Abel and A. Sarat (1980) 'The emergence and transformation of disputes: naming, blaming, claiming ...', *Law and Society Review*, special issue on dispute processing and civil litigation, 15(3/4): 631–54.

Halford, S. J. (1949) *The Griquas of Griqualand: A Historical Narrative of the Griqua People, Their Rise, Progress, and Decline*, Cape Town: Juta and Company.

Hamilton, C. (1999) 'Where is the border now? The new politics of identity in South Africa', in

M. Roesler and T. Wendl (eds), *Frontiers and Borderlands: Anthropological Perspectives*, Oxford: Peter Lang.

Hershkoff, H. and D. Hollander (eds) (2000) *Rights into Action: Public Interest Litigation in the United States. Many Roads to Justice – The Law-Related Work of Ford Foundation Grantees around the World*, Ford Foundation, USA.

Houtzager, P. P. (2005) 'The Movement of the Landless (MST) and the juridical field in Brazil', IDS Working Paper 248, Brighton: IDS.

Hvalkof, S. (2002) 'Beyond indigenous land titling: democratising civil society in the Peruvian Amazon', in J. Chase (ed.), *The Spaces of Neo-Liberalism*, Bloomfield, IN: Kumarian Press.

Jasanoff, S. (1995) *Science at the Bar*, Cambridge, MA: Harvard University Press.

Joshi, A. (2005) *Do Rights Work? Law Activism and the Employment Guarantee Scheme*, Centre for the Future State, Research Summary no. 13, Brighton: IDS.

Kazan-Allen, L. (n.d.) *South Africa: The Asbestos Legacy*, International Ban Asbestos Secretariat, www.btinternet.com/~ibas/Frames/f_lka_sa_leg.htm, accessed 14 December 2006.

Keck, M. and K. Sikkink (1998) *Activists beyond Borders: Advocacy Networks in International Politics*, London: Cornell University Press.

Laclau, E. and C. Mouffe (1985) *Hegemony and Socialist Strategy: Towards a Radical Democratic Politics*, London: Verso.

Legassick, M. (1979) 'The Northern Frontier to 1820: the emergence of the Griqua People', in R. El-

phick and H. Giliomee (eds), *The Shaping of South African Society 1652–1820*, Cape Town: Maskew Miller Longman.

Martin, D. M. (1998) 'What's in the name "coloured"?', *Social Identities*, 4(3): 523–40.

McCulloch, J. (2002) *Asbestos Blues: Labour, Capital, Physicians and the State in South Africa*, Oxford: James Currey.

McEachern, C. (1998) 'Mapping the memories: politics, place and identity in the District Six Museum, Cape Town', *Social Identities*, 4(3): 499–521.

Meeran, R. (2003) 'Cape Plc: South African mineworkers' quest for justice', *International Journal of Occupational and Environmental Health*, 9(3): 218–29.

Melucci, A. (1996) *Challenging Codes: Collective Action in the Information Age*, Cambridge: Cambridge University Press.

Morris, D. (1982) *The Griqua of Campbell: Questions of History and Identity*, Third-year fieldwork project, Department of Social Anthropology, University of Cape Town.

Mossman, B. T. and B. L. Gee (1989) 'Asbestos-related diseases', *New England Journal of Medicine*, 320: 1721–30.

Myers, J. (1981) 'The social context of occupational disease: asbestos and South Africa', *International Journal of Health Services*, 11(2): 227–45.

Newell, P. (2001) 'Managing multinationals: the governance of investment for the environment', *Journal of International Development*, 13(7): 907–19.

Nurse, G. T. (1975) 'The origins of the Northern Cape Griqua', Institute for the Study of Man Paper 34, pp. 2–21.

President's Commission (1983) *Report of the Constitutional Committee of the President's Council on the Needs and Demands of the Griqua*, Cape Town: Government Printer.

Ross, R. (1974) 'Griqua government', *African Studies*, 33(1): 25–42.

— (1976) *Adam Kok's Griqua*, Cambridge: Cambridge University Press.

— (1996) 'The self-image of Jacob Adams', in P. Skotnes (ed.), *Miscast: Negotiating the Presence of the Bushmen*, Cape Town: University of Cape Town Press.

— (1999) *Status and Respectability in the Cape Colony, 1750–1870: A Tragedy of Manners*, Cambridge: Cambridge University Press.

Schoeman, K. (1996) *Griqua Records: The Philippolis Captaincy*, Cape Town: Van Riebeeck Society.

Scott, A. (1991) 'Action, movement and intervention: reflections on the sociology of Alain Touraine', *Canadian Review of Sociology and Anthropology*, 28(1): 30–45.

Shipton, P. (1989) *Bitter Money: Cultural Economy and Some African Meanings of Forbidden Commodities*, American Ethnological Society Monograph Series no. 1, Washington, DC: American Anthropological Association.

Sonn, J. (1996) 'Breaking down the borders', in W. James, D. Caliguire and K. Cullinan (eds), *Now That We Are Free: Coloured Communities in a Democratic South Africa*, London: Lynne Rienner.

Touraine, A. (1988) *Return of the Actor: Social Theory, in Postindustrial Society*, University of Minneapolis Press.

Vail, L. (1989) 'Introduction', in L. Vail (ed.), *The Creation of Tribalism in Southern Africa*, London: James Currey.

Waldman, L. (2006) 'Klaar Gesnap as Kleurling: the attempted making and remaking of the Griqua People', *African Studies*, 65(2): 175–200.

— (2007) 'When social movements bypass the poor: asbestos pollution, international litigation and Griqua cultural identity', *Journal of Southern African Studies*, 33(3): 577–600.

Waldman, P. L. (1989) *Watersnakes and Women: A Study of Ritual and Ethnicity in Griquatown*, BA (Hons) dissertation, University of the Witwatersrand, Johannesburg.

Walker, H. and A. D. LaMontagne (2004) *Work and Health in the Latrobe Valley: Community Perspectives on Asbestos Issues*, Melbourne: Centre for the Study of Health and Society.

Ward, H. (2002) 'Corporate accountability in search of a treaty: some insights from foreign direct liability', Royal Institute of International Affairs Briefing Paper 4, pp. 1–11.

Warren, K. (1998) *Indigenous Movements and Their Critics: Pan Maya Activism in Guatemala*, Princeton, NJ: Princeton University Press.

Worsley, P. (1957) *The Trumpet Shall Sound: A Study of 'Cargo' Cults in Melanesia*, London: Macgibbon and Kee.

TWO | Social movements and global development discourses

5 | Water and rights: state management in South Africa and India

LYLA MEHTA, LISA THOMPSON AND
NDODANA NLEYA

This chapter examines the relationship between citizens mobilizing for their rights to water in South Africa and India and the ways in which state policies may hinder the acquisition of socio-economic rights, even where the policies themselves are ostensibly aimed at promoting the socio-economic interests of the poor. As discussed in the introductory chapter, the ways in which poor communities mobilize to claim rights is essential to understanding how socio-economic rights make a difference to the lives of the poor, but the other side of the equation is what state actors' responses are to different types of mobilization in relation to problems of policy implementation. This chapter illustrates that even when such rights are upheld by international laws, as well as national policies, they may still have to be fought for by ordinary citizens, and may be denied by the state in a number of ways. We refer here to the relationship between what Mehta (2006) has called 'sins of omission' and 'sins of commission' on the part of governments upholding rights in legal terms as well as in the ways they mediate citizens' claims for both negative and positive rights.[1]

In this regard, *sins of omission*[2] are understood as situations in which governments may by default deny citizens access to social and economic rights. It is well known that poor states may not prioritize the imperative to provide education, water and housing for all. Also, many developing countries may lack the resources to provide rights to all citizens to live a life in dignity or else may lack the institutional capacity to provide these rights. Similarly, citizens may not be aware of rights and may not have the capacity to mobilize around them, or may mobilize in fragmented and unorganized ways that do not significantly impact on government policies or behaviour. It is well known that social movements are generally discouraged by governments in the South (see Thompson and Mahmud, this volume, as well as Bond et al. 2001). This relates to what Mehta (2006) describes as *sins of commission*. Here states or international non-governmental actors such as the World Bank may knowingly put vulnerable people's rights at risk or even violate them for a variety of reasons. For example, the freedom of speech and right to protest are severely restricted in times of dictatorships. Rights may also be violated in the name of 'development'. This chapter demonstrates how in the case of India, dam-building causes forced displacement which infringes on displaced people's rights to livelihood, land, water, and so on. Moreover, in the South African case, a combination of sins of omission and commission play themselves out owing largely to an uneasy mix of official socio-economic entitlements to water which are in conflict with broader macroeconomic policies.

Mobilization often occurs around citizens' demands for rights bestowed on them constitutionally and in terms of both national and international norms and policy declarations. This chapter examines the linkages between rights 'on paper' and rights 'in practice' by focusing on the sins of omission and commission that have taken place in the relation to how Indian and South African governments have mediated their constitutional and policy commitments to the right to water in relation to the claims of poor communities, as well as how communities have mobilized to claim back these rights.

In 2002, the UN Economic, Social and Cultural Council gave a lot of prominence to the right to water through its General Comment No. 15, which is an authoritative interpretation of the International Covenant on Economic, Social and Cultural Rights, 1966, which implicitly points towards the recognition of the right to water. The Comment, a non-legally binding document, stated explicitly that the right to water is a human right and that responsibility for the provision of sufficient, safe, affordable water to everyone, without discrimination, rests with the state. Still the right to water is very controversial on many fronts. While in principle it is accepted that there is an 'indivisibility' of civil and political rights on the one hand, and economic, cultural and social rights on the other, in practice there is still no equal recognition, and there is the assumption that economic and social rights can be realized only once the so-called first generation of rights are realized. Furthermore, in the water debate, dominant narratives, especially with the passage of the four so-called 'Dublin principles' (ICWE 1992), more often see water as an economic good rather than as a human right. South Africa, however, stands out in this regard and is among the seven countries with a constitutional right to water, alongside Ethiopia, Uganda, Gambia, Uruguay, Panama and Zambia (COHRE 2006, in Anand 2007; Gowlland-Gualtieri 2007). The case study examples discussed here show that there is no direct relationship between rights 'on paper' and rights 'in practice'. Nor is there necessarily a causal relationship between mobilization and achieving rights, especially socio-economic rights. In the South African case, the role of mediating social movements like the Coalition against Water Privatisation has enabled marginalized communities to mobilize for their rights, and in India social movement activity has also helped to frame rights discourses more effectively. Yet the Indian case also calls into question the ability of social movement activity to change the course of government policy, especially where sins of commission have taken place.

South Africa's policies relating to the provision of water examine how sins of omission largely prevent many vulnerable groups from having access to the right to water in South Africa, where the lack of financial resources, poor institutional capacity and very little knowledge of rights prevent them from being realized and claimed by citizens. The sins of commission relating to the clash of free basic water (FBW) policies with privatization and cost recovery, which put basic rights at risk, are also discussed. The chapter also examines the ways in which the state mediates the socio-economic claims of citizens through various forms of participation and mobilization, and in so doing sometimes acts in contradictory ways, for example in the South African case, on the one hand enforcing socio-economic entitlements (FBW) and on the other hand undermining these rights (through the installation of water meters, for example).

The Indian case examines government sins of commission where displaced people's rights are both put at risk and blatantly violated through processes of forced displacement as a consequence of dam-building. It focuses on how states and agencies such as the World Bank knowingly put both negative and positive rights at risk in the name of 'development'. Even though policy safeguards are in place to ostensibly mitigate the risks of forced displacement, the history of dam-building is characterized by a string of human rights violations, as well as depriving communities of their livelihoods. These issues are examined by looking at the case of the Narmada dams in India and by asking how and whether agencies such as the Indian government and the World Bank can be held accountable, in particular how communities and globally based social movements help to channel rights claims and accountability issues.

Both South Africa and India experience challenges of water provision to the poor and periods of water shortage. Post-apartheid South Africa has one of the world's most dynamic water ministries committed to overcoming the problems of poor water access and provision and water scarcity, and is striking in explicitly recognizing the human right to water.

South Africa has also experienced controversial and rather contradictory experiences of cost recovery and privatization along with its more rights-based approaches to water. India, by contrast, has over fifty years of water management experience, and its water management approaches have until very recently focused primarily on technocratic and engineering solutions in a supply-driven framework, with social, institutional and rights-based issues only recently coming to the fore. While India also recognizes the constitutional right to water, it does not have a specific rights-based policy on water equivalent to South Africa's. Both have vibrant citizen action in terms of water issues (in particular, over dam technologies in India and privatization issues in South Africa). Both experience variability in river flow and a highly geographically skewed occurrence of both rain and groundwater in the country. In both countries, water management policies and practices have been shaped by international financial institutions (IFIs) such as the World Bank and the International Monetary Fund – we refer to these in the cases that follow. Both cases, in different ways, thus help us to highlight the dilemmas of assuming a direct relationship between the policy framings of rights discourses and the lived realities of poor communities.

The right to free basic water in South Africa: the ideal and the reality

South Africa is one of only seven countries that recognize the human right to water at both the constitutional and policy level. Moreover, its FBW policy goes against the grain of conventional wisdom in the water sector, which stresses cost-recovery mechanisms and shies away from endorsing the human right to water (Mehta 2004). The provision of free water to consumers was under consideration at the Department for Water Affairs and Forestry from early 2000, and gained impetus when the ANC included it as part of its manifesto for the local government elections in September 2000. In February 2001, the government announced that it was going to provide a basic supply of 6,000 litres of safe water per month to all households free of charge (based on an average household size of eight people).[3] The Water Services Act 108 of 1997 states that a basic level of water should be provided to those who cannot pay, and the FBW policy emanates from the legal provisions of the act. The main source of funding for this initiative is the 'Equitable Share', an annual grant from the central government to local authorities.[4]

While the endorsement of the right to water in the constitution was groundbreaking, South African policies continue to be informed by several contradictory dominant framings in water management, which include an emphasis on cost recovery, commercialization and privatization, with the receding state assuming a regulatory role. This policy thrust draws on a quasi-consensus among multilateral and bilateral agencies that have manifested themselves in both poor and middle-income countries like South Africa (ibid.). Thus, alongside the remarkable commitments to providing free water, World Bank-induced policy changes have also been introduced in the last decade, most notably water disconnections to non-paying customers, a move that has been linked to dire health consequences such as cholera and other conditions (Pauw 2003; Bond et al. 2001; McDonald 2002). From 1997, municipalities began widespread cut-offs of basic services to non-payers, and even with the introduction of FBW in 2001, many households using more than the FBW allocation were unable to pay and were disconnected. This has led to widespread protest action throughout South Africa in the past decade, with limited impact on local government policies (Thompson and Nleya 2008).

One form of cost recovery that has been flagged as a way out of the politically contentious area of water cut-offs is through the installation of water meters, which, while also controversial, has been envisaged as a way of curbing the indebtness to local government in poor communities. The Coalition against Water Privatisation, a social movement linked to the environmental movement and the anti-privatization movement, has played the principal role in resisting government initiatives on water meters (Bond et al. 2001; Bond 2002).

In relation to the above, the recent and perhaps most far-reaching protest action on water services in South Africa is the social movement resistance that led to the case of *Mazibuko and Others* v. *City of Johannesburg and Others*, also known as the Phiri case (2008). The application was brought by five unemployed applicants, all living in conditions of abject poverty, on their own behalf as well as that of all residents of Phiri with the assistance of Coalition against Water Privatisation, supported by the Centre for Applied Legal Studies at the University of the Witwatersrand and the Freedom of Expression Institute (IDASA 2008; WaterAid et al. 2008). The applicants asked the court to declare prepaid meters unconstitutional and to require the installation of a credit-metered supply at the cost of the City of Johannesburg. Furthermore, they challenged the provision of only 6,000 litres per month per household for free, asking the court instead to double the allocation from the 25 litres per person per day to 50 litres per person per day. Judge Tsoka found that 'prepayment meters have no source in law. They are unconstitutional.' Furthermore, the judge found that prepaid meters do not afford people a reasonable time to make representations about their financial status while residents of middle-class areas are given ample time to make arrangements. This was found to be 'unreasonable, unfair and inequitable ... discriminatory solely on the basis of colour'. The court upheld the contention that 25 litres per person per day was insufficient and recommended that 50 litres per person per day be implemented. Although this case is under appeal, the courts have thus demonstrated their willingness to protect the right to water. The case also underlines that citizen agency and mobilization strategies, especially in this case as upheld by the justice system, can be used to overturn unjust and inequitable administrative decisions.

Understandably as a result of the Phiri court case, there has been a large fallout from the decision, with Johannesburg mayor Amos Masondo arguing that the judge was usurping the role of the executive: 'Judges are not above the law. We don't want judges to take the role of Parliament, the role of the national council of provinces, the role of the legislature and the role of this council. Judges must limit their role' (Shoba 2008).

The complaint by Masondo reflects on the basis that socio-economic rights are not justiciable as they require courts to enter into distribution of resources, an area that is a traditional reserve of the executive (see Francis 2005). It is important to note, however, that in previous judgments, the Constitutional Court broke away from traditional international human rights jurisprudence, which considers socio-economic rights as non-justiciable (Gabru 2005; Francis 2005), as ruling on them requires the courts to direct the distribution of state resources, something that is beyond judicial function (Gabru 2005). In its very first judgment, the certification judgment,[5] the Constitutional Court stated:

> Nevertheless, we are of the view that these rights are, at least to some extent, justiciable. As we have stated ... many civil and political rights entrenched in the New Constitution will give rise to similar budgetary implications without compromising their justiciability. At the very minimum, socio-economic rights can be negatively protected from improper invasion.

Nonetheless, Francis (2005) notes that the Constitutional Court has shown its reluctance to interfere in fiscal responsibilities of the executive. Ruling on this, Judge Yacoob said:

> I am conscious that it is an extremely difficult task for the State to meet these obligations in the conditions that prevail in our country. This is

recognized by the Constitution which expressly provides that the State is not obliged to go beyond available resources or to realise these rights immediately. *I stress however, that despite all these qualifications, these rights and the Constitution oblige the State to give effect to them.* This is an obligation that courts *can, and in appropriate circumstances, must enforce.* (Emphasis added)

The first emphasis above highlights that the courts hold that the state has an obligation to fulfil the requirements of the constitution and the second emphasis that the courts are willing to hold it to account in *appropriate circumstances.* The conditionality of circumstances is perhaps linked to the reluctance identified by Francis (ibid.). On the same point, a reading of the Treatment Action Campaign judgment on state provision of antiretrovirals emphasizes that courts can indeed require the state to comply.

The primary duty of the courts is to the Constitution and the law ... Where state policy is challenged as inconsistent with Constitution, courts have to consider whether in formulating and implementing such policy the state has given effect to its constitutional obligations. If it should hold in any given case that the state has failed to do so, it is obliged by the Constitution to do so.[6]

It is clear that in relation to FBW there is a positive relation between how government has bestowed rights and how rights are interpreted and deployed by local people. In spite of both sins of commission and omission on the part of government, communities are asserting and mobilizing for their right to water in South Africa, especially in urban areas. Protests against water disconnections and prepaid meters are widespread, and the use of the courts to enforce socio-economic rights is becoming more regular, largely thanks to the involvement of social movements such as the Coalition against Water Privatisation.

Violations of rights in India's Narmada Valley: state policies and community responses

In recent decades, India has witnessed the emergence of new social movements questioning conventional 'development' models and the role of the state in decision-making processes concerning access to and control over natural resources. Nowhere is this more evident than with the construction of large dams. While large dams may have made some parts of the desert bloom and led to full granaries and enhanced food security, they have not been without high social and environmental costs (cf. McCully 1996; Goldsmith and Hildyard 1992). While the attractiveness of electricity, water supplies and improved food security in industrial economies is often difficult to contest, it is important to reflect on the adverse effects of large dams, especially the displacement of people from ancestral homes and concomitant homelessness. Indeed, since independence, around thirty to fifty million Indians – mainly from *adivasi* (tribal)[7] and low-caste communities – have lost their lands and livelihoods owing to the forced displacement caused by the reservoir flooding of large dams (Thukral 1992; Roy 1999). Displacement and resettlement have been traumatic and protracted processes that have uprooted people from their familiar environment with drastic effects on economic, sociocultural and livelihood capabilities (Thukral 1992; Fernandes and Thukral 1989; Morse and Berger 1992). Of these, the Narmada Project is a good example of the clash between state-framed development policy objectives and the ways in which indigenous people express their socio-economic rights.

The Narmada Project comprises two megadams, thirty large dams, 135 medium dams and 300 small reservoirs and dams. All these projects, if realized, will most certainly totally transform the Narmada river, India's holy and last free-flowing river. One of the megadams, the Sardar Sarovar Project, is supposed to bring water to some thirty million people and irrigate 1.8 million hectares of land with a capacity of 1,450 megawatts of power (Raj 1991). The 163-metre dam project will negatively affect the homes, lands and livelihoods of about a million people in addition to the ecosystem effects. In 1992, the report of an independent review set up by the World Bank, also known as the Morse Report, found that the World Bank and the government of India had violated the provisions of the Bank's resettlement, tribal peoples and environmental policies (Morse and Berger 1992). In 1993, the World Bank withdrew its funding from the project owing to national and international criticism. The project stalled during the 1990s after a stay of construction ordered by the Supreme Court was later overturned in a controversial Supreme Court judgment.

The dams on the Narmada river also stand out with regard to their high social costs. Moreover, they are also notorious owing to the activism spearheaded by the Narmada Bachao Andolan (Save the Narmada Movement, henceforth Andolan). The Andolan has successfully highlighted and brought home to millions all over the globe the plight of the displaced peoples affected by the Narmada dams and the dark sides of top-down projects such as large dams. It has also inspired several social and environmental struggles on the Indian subcontinent and raised questions important for India's future concerning, for example, sustainable development, participation, the rights of indigenous peoples, the viability or non-viability of large top-down centralist projects, and the mobilization of protest. Over the years, the Andolan adopted a strategy of non-cooperation, mass mobilization and non-violent forms of protest, including rallies, picketing, sit-ins, fasts and the more extreme case of *jal samapan* (save-or-drown actions). Enacting the slogan 'We will drown, but not move', activist villagers have refused to vacate their ancestral homes. As a result they have resisted and faced police atrocities and repressive tactics including mass arrests, harassment, the molesting of women and the clear felling of their forests (see Mehta 2000). Also striking is the international attention that the protest has received, in particular in the 1980s and 1990s. This is largely due to powerful transnational alliances that have been forged with environmental and development non-governmental organizations (NGOs) all around the world, which have often, with success, lobbied their governments to withdraw financial support and aid to these dam projects.

Since 1991, tribal villages have been partially submerged by the swollen waters of the Narmada river every year during the monsoon season, an irony for a river known locally as 'Mother'. Resettlement and rehabilitation must follow the procedures set by the following: the Narmada Water Disputes Tribunal Award; the directions of the Indian Supreme Court of 2001;[8] the rehabilitation and resettlement policies of the states of Gujarat, Madhya Pradesh and Maharashtra; and World Bank policies, as well as India's human rights obligations.[9]

The World Bank policies were in force when the 1985 loan to the Sardar Sarovar was approved. According to legal specialists, these World Bank policies will continue to apply to the project until the loan is repaid. The most relevant policy includes the Involuntary Resettlement Policy (OM S233, issued February 1980), which clearly states that settlers' living standards need to at least match those before resettlement and that the Bank will avoid or minimize involuntary resettlement wherever feasible (Clark and Bhardwaj 2003: 7). Furthermore, the tribal people's policy (OM S 234, issued 1982) clearly states that wherever tribal people are involved, projects must be designed to safeguard their special interests and well-being. Even though the World Bank is no longer involved in the project, according to advocacy groups the Bank should not be absolved of its responsibility for ensuring that the project continues in compliance with its policies and safeguards, a position clarified (albeit by inference) by the World Bank's general counsel that the government of India is legally obligated to carry out its obligations under the original loan agreement (Clark 2003).

This is paradoxical, since it was the protest in the Narmada Valley which led to the constitution of the first ever World Bank independent review and also of the Inspection Panel and the convening of the World Commission on Dams. Thus, while the protest movement has had significant victories with respect to the creation of new policies and institutions, their lot on the ground has not improved significantly. Moreover, increases in the dam's height have not proceeded hand in hand with rehabilitation of affected people (Clark 2003; Clark and Bhardwaj 2003). In 2002, flood waters during the monsoon of September submerged homes, crops and livestock across the Narmada Valley. People had to be pulled out of hip-high water by the police. People stood in rising waters in their homes and the police arrived to arrest them. In 2002, a young *adivasi* woman from Madhya Pradesh told a gathering:

> A few months ago, a team surveyed the whole village, the lands, the assets and the resettlement package. The team assured us that they would not allow any submergence to take place until the resettlement process was completed. But still on the day when the water came, 5,000 police personnel came to the village with only four women police. We asked why so many police had come ... All of a sudden they began dragging us out of our houses. They even dragged out the women who had no clothes with them. They pulled children and even a three-month-old baby who could barely survive without its mother. There was another four-year-old child who was found only after fifteen days. On the one hand, our village was filling with water and on the other hand the police were dumping people forcibly in makeshift camps.

Every year when submergence occurs, there are problems with the availability of food supplies and access to drinking water owing to the destruction of crops and the complete transformation of the river (Clark and Bhardwaj 2003). Furthermore, the Indian government is also known to resort to draconian measures to make protest illegal in order to legitimize mass arrests in contravention of Article 19 of the Indian constitution, which allows people to protest peacefully.

Sit-ins, protest and hunger strikes in state capitals and in Delhi led to ministers and senior bureaucrats and members of the National Human Rights Commission and National Women's Commission making visits to the affected areas and to resettlement villages. In an incremental way, the lot of some oustees improved as a result of these massive protests. Still, despite mass mobilization, high-profile campaigns and media presence, rights continued to be violated with impunity in the Narmada Valley. Moreover, the Narmada Control Authority has often agreed to increases in the dam's height despite illegalities and failures related to resettlement and rehabilitation. The state governments claim that they have already provided resettlement and rehabilitation and that the affected people should address their concerns to the GRA (Grievance Redressal Authority). In relation to this, the central government has found it convenient to pass the buck to the relevant state governments.

Owing to these institutional and accountability failures there are now calls to refocus attention on the role of the World Bank. While most displaced people do not want the World Bank to be involved, they continue to hold it responsible for its role in promoting a project that so clearly violates its own policies as well as international human rights standards, and believe it is therefore obliged to provide reparations to survivors and their families owing to the desperately inadequate living conditions after resettlement. But how can such mechanisms be installed? At the moment, IFIs such as the World Bank disclaim all responsibility. It has been suggested that an international court of arbitration could decide on how the IFIs and borrower countries could share costs in the case of disagreements after complaints are filed by governments, NGOs and the affected people (Bretton Woods Project 2004).

The linkage between 'bestowed' rights and 'claimed' rights

The discussion thus far has examined how rights framed in policy may be denied at policy implementation, in spite of democratic institutions aimed at enforcing such rights. Both South Africa and India have progressive constitutions and legislation in place to cement the realization of human rights. Moreover, both countries have human rights commissions that monitor how rights are being violated or realized and which, in both cases, have taken pro-poor stances. In the South African case at least, however, it has been argued that the South African Human Rights Commission is a 'toothless bulldog' which is failing to rein in human rights violations (Matshekga 2002; see also Chabane 2007). The institutional arrangements for adequate follow-up may sometimes be limited. This is particularly true for Narmada, where the monitoring of human rights violations has not necessarily led to a change in the perception that officials can continue to disregard human rights in order to carry on with dam-building activities. As the International Council on Human Rights Policy (ICHRP) rightly says, 'while national human rights commissions can promote and validate a human rights culture in the right circumstances, they can equally remain ineffectual when they operate in a political culture that ignores or is antagonistic to human rights' (ICHRP 2004: 42).

As also highlighted by the chapter by Simpson and Waldman in this book, judicial activism has enhanced the voice of the poor and played a constructive role in ensuring the realization of rights (Goetz and Jenkins 2004). Indeed, the litigation cases mentioned in South Africa have demonstrated how judges' constitutional interpretations can expand the scope of rights and thus increase the state's obligations to citizens. In India, too, much is made of judicial activism and the role of the Supreme Court in enhancing voice. But the Narmada judgment changed this perception. The controversial 2000 Supreme Court judgment is considered by many to be a highly emotive and non-judicial judgment, making many in India now cautious about the litigation route. In the Narmada case, the law turned out to be highly arbitrary, influenced by powerful vested interests and narratives. It would be a mistake to argue that social activism can rely on litigation as a panacea for resolving ongoing injustices with regard to breaches between constitutionally enshrined rights, including socio-economic rights, and policy decisions.[10]

In the case of Narmada, despite many victories and the establishment of several new institutional processes that should enhance the rights of displaced people around the world (e.g. the Inspection Panel, World Commission on Dams, GRAs), human rights continue to be violated with impunity in India. The World Bank also has no mechanisms to ensure that borrowers comply with loan regulations and standards and tends to pass the buck to borrower countries. While human rights commentators such as the ICHRP (2004) talk of creating a favourable institutional environment in which to realize human rights and seek accountability, often the institutional mechanisms in place may not end up being very pro-poor in their outcomes. In instances such as this, even robust forms of social mobilization and social movements are unable to transform the status quo.

Conclusions

The South African examples highlight problems stemming from adequate financial resources to extend the rights to water as well as contradictions of market-based and rights approaches. Negotiating this contradiction requires active citizen lobbying and even judicial enforcement, as demonstrated in the various South African cases. In the Indian case of oustee displacement, there is a marked lack of official endorsement to shift from programmes that merely seek to ameliorate the impacts and risks of displacement to upholding the rights of the displaced. For example, the World Bank, despite being one of the founding members of the World Commission on Dams (WCD), declined to adopt WCD recommendations that, among other things, a decision-making process should strive towards balancing the rights and risks of all stakeholders, and in particular protect the rights of groups such as indigenous peoples. In sum, 'access to the rights to those at the bottom of the pile can only be achieved by radical policy changes backed up with financial support' (ibid.: 39). To do this, strong commitments towards furthering the interests of the weak and marginalized are urgently required, a commitment that appears to be lacking on the part of IFIs such as the World Bank.

This chapter has examined why citizens are denied economic and social rights through sins of omission and commission, and the efforts made by poor communities to claim what is rightfully theirs. Clearly, not having access to rights does not mean that the rights do not exist, yet the extent to which rights are abstract conjectures existing only in statute books that cannot be enforced owing to various obstacles such as those outlined in this chapter may create the impression of superficiality and irrelevance of the rights framework. While, in a number of instances, supreme courts in South Africa have ruled in favour of those denied access to socio-economic rights, these successes have not transformed livelihoods of poor South Africans owing to limiting clauses that form part of rights clauses in the constitution. This should not detract from the fact that rights do and should matter.

The success, albeit limited, of high-profile resistance activities such as those against the Narmada dams depends on transnational alliances of NGOs, campaigns and movements, while the ability of activist social movements such as the Coalition against Water Privatisation in court cases in South Africa demonstrates the importance of having a codified form of rights, although the Indian example shows willingness by government to subvert laws in pursuit of certain ends. Yet even where success has been more symbolic than material, rights claims on the part of social movements have often transformed public and political attitudes as well as unleashed debates about social justice. These successes are in turn mediated by global economic discourses that emphasize economic development, which may run counter to pro-poor rights-based policies in the South.

Notes

1 Advocacy for positive rights – such as access to water, food and shelter – marks a sharp change from the negative or liberal understanding of rights that underpins notions of liberal democracy. Neoliberal thought has traditionally viewed negative civil and political rights as essential to understanding what constitutes citizenship. Yet these traditions have been reluctant to award the same widespread attention to social and economic rights, because such rights have strong links to social justice and imply moving away from the neoliberal notion that people's socio-economic status is determined by the market (Plant 1998: 57–8).

2 This distinction is not new. This chapter, however, seeks to tease out the conceptual and practical implications.

3 This is based on the World Health Organization recommendation for water supply sufficient to promote healthy living set at 25 litres of safe, clean water per person per day within 200 metres of homes.

4 Department of Water Affairs and Forestry official, personal communication by email, 16 May 2005.

5 Certification of the Constitution of South Africa 1996 1996 4 SA 744 (CC).

6 Ibid.

7 *Adivasi* literally means 'original/ earliest settler'. This term is used to designate the indigenous peoples of India, officially known as 'scheduled tribes', who make up about 7 per cent of the entire population.

8 In October 2001, the Supreme Court of India issued directions in relation to the Sardar Sarovar Project, including the obligation to comply with the relief and rehabilitation work, and 'take the necessary ameliorative and compensatory measures for environmental protection' (Clark and Bhardwaj 2003: 9).

9 India has signed various international human rights treaties which recognize, among others, the right to life, to freedom of movement and to choose one's residence, and to an adequate standard of living, including adequate food, clothing and housing. The Covenant on Economic, Social, and Cultural Rights requires, for instance, that procedural guarantees be offered by the government, including 'genuine consultation with the project-affected people, the issue of adequate notice to all affected persons prior to the date of eviction, and the provision of legal remedies and legal aid where applicable' (Cullet 2000).

10 Even the ICHRP notes that when indigenous peoples use the Supreme Court the outcomes can be variable. For example, Oaxaca Indians found that the Mexican Supreme Court refused to accept their evidence (ICHRP 2004: 22).

References

Anand, P. B. (2007) 'The right to water and access to water: an assessment', *Journal of International Development*, 19: 511–26.

Bond, P. (2002) 'Local economic development debates in South Africa', Occasional Papers Series 6, Cape Town: Municipal Services Project.

— (2003) 'Privatisation, participation and protest in the restructuring of municipal services: grounds for opposing World Bank promotion of "public–private partnerships"', *The Water Page*, www.thewater

page.com/ppp_debate1.htm, accessed 16 November 2003.

Bond, P., D. McDonald, G. Ruiters and L. Greeff (2001) *Water Privatisation in Southern Africa: The State of the Debate*, Cape Town: Environmental Monitoring Group.

Bretton Woods Project (2004) 'World Bank accountability: demand for reparations won't go away', *Bretton Woods Update*, London.

Chabane, P. E. (2007) *Enforcement Powers of Human Rights Institutions: A Case of Ghana, South Africa and Uganda*, LLM thesis, University of Pretoria.

Clark, D. (2002) 'Overview of revisions to the World Bank resettlement policy', in L. Mehta (ed.), *Gender and the Politics of Displacement*, New Delhi: Sage Publications.

— (2003) *International Accountability Project*, Berkeley, CA, www.narmada.org/resources/DanaWBLetter. pdf, accessed 9 February 2005.

Clark, D. and S. Bhardwaj (2003) *The Impact of the 2002 Submergence on Housing and Land Rights in the Narmada Valley: Report of a Fact-Finding Mission to Sardar Sarovar and Man Dam Projects*, Habitat International Coalition, Housing and Land Rights Network, www.hic-sarp.org/documents/narmada. pdf, accessed 9 February 2005.

CLC (2002) South African Cases: High Court Cases: *Residents of Bon Vista Mansions* v. *Southern Metropolitan Local Council* 2002 (6) BCLR 625 (W), Community Law Centre, Socioeconomic Rights Project, www.communitylawcentre.org. za/ser/casereviews/2002_6_BCLR_625.php, accessed 18 March 2005.

COHRE (2004) *Legal Resources for the Right to Water: International and National Standards*, Geneva: Centre on Housing Rights and Evictions.

Cook, P. and M. Minogue (2003) 'Regulating for development', id21 Insights 49, Brighton: Institute of Development Studies.

COSATU and SAMWU (2003) *Joint Submission by COSATU and SAMWU on the Draft White Paper on Water Services Presented to the DWAF*, Congress of South African Trade Unions and South African Municipal Workers' Union, www.queensu.ca/msp/pages/Project_Publications/Reports/CosatuSamwu.pdf, accessed 18 March 2005.

Cullet, P. (2000) 'Narmada dams and human rights', *Frontline*, 17(14), www.ielrc.org/content/n0003.htm, accessed 18 March 2005.

Donnelly, J. (1999) 'Human rights, democracy and development', *Human Rights Quarterly*, 21: 608–32.

Dreze, J., M. Samson and S. Singh (eds) (1997) *The Dam and the Nation: Displacement and Resettlement in the Narmada Valley*, Delhi: Oxford University Press.

DWAF (2005) *Free Basic Water Project, Implementation Status*, Department of Water Affairs and Forestry, www.dwaf.gov.za/FreeBasicWater/Defaulthome.asp, accessed 18 March 2005.

— (2008) *Free Basic Water Project, Implementation Status*, Department of Water Affairs and Forestry, www.dwaf.gov.za/freebasicwater/Default.asp?ServiceType=1, accessed 5 June 2008.

Fernandes, W. and E. G. Thukral (eds) (1989) *Development, Displacement, and Rehabilitation*, New Delhi: Indian Social Institute.

Francis, R. (2005) 'Water justice in South Africa: natural resources policy at the intersection of human rights, economics and political power', *Georgetown International Environmental Law Review*, 18(1): 149–96.

Gabru, N. (2005) 'Some comments on water rights in South Africa', *PER*, 1.

Goetz, A. and R. Jenkins (2004) *Reinventing Accountability: Making Democracy Work for Human Development*, Basingstoke: Palgrave Macmillan.

Goldsmith, E. and N. Hildyard (eds) (1992) *The Social and Environmental Effects of Large Dams*, vol. III: *A Review of the Literature*, Cornwall: Wadebridge Ecological Centre.

Gowlland-Gualtieri, A. (2007) *South Africa's Water Law and Policy Framework*, Geneva: International Environmental Law Research Centre, www.ielrc.org/content/w0703.pdf, accessed 30 May 2008.

Häusermann, J. (1998) 'A human rights approach to development', *Rights and Humanity*, London: Department for International Development.

ICHRP (2004) *Enhancing Access to Human Rights*, Versoix: International Council on Human Rights Policy.

ICWE (1992) *The Dublin Statement and Report of the Conference*, International Conference on Water and the Environment: Development Issues for the 21st Century, 26–31 January, Dublin.

IDASA (2008) *Residents Win a Court Battle in the Struggle for Free Basic Water*, www.idasa.org.za/index.asp?page=output_details.asp%3FRID%3D1454%26oplang%3

Den%26Pub%3DY%26OTID%3D5, accessed 6 June 2008.

INTRAC (2003) 'Viewpoint: rights or values?', Newsletter of the International NGO Training and Research Centre, Oxford.

Jackson, B. (2002) 'Free water – what are the chances of serving the poor', Mimeo, Johannesburg.

Jayal, N. G. (1999) *Democracy and the State: Welfare, Secularism and Development in Contemporary India*, New Delhi: Oxford University Press.

Kasrils, R. (2003) 'Minister Kasrils responds to false claim of 10 million cut-offs', www.dwaf.gov.za/Communications/Articles/Minister/2003/Cutoffs%20article%20WEBSITE.doc, accessed 4 May 2004.

Kidd, M. (2003) 'Not a drop to drink: disconnection of water services for nonpayment and the right of access to water', Paper delivered at the Water Institute of South Africa Management and Institutional Affairs Division Conference: Managing Change in the Water Sector, Sandton, www.law.wits.ac.za/sajhr/2004/kidd.pdf, accessed 18 March 2005.

Kihato, C. and T. Schmitz (2002) 'Enhancing policy implementation: lessons from the water sector', Research Report 96, Social Policy Series, Johannesburg: Centre for Policy Studies.

Manor, J. (2001) 'Local government in South Africa: potential disaster despite genuine promise', SLSA Working Paper 8, Brighton: Institute of Development Studies.

Manqele v. Durban Transitional Metropolitan Council (2001) JOL 8956 (D).

Matshekga, J. (2002) 'Toothless

bulldogs? The Human Rights Commissions of Uganda and South Africa: a comparative study of their independence', *African Human Rights Law Journal*, 2: 68–91.

Mazibuko, L. & Others v. *City of Johannesburg and Others*. Case No. 03/13865. Witwatersrand Local Division of the High Court of South Africa (2008) (unreported case).

McCully, P. (1996) *Silenced Rivers: The Ecology and Politics of Large Dams*, London: Zed Books.

McDonald, D. (2002) *The Bell Tolls for Thee: Cost Recovery, Cut-Offs and the Affordability of Municipal Services in South Africa*, Municipal Services Project, qsilver.queensu. ca/~mspadmin/pages/Project_ Publications/Reports/bell.htm, accessed 12 December 2003.

McKinley, D. (2003) 'Water is life: the Anti-Privatisation Forum and the struggle against water privatisation', *Public Citizen*, www.citizen.org/cmep/Water/ cmep_Water/reports/southafrica/ articles.cfm?ID=10554, accessed 12 December 2003.

Mehta, L. (2000) 'Women facing submergence: displacement and resistance in the Narmada', in V. Damadoran and M. Unnithan (eds), *Identities, Nation, Global Culture*, New Delhi: Manohar.

— (2004) 'From state control to market regulation: behind the border policy convergence in water management', IDS Working Paper 233, Brighton: Institute of Development Studies.

— (2005) *The Politics and Poetics of Water: Naturalising Scarcity in Western India*, New Delhi: Orient Longman.

— (2006) 'Do human rights make a difference to poor and vulnerable people? Accountability for the right to water in South Africa', in P. Newell and J. Wheeler (eds), *Rights, Resources and the Politics of Accountability*, London: Zed Books.

Mehta, L. and Z. Ntshona (2004) 'Dancing to two tunes: rights and market based approaches in South Africa's water domain', Sustainable Livelihoods in Southern Africa Research Paper 17, Brighton: Institute of Development Studies.

Morse, B. and T. Berger (1992) *Sardar Sarovar: Report of the Independent Team*, Ottawa: Research Futures International.

Muller, M. (2007) 'Parish pump politics: the politics of water supply in South Africa', *Progress in Development Studies*, 7: 33–45.

— (2008) 'Free basic water: a sustainable instrument for a sustainable future in South Africa', *Environment and Urbanisation*, 20(1): 67–87.

National Treasury (1999) 'Provincial and local government finances', *National Budget Review 1999*, ch. 4, Republic of South Africa, www.treasury.gov.za/documents/ budget/1999/review/chapter_4. pdf, accessed 7 May 2004.

— (2004) 'Provincial and local government allocations', *National Budget Review 2004*, ch. 7, Republic of South Africa, www.finance. gov.za/documents/budget/2004/ review/Chapter%207.pdf, accessed 7 May 2004.

NCA (2005) *Provisions of NWDT Award and States Resettlement and Rehabilitation (R&R) Policies*, Narmada Control Authority, www.ncaindia.

org/rnr_prov.htm, accessed 18 March 2005.

Nleya, N. (2008) 'Development policy and water services in South Africa: an urban poverty perspective', *Development Southern Africa*, 25(3).

Olver, C. (1998) 'Blueprint for the business of running efficient cities', *Sunday Times* (South Africa), 14 June, www.suntimes. co.za/1998/06/14/insight/in04. htm, accessed 28 May 2004.

Parasuraman, P. (1997) 'The anti-dam movement and rehabilitation policy', in J. Dreze, M. Samson and S. Singh (eds), *The Dam and the Nation: Displacement and Resettlement in the Narmada Valley*, Delhi: Oxford University Press.

Pauw, J. (2003) *Metered to Death: How a Water Experiment Caused Riots and a Cholera Epidemic*, Centre for Public Integrity, www.icij.org/water/report. aspx?sID=ch&rID=49&aID=49, accessed 11 November 2003.

Plant, R. (1992) 'Citizenship, rights and welfare', in A. Coote (ed.), *The Welfare of Citizens: Developing New Social Rights*, London: IPPR.

— (1998) 'Citizenship, rights, welfare', in J. Franklin (ed.), *Social Policy and Social Justice*, Cambridge: Polity Press.

Raj, P. (1991) *Facts: Sardar Sarovar Projects*, Gandhinagar: Narmada Nigam Ltd.

Rajagopal, B. (2000) *Human Rights and Development*, World Commission on Dams Submission, www. dams.org/kbase/submissions/ showsub.php?rec=INS206, accessed 18 March 2005.

Residents of Bon Vista Mansions v. Southern Metropolitan Local Council 2002 (6) BCLR 625 (W).

Robinson, C. (2003) 'Risks and rights: the causes, consequences, and challenges of development-induced displacement', Occasional Paper, SAIS Project on Internal Displacement, Washington, DC: Brookings Institution.

Roy, A. (1999) 'The greater common good', *Frontline*, 16(11), www. flonnet.com/fl1611/16110040. htm.

Schoonakev, B. (2004) 'Treated with contempt', *Sunday Times*, 21 March.

Scudder, T. (1996) 'Development-induced impoverishment, resistance and river-basin development', in C. McDowell (ed.), *Understanding Impoverishment*, Providence, RI, and Oxford: Berghahn Books.

Shoba, S. (2008) 'Masondo takes on "water" judge', *Business Day*, 15 May, www.businessday. co.za/articles/topstories. aspx?ID=BD4A766825, accessed 6 June 2008.

Social Watch (2003) *Social Watch Report 2003: The Poor and the Market*, Montevideo: Instituto del Tercer Mundo.

Statistics South Africa (2002) *Measuring Rural Development: Baseline Statistics for the Integrated Sustainable Rural Development Strategy*, Pretoria: Statistics South Africa.

— (2007) *Community Survey 2007: Methodology, Processes and Highlights of Key Results*, Pretoria: Statistics South Africa.

Sunday Independent (2003) 'Attack the problem not the data: report on the number of people affected by water cut-offs was based on sound methodology', 15 June.

Thompson, L. and N. Nleya (2008) 'The policy implications of the Millennium Development

Goals and service delivery at the national and local levels', *Africanus*, December.

Thukral, E. (1992) *Big Dams, Displaced Peoples: Rivers of Sorrow, Rivers of Joy*, Delhi: Sage Publications.

WaterAid, Rights and Humanity, and FAN (2008) *Challenging the Adequacy of Free Basic Water in Phiri, Soweto, South Africa*, www.

righttowater.org.uk/code/legal_6. asp, accessed 6 June 2008.

World Bank (2004) *World Bank Operational Manual, 2001 (revised 2004): Operational Policies: Involuntary Resettlement*, wbln0018.worldbank.org/Institutional/Manuals/OpManual.nsf/whatnewvirt/CA2D01A4D1BDF58085256B19008197F6?OpenDocument, accessed 18 March 2005.

Water rights and state management

6 | Environmental activism in Brazil: the rise of a social movement[1]

ANGELA ALONSO, VALERIANO COSTA
AND DÉBORA MACIEL

Environmental mobilizations have been widely studied over the past few decades as part of a broad class of social movements. Competing perspectives in the field have emphasized their different analytical dimensions: political opportunities and mobilizing structures (political process), and on the other hand symbolic and cognitive features and collective identity-building processes (NSMs).

Recently, some scholars have produced a synthesis of these perspectives to accommodate both dimensions, strategy and identity, that each school had tended to focus on separately. In this vein, Diani (1995) argues that social movements are informal organizations whose existence depends both on activists sharing experiences and on mobilizing resources and strategies. Diani even redefines social movements in order to put the symbolic and material dimensions together as central features of the phenomenon. At the same time, he and other contemporary analysts consider the material and strategic dimensions stressed by political process theory as well as the symbolic dimensions emphasized by the NSM theoreticians, such as micro-mobilization contexts (Gamson 1982) in which collective identities and frames are created.

In this chapter the same blend of concepts helps explain why the Brazilian environmental movement appeared when and as it did, how the activists gathered in groups and networks, and which frames and strategies they built in order to mobilize. 'Political opportunity structure' (POS) describes the 'consistent – but not necessarily formal, permanent, or national – dimensions of the political struggle that encourage people to engage in contentious politics' (Tarrow 1998: 20). Being a middle-range concept, POS makes it possible to revive the political national conjunctures, which NSM theories frequently neglect (Kriesi 1995) – in our case, the Brazilian political conjuncture through which an environmental movement was formed.

The notion of 'micro-mobilization contexts' brings into our analysis the micro-dimensions of activism that macro-structural analyses usually lose, such as the local contexts where mobilization first arises. Socio-economic extraction is not enough to explain why ordinary people mobilize around specific issues. As Mueller (1992: 10) argues, activism arises from micro-mobilization contexts, such as educational and professional institutions, cultural groups, and friendship and neighbourhood networks, in which activists live their everyday lives and engage with others. It is within micro-contexts of social interaction that isolated ordinary citizens gather in shared collective action, building a new identity as 'environmental activists'. Hence, this latter aspect is key to understanding how the identities of distinct environmental groups developed in Brazil.

Collective action also depends on activists' ability to build up shared interpretations. Activists interpret the situations they live in on the basis of their own experiences and perceptions, including even the most stable features of POS. This process occurs through frame production and alignment, as Snow and Benford (1992) demonstrate. This was the mechanism used by groups of activists with particular experiences to shape some aspects of the Brazilian social reality into environmental problems, comprising distinctive frames. These environmental frames have been adjusted to variations in POS, competing among themselves to prevail as the frame of the movement as a whole.

Social movements require organizational bases and strategies to support mobilization. Since social movements are not always institutionally based, activists have to appropriate or even create channels to achieve collective action from what is available (Tilly 1978). Mobilizing structures helps solidarity among members and collective identities arise (Diani 1995). Accordingly, to explain the formation of the Brazilian environmental movement, both the structured and fluid dimensions of collective action must be taken into consideration. All of these dimensions – POS, collective identity, micro-mobilization contexts, framing processes and mobilizing strategies – configured the Brazilian social movement.

In the following sections we argue that the Brazilian environmental movement is a network of different activist groups that became mobilized, originally, for different purposes in specific settings, following their own focal mobilizing routines. In specific POSs, challenges from opponents or specific opportunities for introducing issues on the public agenda strengthen ties among the groups and facilitate joint mobilization, helping to build common frames and mobilizing strategies and shaping 'movement identity' (Jasper 1997).

This chapter relies on a theoretical blend that uses the strengths of both approaches, relying on concepts derived from NSM theories, such as 'collective identity', as well as from POS, from the theories of political process. Based on this combination, we argue here that three POSs – redemocratization, the Constituent Assembly and the United Nations Conference on Environment and Development (Rio '92) – were decisive in the formation of the Brazilian environmental movement, as they brought to the fore the activists' problems concerning the coordination of their collective action. They were the context for the environmental activists' symbolic and strategic choices, substantially affecting the movement's make-up. The POSs also made possible the pivotal articulation between the vertical connections activists built inside the 'formal invited spaces', even in Congress, and the horizontal connections activists worked out among themselves by means of framing strategies and coalition-building.

Formation of environmental groups (1970–85)

Political opportunity structure of redemocratization Political process theory points out that social movements usually arise when changes in political opportunities increase the possibilities for making claims by opening up existing channels or creating new ones. This can occur in three main directions. First, political and administrative institutions can become more receptive to claims from civil society owing to crises in the coalition of the political elite. Second, the style of political interactions between the state and social movements can change, especially when the repression of mobilization is reduced. Third, potential allies may become available, such as other social movements, political parties, media or dissident elites (Kriesi 1995). These factors enhance the channels for dissatisfied social groups to express their demands in the public arena. In situations where many groups are organizing themselves to express grievances, a cycle of protests arises (Tarrow 1983). The formation of an environmental movement in Brazil was possible only thanks to the new POS in the late 1970s, which matched the above three conditions. The authoritarian regime, which had been in power since 1964, began to fall apart and the redemocratization process began.

The rise of environmental protests and groups during the authoritarian regime was made possible by a couple of peculiarities of the Brazilian dictatorship. Despite being politically and administratively very centralized and repressive of opposition groups,[2] the authoritarian regime kept some democratic features (Linz 1973). Electoral competition was also maintained, although limited to two official parties: ARENA (the National Renewal Alliance), comprising civil society supporters of the military regime, and the MDB (Brazilian Democratic Movement), a grouping of the moderate opposition (Kinzo 1988). Minimal democratic elements provided room for the formation of local, philanthropic and professional associations and also space for local collective protests to occur, even before the regime crisis.

The opportunities for mobilization increased at the end of the 1970s, when the governing coalition suffered a crisis. The more moderate faction won, bringing back some democratic guarantees. Channels for political mobilization were then created in two ways. The ban on political expression was abrogated in 1978 and media censorship was lifted. In 1979, leftist activists, exiled since the beginning of the regime, were given amnesty. A few immediately resumed their political activities. In the same year, the right to create new parties was restored, resulting in many new left-wing parties, which included former social movement activists previously operating under the MDB's umbrella (ibid. 1988; Sallum 1996).

The last outcome of this process was the succession of MDB electoral victories for national representatives (1974), mayors (1978) and state governments (1982). In the last, the opposition ended up with ten governors, including of the three important states of São Paulo, Rio de Janeiro and Minas Gerais. These victories served as incentives to various dissatisfied social groups to express their grievances publicly and collectively by organizing social movements and building up a cycle of protest (Tarrow 1983: 36–9). Although the authoritarian regime was still in charge of the political system and in control of presidential elections, from 1983 on this 'controlled opening was hit by the processes of democratization of society, mainly by the union movement and middle class organizations' (Sallum 1996: 42).

Four dimensions of this POS are fundamental to understanding the appearance of environmental protests in Brazil in the 1970s.

First, there were changes in the style of political interaction between the state and social movements. From the mid-1970s, formal changes to legal-political aspects of the regime, such as amnesty for political prisoners, the return of a rights dispensation and freedom of the press, the possibility of promoting political candidates and public demonstrations, provided openings for environmental protest.

Second, environmental activists found themselves on a rising tide of protest and were able to rely on the potential support of allies that were already organized, such as traditional institutions, including the Catholic Church and the renowned Brazilian Bar Association, and the MDB. They could also count on many sectors of civil society – workers, middle-class liberal professionals, civil servants and residents of the areas on the fringes of the large urban centres – that had previously organized themselves as social movements.

Third, political and administrative institutions were increasingly receptive to civil society claims, including environmental grievances. During the authoritarian regime, bureaucratic organs had been created in this field, such as the Special Secretariat for the Environment (1973), and specific legislation had been introduced regulating the use of the natural environment, especially reserves. This legal-bureaucratic structure, enlarged through the redemocratization process, not only provided activists with new political space and new mobilizing structures to voice their claims, but also opened new career possibilities in government.

Finally, during this period an international environmental agenda was being put together. The organization of large international environmental associations – Friends of the Earth (1967) and Greenpeace (1971) – and green political parties in New Zealand (1972), Great Britain (1973), Germany (1979) and France (1982), offered organizational models and mobilizing strategies for Brazilian activists concerned with the environment. Besides this, the coalition between international environmental protection agencies created after the Second World War – the United Nations Environment Programme (UNEP), the International Union for the Conservation of Nature and Natural Resources (IUCN), the World Wildlife Fund for Nature, WWF – plus US and European civil environmental associations resulted in a call for a meeting on the issue at the UN in 1972. By participating in the UN Conference on the Human Environment in Stockholm, even though defending an anti-environmental position, the Brazilian state brought the matter to a head. This led to the creation of the Special Secretariat for the Environment and the opening up of the public *national* discussion on environmental issues in Brazil.

Together, these dimensions of the POS of the redemocratization process allowed for the formation of environmental groups that became the backbone of the Brazilian movement in the 1980s.

Micro-mobilization contexts and the formation of collective identities
Although the social basis of all Brazilian environmental groups that came into being in the 1970s and 1980s could be described as 'middle class' (Antuniassi 1989), this is not an explanation for their mobilization, since most political mobilization at that time involved activists from the middle class. The reason for the mobilization of environmental groups has to be found in the distinct micro-mobilization contexts in which each one

was formed. What connects activists is, first of all, sociocultural and personal interaction, through which common interpretation, affective ties and communitarian loyalties are built and a sense of membership to the same group is produced (Gamson 1992; Taylor and Whittier 1992). Jasper (1997: 86) adds that '[c]ollective identity consists of perceptions of group distinctiveness, boundaries, and interests, for something closer to a community'. The different genres of social and political experience shared by members end up giving each group peculiar features and distinct styles of environmental activism (Diani 1995). To describe the contexts of social experience in which the Brazilian activists engaged and collective environmental identities were built, we must take into account their professional backgrounds, connections to the political elite and state bureaucracy and contact with other political and cultural movements.

At the roots of Brazilian environmental activism was a pioneering conservationist association called the Brazilian Foundation for the Conservation of Nature (FBCN), founded in 1958 in Rio de Janeiro. Its members came, mostly, from scientific fields; they were agronomists, agricultural engineers and natural scientists who got involved in environmental issues for professional reasons. Many were civil servants and had ties with the Brazilian political elite. This closeness to the state made them favour lobbying instead of public demonstrations as a strategy for mobilization. As employees within the state bureaucracy they worked as an interest group, seeking to influence state decisions directly, rather than building alliances with parties or social movements. Before and during the military regime, this strategy was very successful: the FBCN influenced the creation of environmental laws, organs and policies, and its members rose to important positions in the field. The careers of FBCN's members were intertwined with the setting up of Brazil's own environmental bureaucracy, giving the FBCN the appearance of a parallel governmental organization until the 1970s.[3]

Other groups sprang up in the 1970s and began linking environmental issues to political debates. AGAPAN (the Southern Association for the Protection of the Natural Environment), founded in 1971 in Porto Alegre, is very similar in origin to the FBCN. It also began as an initiative of natural science researchers with a professional interest in ecological matters, many with previous experience in local conservationists' associations. In the early 1970s, like the FBCN it worked on setting up the government's environmental bureaucracy, influencing the development of legislation and implementing public environmental policies, but at a regional level.[4] It differed from the FBCN, however, in using mobilization strategies, such as campaigns, lectures and symbolic forms of demonstration. AGAPAN's most important mobilization at the time was the National Campaign against the Use of Agrotoxins, launched in 1972. It began at local level, but quickly reached a national audience, with AGAPAN's leader, José Lutzenberger, travelling the country disseminating the idea (Bones and Hasse 2002). Actions of this kind brought AGAPAN progressively closer to the redemocratization movement, as it participated in politically oriented collective events at the end of the 1970s.

Another group was MAPE (the Art and Ecological Thinking Movement), formed in São Paulo in 1973. It consisted mainly of artists and some journalists and writers, with ties to countercultural movements, and concerned about urban pollution. MAPE introduced creative and symbolic mobilization strategies devised by new European social movements to the Brazilian environmental movement: artistic happenings, exhibitions, literary displays and entertainments. Its inaugural demonstration was a one-man parade: the Catalan painter Miguel Abellá walked into the centre of São Paulo wearing a gas mask and carrying a poster saying, 'This is my pacifist and solitary protest against cowardly environmental aggression' (O Estado de São Paulo, 8 September 1973). 'Ecological Crusades', a travelling art exhibition designed to attract followers, toured the country. The fact that its members had no technical expertise in the area kept MAPE at a distance from public environmental positions and more oriented towards civil society, including the redemocratization movement.

Also in São Paulo, the APPN (São Paulo Association for Natural Protection) was set up in 1976. Its members were liberal professionals and small businessmen with previous political and organizational experience. The APPN arose from a communitarian reaction against government works that impacted on its members' residential area. The APPN's main campaign was against the building of an international airport in the south-western region of São Paulo, where most of its activists lived. APPN mobilized the residents in the neighbourhood potentially affected. Since this neighbourhood included the University of São Paulo, however, leftist intellectuals quickly joined the protest, opening a connection with members of the MDB political party (Antuniassi 1989: 26). The association thus engaged with the opposition to the military regime's 'model of development'. Consequently, the protest ultimately took on national proportions quite by accident, through being adopted and supported by the movement for redemocratization and attracting intellectual, artistic and political activist groups. The APPN's mobilization strategies were also the classic ones: public protests, petitions and open letters to the authorities. It strengthened the previously weak links between environmental activism and the movement for redemocratization.

In each of these micro-mobilization contexts, isolated individuals gathered into small groups of environmental activists and specific kinds of environmental identities were built (Sainteny 1999): one technical, based on professional links among natural scientists previously connected with the state bureaucracy; the other political, relying on a humanistic background and connections with the redemocratization movement. It was from these micro-mobilization contexts that distinctive collective identities as 'environmentalists' were born.

Environmental frames Frames work as cognitive components that question a given social situation seen before as non-problematic, blame groups or authorities as responsible for that situation and point out strategies – recognized by activists as feasible – for solving it (Gamson 1992; Snow 1986; Snow and Benford 1992). Social movements use frames to indicate problems and attract activists, thus transforming discontentment into collective action. In this sense, frames are guides for collective action (Snow 1986: 464).

Studying the Italian case, Diani (1995: 22) identifies two typical frames concerned with environmental activism. The 'conservationist' one defines the environment exclusively as the untamed natural world and sees any intervention as a technical issue restricted to natural scientists. In doing this, it restricts the debate around environmental issues to technical and scientific experts. The 'political ecology' frame, on the other hand, defines the environmental problem as also related to the urban world and emphasizes its political and social dimensions. The causes of environmental degradation are ascribed to capitalist development and the modern lifestyle. The consequent social and cultural critique of capitalist society pushes the environmental discussion into the political arena. In the Brazilian environmental movement the picture is similar. The variations of micro-mobilization contexts and of perceptions of the POS among Brazilian environmental groups in the 1970s and 1980s led them also to develop two main frames.

The FBCN spread classic conservationism across Brazil. In its content, the FBCN adopted a biocentric viewpoint regarding the relationship between society and nature. The environment was defined as wild nature, untouched and untouchable, to be protected from the destructive actions of social groups through the setting up of national parks and reserves. Science was presented as the natural attitude to the environment and natural scientists as the authorities for defining environmental problems and policies. From both angles, conservationism segregated environmental issues from any social dimension and presented them as apolitical: '[w]e were more concerned with saving animals and creating protected areas; ... reserves should be maintained without use ... by man ... in order to protect biodiversity' (interview with FBCN member, 12 August 2004).

Despite the fact that the POS of redemocratization and changes in the international context have forced the FBCN to incorporate the 'management of natural resources' in forest areas already inhabited by traditional populations, the core of its conservationism has changed very little, keeping its focus on flora and fauna.

Another collective frame surfaced within the redemocratization process: socio-environmentalism, adopted by all the environmental groups formed in the 1970s. It differs from those mentioned above in two ways.

First, the definition of the environmental problem was transferred from the natural to the social sciences. That meant an increasing concern with the relationship between social and natural processes. The scientific approach was balanced by a countercultural humanism. MAPE argued for the restoration of an 'original humanist ethic' with regard to nature, while AGAPAN's discourse mixed natural and social science and demanded 'an ecological ethics, led by a unifying vision of the natural and social world' (Lutzenberger 1977).

Second, the idea of the environment was itself redefined: instead of referring to it as an untamed natural world, the new groups talked about the relationship between natural resources and social groups. All the concerns of these groups incorporated both social and environmental dimensions, which had been neglected by the conservationists.

The social dimensions also came into the debate in a more general way, with reference to Brazil's industrialization during the 1970s. MAPE criticized environmental deterioration caused by the expanding consumer society (Peco Bulletin 1978). The APPN associated these matters with the pattern of capitalism and the Brazilian state, as combined in the 'Brazilian development model'.

As a consequence, the emphasis on technical solutions to environmental issues shifted to changes in lifestyle to be achieved through public debate. In this way, the issue was reassigned from natural scientists to civil society and to the political arena. By doing this, the new groups associated environmental problems strongly with political matters. The point is clear in a joint manifesto from AGAPAN and APPN: '[W]e need a real democratic opening, citizenship participation, administrative de-centralization, real federalism and actual power division, and a maxim of self-sufficiency and self-governing' (AGAPAN and APPN 1978).

By the end of the 1970s, Brazilian environmental groups had worked out two main ways of defining and solving environmental problems: the conservationist and the socio-environmentalist frames. Which was more successful at different phases of the formation of the environmental movement depended on the issue at stake on the public agenda and on activists' ability to link either one or the other to elements that became available in each POS.

The formation of the Brazilian environmental movement

By drawing activists together and building distinct collective identities, the environmental groups formed during the 1970s established the basis for a nationwide movement. But a cohesive social movement could be formed only when these groups began to coordinate so that collective action could effectively emerge. A social movement requires not just a set of activists, but 'networks of informal interactions between a plurality of individuals, groups and/or organizations, engaged in political or cultural conflicts, on the basis of shared collective identities' (Diani 1995: 13). From their very beginning as a number of autonomous groups with distinct frames and mobilizations to their manifestation as a unique social movement, the Brazilian environmental groups created during the 1970s had a long way to go.

Although the groups that emerged in the 1970s knew of each other, they remained quite independent in conceptions and action until late in the decade. To act as a social movement, these groups had to solve three successive problems of coordinating collective action. They had to, first, create a network of groups from the fragile connections between them; second, agree on common mobilizing strategies; and third, develop a frame capable of unifying their approaches.

Each of these problems was solved during three decisive POSs: the redemocratization process in the late 1970s, the Constituent Assembly in the mid-1980s, and the United Nations Conference on Environment and Development in 1992. In each of these POSs, cycles of protests arose and the Brazilian environmental groups defined a minimum set of common patterns of thinking and acting. Those choices configured the collective identity of the whole environmental movement.

Cycle of protests for redemocratization (1970s) The first coalition among

Brazilian environmentalists occurred in the midst of the political process related to redemocratization, which began at the end of the 1970s. The redemocratization process fed a huge cycle of protests. Social groups, until then oblivious to the political universe, became organized and began collectively and publicly to voice their demands. Besides unionism and popular movements, an important part of these mobilizations had as a social base a new urban middle class (Boschi 1989): university professors, civil servants, liberal professionals, lawyers and students. These diverse movements gathered with the official opposition party, the MDB, for large-scale campaigns against the authoritarian regime and to focus on economic issues as well as to support the national movement for redemocratization.

Although somewhat tangential, the presence of environmental issues in the cycle of protests motivated the previously organized environmental groups to articulate a common participation in the public debate. Thus, an environmental network came about in the form of joint campaigns. Since the central matter on the public agenda was redemocratization, the incipient environmental network became mobilized around matters that could possibly be absorbed by the broader public debate. The result was the almost immediate politicization of environmental problems and, consequently, more connections between the environmental protest groups and the redemocratization movement.

This link was made possible by the socio-environmentalist frame, which brought together social and environmental matters, associating environmental damage with the authoritarian regime's development policies. This matched the emphasis of the redemocratization movement on the Brazilian 'social problem', thus paving the way for an alliance that could be seen in the three first national protests organized by environmental groups hand in hand with the redemocratization movement.

The Campaign in Defence of the Amazon, which began at the end of 1978, opposed the federal government's plan to draw up contracts with international companies for the exploration of the Amazon forest (Hochstetler and Keck 2007). The political connotation of this campaign was clear from the outset, since the opposition party, the MDB, was also involved. Led by the APPN, and including AGAPAN and MAPE, the campaign became the Movement in Defence of the Amazon and was organized through local committees in more than eighteen states and in the Federal District. On 15 January 1979, a public demonstration in São Paulo attracted close to 1,500 people and spawned the 'Open Letter to the Brazilian Nation' against the internationalization of the Amazon and in defence of the lifestyle of traditional communities living in the area (ibid.).

Another important coalition that used a similar style was the Campaign against the Use of Nuclear Energy, which began in 1980. The same associations from the previous campaign were involved, backed by smaller, recently formed environmentalist groups – like Oikos, Friends of the Earth (1982) and the SAP Ecology Group (1980). The issue attracted a larger spectrum of supporters from the redemocratization movement: the student movement, popular social movements, cultural movements, scientists, politicians, artists and religious leaders (Urban 2001).

The third campaign articulated by environmental groups was the 'Goodbye, Seven Falls' campaign, led by MAPE and including AGAPAN, APPN and other smaller associations, such as SAP Ecology and the Green Collective (1985) (a group of countercultural artists and intellectuals from Rio de Janeiro's elite, exiled during the military regime).

In all of these campaigns, the proximity with the redemocratization movement facilitated building a network of environmental activism. It was through the campaigns that the outline of relatively durable connections among environmental groups came into existence.

These mobilizations motivated the formation of new associations. In 1985, there were about four hundred organized environmental groups (Viola 1992: 57). They also enhanced the debate around the best mobilizing strategy for voicing environmental demands. Each group presented its own solution.

MAPE proposed a Brazilian environmental federation as a way to formalize a coalition among the various activist groups and also to keep activism directed at civil society. The fear of centralizing the movement led MAPE to prefer a looser network that limited its coordination to the regional level: the Permanent Assembly for the Defence of the Environment in São Paulo (APEDEMA), created in 1983.

The APPN, which from the beginning was committed to politicizing the issue of the environment, went back to discussing the coalition between the network of environmental associations and other groups mobilized in civil society and the opposition party, the MDB. Internal conflicts regarding the proposal to form a political party and launch green candidates resulted, however, in the fragmenting of the association into small groups.

Meanwhile, AGAPAN adopted the strategy of propelling its main activist, José Lutzenberger, to the status of a national leader. The group succeeded in acting as a broker among the diverse groups and achieving a central position in the network of environmental activism. The reason was twofold. First, AGAPAN's definition of the socio-environmental frame included all other movements' themes, ranging from strict natural protection, as in FBCN models, to urban environmental matters and countercultural topics. Second, it combined the traditional mobilizing strategies of conservationist groups, such as lobbying and access to state bureaucracy, with the public manifestations preferred by other environmental groups. AGAPAN thus became the main broker of 1970s environmental groups.

By the mid-1980s, the first stable coalition among environmental activist groups had emerged. The joint campaigns, and even the competition among groups, indicated the establishment of an environmental field, with its own leaders and agenda.

As a result of the redemocratization cycle of protests, environmental groups also ended up with a dominant frame. The FBCN conservationists lost their hegemony in the definition of the Brazilian environmental agenda. The redemocratization agenda helped consolidate a politicized approach to the environmental question: namely, socio-environmentalism. Throughout the 1980s, this frame oriented the nationalization of the environmental movement, bridging the discourse of the previously independent protest groups. And, most important, it connected the environmental groups to the redemocratization discourse. It was by these means that a national environmental mobilization surfaced in Brazil.

Cycle of protests for the Constituent Assembly (1980s) The final period of redemocratization, 1984 and 1985, is the second POS relevant to understanding the formation of the Brazilian environmental movement. If, in the previous POS, it was only coalitions on specific issues which allowed us to speak of an environmental movement, the perspective of a Constituent Assembly necessitated forming more stable coalitions as a strategy for including environmental issues in the new constitution.

The network had to solve two problems regarding collective action. On one hand, the groups had to decide which mobilizing strategy to opt for. The redemocratization process had reached the stage of general elections for a national Constituent Assembly, which forced the movement to choose whether to maintain its mobilizations at civil society level or to form a political party in the institutional arena. On the other hand, in order not to fragment environmental demands, the groups had to find common ground so as to set up minimum consensual points to constitute the environmental agenda.

The new POS confronted the environmental groups with the problem of choosing the most suitable mobilizing strategy in two stages: the discussions about the calling of a Constituent Assembly and then its actual functioning. At first, two forms of assembly were under debate. Social movements and the left-wing parties, headed by the Workers' Party (PT) created in 1980, proposed an assembly elected with the exclusive purpose of drawing up a constitution and open to direct participation by civil society. The moderate opposition, mainly the MDB, and the dissident groups from the military regime, proposed an assembly elected through parties, which would function simultaneously as a house of representatives. During this debate, coalitions among environmental groups were formed around a number of different strategies.

First, with the end of the democratic transition and the demobilization of civil society, some environmental activists opted to consolidate protest groups in specialized professional organizations, keeping just a tangential relationship with the broader political process, mainly through lobbying. SOS Mata Atlântica was constituted in 1986 on this basis, combining activists from previous groupings, such as APPN and FBCN, besides attracting business groups that, until then, had not been involved in environmental issues. In the Constituent Assembly, SOS Mata Atlântica, FBCN, AGAPAN and other newly formed conservationist associations preferred lobbying or supporting independent candidates for any party that included green proposals.

Second, the groups that aimed at lifestyle changes, such as MAPE and SAP Ecology, proposed to continue demonstrations at the civil society level and launch independent candidacies of environmental movement activists or supporters, but without connections to any party.

The third possibility was to launch or support candidacies within the recently organized left-wing parties and use nationwide campaigns as a way to disseminate their electoral platforms. Oikos, one of the APPN's dissident groups, invested in this alternative. The fourth option was to form a party as a channel for the political representation of the environmental movement.

Not all the alternatives were feasible. The congressional assembly format won out at the end of 1985. Independent candidates not belonging to parties were banned, so the option of taking part in the Constituent Assembly process outside parties fell away. There was no consensus on the two remaining possibilities. The environmental groups that took part in the elections for the Constituent Assembly were divided between two mobilizing strategies.

One coalition, headed by the Green Collective, opted for the creation of a Green Party (PV) in January 1986, gathering isolated activists from small associations, especially in Rio de Janeiro (Zhouri 1992: 66). Since then, the PV has led a small coalition that puts up its own candidates.

Another strategy was to support candidates from several parties, as long as they were committed to a list of green proposals. As a result, another problem appeared: how to coordinate the broad set of themes present in the coalition? This did not become a big issue, however. A detailed debate around the topics to be considered part of an environmental agenda was postponed. The building of a common agenda was solved by simply aggregating the various agendas. To keep the focus on the strategy, the provisional solution was just to put together socio-environmentalist issues (present in the discourse of almost all the groups) and conservationist ones (the FBCN's focus) with hints of counterculture, in a 'Green List'. At the beginning of 1986, the Interstate Ecologist Coordination for the Constituent Assembly (CIEC) was born and made responsible for this first nationwide attempt to coordinate the frames orienting the diverse environmental groups.

The Green List succeeded. Fábio Feldmann, the main Oikos activist committed to it, became the only candidate for election supported by environmental groups. In this sense, the electoral process for the Constituent Assembly consolidated the associative structure as the more efficient mobilizing strategy for voicing the movement's demands. The creation of an environmental party therefore did not work.

Once the Constituent Assembly began work in 1987 and 1988, environmental groups faced other problems. Pressure from leftist sectors of the redemocratization movement resulted in the Constituent Assembly operating without a preliminary agenda and with a decentralized structure of sub-commissions (Souza 2003). The absence of a previous structure made the Constituent Assembly susceptible to protest and interest groups, which pressed for the creation of sub-commissions on topics related to their agendas (Kinzo 2001). These organized groups and social movements were also allowed to participate through 'Popular Initiatives': amendments supported by at least thirty thousand signatures, which could be introduced directly for consideration by the Constituent Assembly, without the intermediation of an elected representative.

Consequently, informal mobilizing strategies, such as petitions and supporting bills, became more efficient means for pushing the environmental agenda than the PV. Using these strategies, activists also succeeded in obtaining the signatures required for three of the eighty-three Popular

Initiatives accepted into Constituent Assembly debate. This kind of pressure, added to Feldmann's statements in Congress, led to the formation of the Sub-commission for Health, Social Security and the Environment, under the jurisdiction of the Committee on Social Order. When this sub-commission was up and running, Feldmann situated himself as a broker between the two arenas of environmental mobilization: demonstrations within civil society and institutional negotiation in Congress. This mix of strategies resulted in the proposition for a chapter in the constitution devoted to the environment.

A reactionary bloc of centre and right-wing representatives led by the president, however – the 'Big Centre' – blocked the influence of organized civil society groups in drafting the constitutional text. It opposed the approval of many leftist bills. In the environmental area, it blocked the prohibition on the use of nuclear energy and criminalization of environmentally damaging acts.

These obstacles led environmental groups, even those excluded from the coalition that had elected Feldmann, to unite again and form a national coalition, thereby broadening alliances outside the movement. Under Feldmann's leadership, the National Front for Ecological Action, a congressional bloc supporting environmental proposals, was born.[5] This was the peak of environmentalist mobilization in the Constituent Assembly period. The National Front's strategy was to apply direct pressure on representatives by promoting visits to potential conservation areas. In doing this, it got support from liberal and even conservative representatives on some issues, which were included in the 1988 constitution in the chapter on the environment. This coalition made possible the approval of protection measures for the Amazon forest, the Atlantic rainforest, the Pantanal (a wetland area in central west Brazil) and the coastline, as well as for Brazil's genetic diversity. The ecological management of species and ecosystems, environmental education and environmental impact assessment for economic activities, including the location of nuclear plants, were also achieved (*O Estado de São Paulo*, 26 May 1988).

Mobilization around the Constituent Assembly had important outcomes for the formation process of the Brazilian environmental movement.

Regarding the mobilizing strategies, the Constituent Assembly demonstrated a common solution to the problem of coordinating environmental collective action: associations proved the most efficient basis for mobilization, for several reasons. First, the electoral process and the Big Centre's blocking actions in the Constituent Assembly showed the limitations of acting through a single party and the advantages of being

147

able to form alliances with many parties. Second, the constitution itself made lawsuits possible. This powerful legal instrument made it possible for environmental organizations to access institutional channels without being parties. Third, the fact that they were more influential as 'environmentalists' than as professional politicians in the Constituent Assembly made all activists ponder deeply the symbolic power of their technical and scientific expertise – something previously restricted to the pioneer conservationist group, the FBCN. From then on, they systematically used this power as a very efficient mobilizing strategy for legitimizing their claims in the political arena. This was the first step in the professionalization of environmental associations, such as the SOS Mata Atlântica, in the late 1980s.

Another impact concerns the frames of collective action. The chapter on the environment in the constitution was achieved by means of commitment. The National Front for Ecological Action opted for items on the Green List that were more palatable to non-environmental representatives, many of whom were right-wing politicians. The social or countercultural issues, previously at the top of the Green List, were discarded, while the conservationist items, such as the protection of ecosystems, were approved. The same change occurred with the agendas of environmental groups: the dominance of the socio-environmental frame, which focused on the damaging effects of capitalist development on the lifestyles of the middle and lower classes, and which had achieved prominence during the cycle of protests for redemocratization, dissolved. Conversely, conservationist issues went from the margins, where they had remained during redemocratization, to the centre of the environmental movement's agenda after the promulgation of the constitution.

In short, the POS of the Constituent Assembly was decisive in advancing the environmental movement's formation. Through the whole process, environmental groups had to consolidate ties and make agreements among themselves in order to act together. The existence of a common enemy and the necessity of finding allies were crucial in overcoming previous fragmentation among autonomous groups with their own agendas. The Big Centre forced the environmental groups to put aside their differences, which in turn gave them the capacity to influence the legal regulation of environmental questions. At least momentarily, they transcended their identities as groups in search of a common identity as an environmental 'movement': '[I]t was a great moment when there was true union [among environmental groups] in favor of progress in the Constitution. ... In a way, the divergences were overcome and we made it'

(Oikos member, interviewed 6 September 2004). As a result, the previously independent groups became a relatively stable national coalition. In this sense, the POS of the Constituent Assembly necessitated the solidification and nationalization of the network of environmental activism that had emerged from the redemocratization process.

Cycle of protests in Rio '92 The UN's decision to hold the second world Conference on Environment and Development in Brazil in 1992 changed, once again, the POS in which the Brazilian environmental activist network could act. It was a decisive event in the network's nationalization, consolidating a common environmental frame and even the Brazilian environmental movement itself.

The agenda of the UN conference linked the issue of the environment to the problem of development, in two ways. On one hand, it proposed the notion of 'sustainable development': new technology and rational methods of managing natural resources were presented as the way to reconcile development and environmental preservation – an alternative to the idea of 'reserves'. On the other hand, the notion of 'biodiversity' was concerned with preserving forms of life and genetic heritage that were at risk of disappearing. In both ways, the conference merged conservationism, which had been dominant in the early 1970s, and socio-environmentalism, which had gained the upper hand during the Constituent Assembly, in a new frame, neoconservationism.

Rio '92 also happened when the Brazilian POS was particularly unfavourable to the environmental movement. The alliances with leftist groups during redemocratization and in the Constituent Assembly had increased activists' expectations of jobs in the environmental bureaucracy. The victory of the right-wing candidate in the presidential elections in 1989, however, thwarted this possibility. With no access to the state and democratic normality flourishing, environmental groups of the 1980s either disappeared or professionalized their associations, giving them a businesslike image. Hence, Rio '92 came about in a national context in which the movement was far removed from the political arena and had little capacity to lobby the government.

The government, in turn, tried to form an alliance with the environmental network by inviting José Lutzenberger, AGAPAN's founder, to be the Special Secretary of the Environment.[6] Lutzenberger, however, had lost his status as a movement leader in the previous decade. He had left AGAPAN and was marginally involved in mobilizations involving the Constituent Assembly. With no support from the movement and no experience in party politics, he was unable to remain in the political arena. He was thought distant from the decision-making process regarding preparations for the conference, and was actually dismissed before it began. As a result, the doors of the national environmental bureaucracy remained closed to activists during preparations for the conference.

In fact, Rio '92 opened spaces for new kinds of national leaders to emerge: it professionalized organizations, such as SOS Mata Atlântica, which used the global conference as an arena to build alliances with global civil society organizations, mainly the WWF (SOS Rain Forest Foundation 1992). Environmental groups' distance from the Brazilian government, as well as the participative format of the conference, motivated them to reinforce once more their choice of civil society coalitions as a way of coordinating collective action, even seeking supporters in other civil society groups. Activist networks with this goal were formed both prior to and during the conference.

During the preparations for Rio '92, initiatives for the national coordination of the movement came from the coalitions formed in the Constituent Assembly. The National Front for Ecological Action, led by SOS Mata Atlântica, regrouped the conservationist formations while the PV launched the movement Pro-Rio '92, with a socio-environmental outlook, including Labour Party members, local community groups, popular social movements and even business groups (*Jornal da Tarde*, 6 September 1987).

Much the same as with the Constituent Assembly, none of the coalitions could articulate the range of issues that the whole movement represented. This is explained by the limited scope of their frames: the National Front was confined to conservationist associations, while Pro-Rio '92 did not go beyond socio-environmentalism. Such exclusive perspectives did not match the UN's agenda for Rio '92, systematized in the Brundtland Report of 1987, which includes both issues. In this way, it was the new POS which compelled environmental groups to seek allies capable of complementing their agenda, even outside the movement. Besides this, the Brazilian environmental movement was small and needed allies to make it more substantial in public debate.

SOS Mata Atlântica adopted a strategy very much in accordance with the new POS. It formed a new national coalition between environmental associations and other social movements that until then had not been involved in the environmental area, but 'whose struggles had direct implications on the environment' (invitation letter, cited in Santos 1994). This is how the Brazilian Forum on NGOs and Social Movements for the

Environment and Development came about in 1990. Some 1,100 associations developed a national network (Landim 1993). From then on, the forum became the focal point and the main mobilizing structure of the environmental movement during the conference.

Its broad network increased the debate on the movement's agenda and frames. As seen before, the Green List created for the Constituent Assembly relied on a patchwork of specific group agendas, emphasizing the social dimensions of environmental problems. In the Constituent Assembly this dominance was reversed and the conservationist frame was reinstated. The network organized by SOS Mata Atlântica broadened the conservationist frame during Rio '92 because the allied social movements arrived carrying socio-environmental agendas focused on two points: on one hand, the denunciation of social inequality, especially of the living conditions of the poor, and the unfair distribution of environmental risks; and on the other, criticism of the 'global model for economic development', particularly of the hierarchy between industrialized and non-industrialized countries, and a radicalization of the claim for a new paradigm of modernization, namely 'sustainable development', already present in the conference proposal.

The revival of the socio-environmental frame was enough to maintain the alliances constructed by the movement with other groups in civil society. This did not, however, restore that frame's dominance. SOS Mata Atlântica, the leading coordinator of the environmental groups, orchestrated a unification of the two frames, which had originally been set in contrast with one another. This was achieved through the dilution of both.

On one side, the socio-environmentalist frame was diversified, moving towards conservationism. The notion of 'sustainable development' was compatible with the simultaneous defence of environmental protection and socio-economic development. Besides this, the macroeconomic dimension of environmental problems was retained, but the emphasis on urban issues, typical of socio-environmentalism in the 1970s, was redirected to the living conditions of social groups interacting with the natural environment, whether in the countryside (indigenous groups) or in the forest (extractive groups – those using the forest for economic gain through extraction of resources).

In another way, the conservationist frame was redefined by replacing the idea of 'ecosystem' with that of 'biodiversity'. This notion sought to extend protection, originally restricted to the habitat of animal and vegetable species, to include social groups living in forest areas, as long as they had lifestyles with 'low environmental impact'. In this way, the genetic and cultural heritage of indigenous communities and traditional populations, such as extractive groups, became the aim of environmental preservation, and forests, a typical topic of classic conservationism, became the locus of biodiversity. This inclusion of non-urban dimensions of the socio-environmental agenda differentiated the reformulated conservationist frame from the conservationist tradition.

In this way, socio-environmental and conservationist frames went through a process of diversification and reconciliation. This unification had two consequences for the environmental movement.

First, a common frame for the entire movement emerged for the first time. Notions of sustainable development and biodiversity allowed groups with divergent agendas to give their own focus to the same categories, producing a discursive agreement. Through these means, a new frame came about: neoconservationism. Incorporating local social issues typical of the socio-environmental agenda and green matters from the global agenda, neoconservationism became the common language among environmental groups, ranging from the 1970s pioneers to the 1990s newcomers. Thus the new frame consolidated coalitions around meanings among environmental groups that until then had been merely strategic.

Neoconservationism manifested itself in the form of an agreement that emerged from Rio '92: Agenda 21. In this document, global environmental issues concerning the conservationist agenda, such as forest protection (Chapter 11) and biological diversity (Chapter 15), merged with socio-environmental topics, such as the preservation of a local social group's way of life while turning it towards sustainable economic activity (Chapter 3). Agenda 21 also stressed participatory decision-making processes as the best way to deal with planning and implementing environmental policies. This model required the big national and international environmental associations to coordinate with the smallest ones that worked only at the local level. In doing so, links among environmental associations at all levels were strengthened.

The new frame brought a new way to formulate environmental issues. Neoconservationism related to social groups living in conservation areas. It incorporated socio-environmentalism, but the political focus of the frame was replaced by a technical approach, formulated by new environmental experts coming from the professional associations of the 1990s. Neoconservationism displaced the issue of the environment from the city, where socio-environmentalism had established it, to the countryside. The lifestyle of the urban middle classes was no longer the focus of activism.

This was clear from the concentration in the 1990s of the efforts of the large environmental associations, such as SOS Mata Atlântica and the ISA (Socio-environmental Institute), created just after Rio '92, in 1994 (ISA member, interviewed 31 August 2004), in forest areas. Urban environmental issues, such as sanitation and air pollution, the main topics in the 1970s, became secondary matters. Thus change in the Brazilian environmental movement's position paved the way for the removal of environmental issues from the political arena.

Neoconservationism became dominant also because it was compatible with the new international POS related to environmental matters. Meanwhile, the Amazon had become an international environmental symbol, directing resources and public attention to protected areas. This opened up the Brazilian environmental agenda to international campaigns, for instance the campaign against genetically modified organisms, in alliance with the large international conservationist associations like Greenpeace and the WWF. The internationalization of the Brazilian environmental network allowed professional environmental associations, such as SOS Mata Atlântica and ISA, to pull in large volumes of resources to manage newly protected areas.

The second impact of the mobilization cycle at Rio '92 on the movement was a new mobilizing strategy. Networks of associations replaced the autonomous groups of the 1970s and 1980s. Environmental networks, as relatively long-lasting coalitions of associations, became the main way to coordinate the movement and the preferred channel for expressing environmental demands in the 1990s. They gave a new structure to the movement in three senses: they became the basis for large-issue campaigns, the route to international and governmental grants and the channel for lobbying for and influencing the formulation and implementation of environmental public policies. These networks meant that Brazilian environmental activists could broaden their initiatives and specialize in specific geographic issues and areas, dividing work among coalitions and associations. As a consequence, the movement gained a decentralized, polycentric and horizontal structure. Although developing a low degree of institutionalization and working by means of cooperation and agreements, the networks came to be a very stable organizational format, sustaining the diversity of groups in the same movement.

The networks did not, however, transcend associations, which are the hub for teaching and learning technical expertise in environmental issues. They supported a new model of activism, professional and specialized, as well as a new relationship with the state as consultants and service providers. Scientific knowledge became activists' most important tool in making themselves heard by the state bureaucracy and civil society as a whole. In this new setting, the environmental agenda became restrictive and not readily compatible with broader political agendas.

During the 1990s, these networks of professional associations were consolidated as the main organizational structure of the movement, reducing the importance of other former options, such as parties. '[I]t is impossible to organize a party and work on the issues, it is either one, or the other. ... This marriage does not work ...' (interview with Oikos member, 6 September 2004).

The POS of Rio '92 was the third step in the formation of the environmental movement. At that point, a new mobilizing strategy, the networks, was adopted and the problem of coordinating groups' distinctive frames into a collective one for the movement as a whole was solved, for the most part. The outcome was the consolidation of a national environmental movement.

Conclusion

In this chapter we have aimed to explain the formation of the Brazilian environmental movement, relying on an approach that sheds light simultaneously on political-institutional dimensions, as usually elucidated by political process theoreticians, and on the aspects addressed by NSM theories, namely the strategic and symbolic features of collective action – features that, until now, have not been taken into account by the Brazilian literature.

The Brazilian case shows that the structural approach NSM theories formulated to accommodate the rise of environmental movements in the North is not always useful in explaining cases in the South. This is because NSM theories do not take into account the national sociopolitical contexts and the way they condition the rise and the dynamics of social movements, dimensions that the POS concept has helped us describe systematically. We have argued that a specific conjuncture, redemocratization, opened avenues into the public arena for environmental groups claiming the right to be represented and to express themselves in the broader public debate. Two other POSs, in turn, opened up two formal participatory spaces through which the environmental activists could influence public policies in the area: Congress, in the form of the Constituent Assembly, and the governmental committees dealing with the global conference on the issue, Rio '92.

The concept of the POS has helped us to describe simultaneously the introduction of environmental issues into the Brazilian public agenda and the process through which an environmental movement came about, gained national stature, and was consolidated in Brazil.

Focusing on micro-mobilization contexts, on the other hand, we argue that it was not as middle-class members that activists gathered, as the NSM approach holds, but because they shared similar genres of social and political experience. Professional background and ties with either bureaucratic elites or other social movements and parties were the common characteristics compelling individuals to build collective identities as environmentalists. The present case shows, however, that political-intellectual counter-elites were more decisive groups in the building of an environment movement in Brazil than the lower social strata, because they had preferential access to the material and symbolic resources that enabled them to mobilize.

We have rejected the main interpretation of the Brazilian environmental movement, which focuses on values as causing mobilization (Viola 1987). Our analysis of framing processes confirms Snow and Benford's (1992) argument about the dynamic and interactional character that the frames of collective action acquire during cycles of protests. The frames brought about by each group were continuously transformed during the movement's formation. The convergence of the two initially independent frames in a new one, that of neoconservationism, produced an interpretation of the environmental problem that could be shared by all environmental activists, making it feasible for the groups to coordinate their actions. This frame convergence process persuaded activists to both work closely with the state and to build alliances with both local and global actors.

In this way, the Brazilian environmental movement shared certain features with the Northern cases described in the literature. Diani (1995) argues that the 1990s were a time of consolidation for environmental frames in Italy after a period of conflict. Rootes (2003) adds that this coincided with a depoliticalization and deradicalization of environmental frames. The same can be said of the Brazilian case. The reconciliation between frames from the 1970s was possible thanks to the rising importance of scientific knowledge and the declining utility of the political approach in the formulation of environmental problems in the Brazilian public debate.

Similarities between the Brazilian and the European cases can also be found in their mobilizing strategies. Most European environmental movements ended up bureaucratizing their associations and professionalizing their activists. As a consequence, direct activism, especially public demonstration, has declined while lobbying has been on the rise (ibid.). In Brazil, the movement also went from politically oriented activism, mainly public protest, to a preference for lobbying through professional organizations, usually based on scientific expertise.

The formation of the Brazilian environmental movement took over two decades. Through a deeply conflict-ridden process, the movement faced and solved its problems of coordination within a framework of collective action. Thematic networks have come to be the main mobilizing strategy while neoconservationism has become the dominant frame. The outcome was the consolidation of a social movement's identity (Jasper 1997).

This does not imply, however, that differences and conflicts among groups have been entirely absent. Disagreements are overcome at crucial moments, so that activists can present themselves publicly as a strong and substantial coalition rather than a fragmented web of autonomous groups. In fact, two levels can be distinguished. There are autonomous groups, with routine focal agendas and strategies of their own, each obeying its internal dynamics. And there are solid networks that emerge only in critical situations. When these networks form, internal disputes are put aside in the name of a core set of common agreements around the issue of the environment and on the ways to push it forward. That is what makes a social movement.

Notes

1 This chapter is based on research developed at the Centro Brasileiro de Análise e Planejamento (Brazilian Centre for Analysis and Planning, CEBRAP) from April 2003 to December 2004, as part of the Science and Citizenship Working Group of the Development Research Centre on Citizenship, Participation and Accountability (CDRC) and published, in a slightly different form, in Institute of Development Studies (IDS) Working Paper 259, November 2005, as 'The formation of the Brazilian environmental movement'. We are grateful to the William and Flora Hewlett Foundation and the CDRC for their grants, to Adriana dos Santos for research assistance and to Ian

Scoones, Lisa Thompson and Peter Houtzager for their suggestions.

2 Institutional Act No. 5, the National Security Law and the Media Law prohibited any public demonstration or political meeting against the political order.

3 From the 1950s to the 1970s, the FBCN's members had positions, including positions of leadership, in most of the governmental bureaus engaged with environmental questions (Urban 1998).

4 The first municipal secretary of the environment was created in Porto Alegre, in 1976 (Bones and Hasse 2002).

5 The Front, created in June 1987, was composed of seventy-one

representatives from environmental associations, as well as nine senators and eighty-two representatives linked to left-wing and centre-left parties (Hochstetler and Keck 2007).

6 The Ministry of Environment, Fluvial Resources and Legal Amazonia was instituted only in 1995.

References

Antuniassi, M. H. (1989) *Movimento Ambientalista em São Paulo: Análise Sociológica de um Movimento Social Urbano*, São Paulo: CERU.

Bones, E. and G. Hasse (2002) *Pioneiros da Ecologia: Breve História do Movimento Ambientalista no Rio Grande do Sul*, Porto Alegre: Já Editores.

Boschi, R. (1989) *A Arte da Associação. Política de Base e Democracia no Brasil*, Rio de Janeiro: IUPERJ/ Vértice.

Diani, M. (1995) *Green Networks: A Structural Analysis of the Italian Environmental Movement*, Edinburgh: Edinburgh University Press.

Gamson, W. (1982) *Encounters with Unjust Authority*, Homewood, IL: Dorsey Press.

— (1992), 'The social psychology of collective action', in C. M. Mueller and A. D. Morris (eds), *Frontiers in Social Movement Theory*, New Haven, CT, and London: Yale University Press.

Hochstetler, K. (1997) 'The evolution of the Brazilian environmental movement and its political roles', in D. Chalmers et al. (eds), *The New Politics of Inequality in Latin America: Rethinking Participation and Representation*, Oxford: Oxford University Press.

Hochstetler, K. and M. Keck (2007) *Greening Brazil: Environmental*

Activism in State and Society, Durham, NC: Duke University Press.

Jasper, J. (1997) *The Art of Moral Protest: Culture, Biography, and Creativity in Social Movements*, Chicago, IL: University of Chicago Press.

Kinzo, M. D. G. (1988) *Oposição e Autoritarismo: Gênese e Trajetória do MDB, 1966–79*, São Paulo: Idesp/Vértice.

— (2001) 'A democratização brasileira: um balanço do processo político desde a transição', *Revista São Paulo em Perspectiva*, 15(4): 3–12.

Kriesi, H. (1995) *New Social Movements in Western Europe: A Comparative Analysis*, Minneapolis: University of Minnesota Press.

Landim, L. (1993) *A Invenção das ONGs: Do Serviço Invisível à Profissão sem Nome*, Rio de Janeiro: Museu Nacional/UFRJ.

Linz, J. (1973) 'The future of an authoritarian situation or the institutionalization of an authoritarian regime: Brazil', in A. Stepan (ed.), *Authoritarian Brazil: Origins, Politics, and Future*, New Haven, CT: Yale University Press, pp. 232–54.

Lutzenberger, J. A. (1977) *Fim do Futuro? Manifesto Ecológico Brasileiro*, Porto Alegre: Editora Movimento.

Mueller, C. M. (1992) 'Building social movement theory', in A. Morris and C. M. Mueller (eds), *Frontiers in Social Movement Theory*, New Haven, CT, and London: Yale University Press.

Pádua, J. (1991) 'O nascimento da política verde no Brasil: fatores endógenos e exógenos', in H. Leis (ed.), *Ecologia e Política Mundial*, Rio de Janeiro: Vozes.

Rootes, C. (ed.) (2003) *Environmental*

Protest in Western Europe, Oxford: Oxford University Press.

Sainteny, G. (1999) 'Logiques d'engagement et logiques de rétribution au sein de l'ecologisme français', *Cahiers Internationaux de Sociologie*, CVI.

Sallum, B., Jr (1996) *Labirintos: Dos Generais a Nova República*, São Paulo: Hucitec.

Santos, S. S. C. H. (1994) 'Entre o heroísmo e a cidadania. O fórum brasileiro de ONG's e movimentos sociais para o meio ambiente e o desenvolvimento (a sociedade civil e o estado: um estudo de caso sobre o exercício da cidadania pelos segmentos intelectualizados das classes médias brasileiras)', PhD thesis, Instituto Universitário de Pesquisas do Rio de Janeiro – IUPERJ.

Snow, D. (1986) 'Frame alignment processes, micromobilization, and movement participation', *American Sociological Review*, 51: 787–801.

Snow, D. and R. Benford (1992) 'Master frames and cycles of protest', in C. M. Mueller and A. D. Morris (eds), *Frontiers in Social Movement Theory*, New Haven, CT, and London: Yale University Press.

Souza, M. T. (2003) 'The decision-making process in the Brazilian Constitution (1988): institutional practices', *Lua Nova*, 58: 42.

Tarrow, S. (1983) 'Struggling to reform: social movements and policy change during cycles of protest', Western Societies Program Occasional Paper no. 15, Cornell University, Ithaca, NY.

— (1998) *Power in Movement: Social Movements, Collective Action and Politics*, New York: Cambridge University Press.

Taylor, V. and N. E. Whittier (1992) 'Collective identity in social movement communities: lesbian feminist mobilization', in C. M. Mueller and A. D. Morris (eds), *Frontiers in Social Movement Theory*, New Haven, CT, and London: Yale University Press.

Tilly, C. (1978) *From Mobilization to Revolution*, Chicago, IL: McGraw-Hill Humanities.

Urban, T. (1998) *Saudade do Matão: Relembrando a História da Conservação da Natureza no Brasil*, Curitiba: Editora da Universidade Federal do Paraná.

— (2001) *Missão (Quase) Impossível: Aventuras e Desventuras do Movimento Ambientalista no Brasil*, São Paulo: Petrópolis.

Viola, E. (1987) 'Movimento ecológico e heterogeneidade política', *Lua Nova*, 3(4), São Paulo: CEDEC.

— (1992) 'O movimento ambientalista no Brasil (1971–1991): da denúncia à conscientização pública para a institucionalização e o desenvolvimento sustentável', in M. Goldenberg (ed.), *Ecologia, Ciência e Política*, Rio de Janeiro: Revan.

Zhouri, A. (1992) *Discursos Verdes: As Práticas da Ecologia: Um Estudo Antropológico da Participação dos Ecologistas Paulistas nas Eleições de 1986*, Master's degree, IFCH – Unicamp.

Interviews

FBCN member interview, 12 August 2004.

ISA member interview, 31 August 2004.

Oikos member interview, 6 September 2004.

Newspapers and reports

O Estado de São Paulo, 8 September 1973, 26 May 1988.

Jornal da Tarde, 6 September 1987.

AGAPAN and APPN (1978) *Manifesto de Curitiba: Declaração de Princípios do Movimento de Luta Ambiental*, Unpublished document, CERU Archive, São Paulo, September.

Peco Bulletin, 1, 1978.

SOS Rain Forest Foundation (1992) *Commemorative Bulletin: 7 years of SOS Rain Forest Foundation*.

Environmental activism in Brazil

7 | The struggle towards rights and communitarian citizenship: the Zapatista movement in Mexico

CARLOS CORTEZ RUIZ

Mexico has a long history of social movements whose actions express the struggle for social justice. But while older movements in rural areas have centred their demands principally on acquiring land, controlling natural resources or receiving funds from government programmes, newer social movements are different in terms of their character, constituency and social composition. These more recent social formations confront social relations directly and challenge the Mexican national development model, particularly the conditions of integration into the globalization process. In recent decades national social movements that incorporate ethnic and cultural demands have grown in importance.

In 1994, a social movement emerged through a struggle demanding changes to the situation of the indigenous population at the national level. The movement was initiated by the Zapatista National Liberation Army (EZLN),[1] and, based on it, in recent years different social actors have established an agenda focused on the recognition of the cultural and political rights of the indigenous populations, including their right to land and territory. Thus, while the EZLN is the organizational core of the movement, other organizations have also joined forces. This collective social action is referred to from this point on as the Zapatista movement. Since 1994 the movement has been mobilizing to transform socio-economic conditions at the local, national and even international levels.[2]

The ascent of the movement was explained initially as the result of government failures to guarantee basic services such as healthcare, education and infrastructure. The basic services situation has been particularly critical in the case of indigenous people, most of whom live in extreme poverty. While these factors were doubtless behind the emergence of the movement, in a broader perspective activism was also the result of a crisis of governance demonstrated by the failure to advance towards a society in which citizenship not only brought the right to vote, but also guaranteed a set of social, economic, political and cultural rights for the whole population.[3]

It is necessary to situate this movement in a perspective that takes into account the influence of the Chiapas social movement and the national experience of social organization, as well as the political and ideological influence of ethnic movements developed in the 1990s to demand indigenous rights in Mexico and other countries. At the beginning of the decade various forms of organization and mobilization were developed around a celebration of what was called '500 years of resistance', from conquest to globalization.

On 12 October 1992, in a massive demonstration, the coming indigenous rebellion was symbolically announced. Thousands of indigenous people marched with bows and arrows in San Cristóbal de Las Casas, Chiapas, a city that symbolized the exclusion and exploitation of indigenous people. But the march was more than symbolic: it was the culmination of a long struggle begun by a Marxist political movement known as the National Liberation Forces (FLN),[4] initiated in 1983 by mestizo activists who arrived in the Lacandon rainforest in Chiapas to prepare for an armed struggle[5] for revolutionary transformation. Their orthodox approach was modified through their interaction with indigenous communities and some leaders, including women, which resulted in the introduction of historical demands for land, justice and cultural rights. In 1993, after consultation with grassroots members in indigenous communities, the decision was taken to declare war on the Mexican state, and preparations began to take over several municipalities in January 1994. This action was predicated on the Mexican constitution, which states that 'national sovereignty resides essentially and originally in the people ... [who] have ... the right to change or modify the form of government'.[6]

The character of the Zapatista movement gave it an international impact that other, even much older, Mexican and Latin American social movements have never had. The success of the Zapatista movement is a result of the combination of two elements: first, the movement's composition reflects the interests of very poor indigenous people who have been demanding profound changes to the character of the national state, and second, the anti-globalization nature of the movement has ensured a common perspective with other, similar social movements around the world.

Since the EZLN became active, the movement has clearly established its normative relationship with the globalization process. The movement itself began on a symbolic date, 1 January 1994, the same day that saw the launch of the North American Free Trade Agreement (NAFTA) between Canada, Mexico and the USA, a fundamental act in the globalization process. In preparation for Mexico's incorporation into NAFTA, the agrarian law was modified and the possibility of acquiring land was definitively closed for many peasants. In the course of time, the movement's critical perspective on the globalization process has been broadened into a critique of capitalism and the idea of progress that it encapsulates. These political definitions and their evolution are concentrated in what are called 'Declarations of the Lacandon Rainforest', from the first one presented when the rebellion was initiated to the sixth one presented in November 2005.

Since the rebellion, the Zapatista movement has provided an impulse towards a more communitarian idea of citizenship understood as critical of the liberal perspective. The communitarian idea expressed through the movement emphasizes cultural identity and the sense of belonging to a common, even collective, purpose, including the management and/or ownership of resources. As expressed through EZLN, this view of citizenship puts limits on individualism and promotes the idea that communitarian purposes will motivate the positive integration of everybody into societal networks.[7]

Over the years the government response to this movement has taken different, sometimes contradictory, phases and forms – ranging, for instance, from accepting that the demands made by the movement are just to accusing it of being manipulated by external interests, and, similarly, from dismissing the activism as just a local movement to accepting the Zapatistas' political credentials to the extent of allowing them to present their position from the tribune of the National Congress in 2001. Yet the dominant perspective has been to put state security uppermost, using valuable resources to maintain political control of the population and to respond to what, in the government's view, is the cause of the rebellion. With the changes to the national and the state governments in 2000, the government perspective was modified and the repression of the movement substantially reduced. A number of initiatives have also been launched by the government, including some original development programmes that are ostensibly designed, at least in terms of their stated objectives, to respond to the causes of the rebellion. During this time, the movement has kept up its resistance to the government's watered-down efforts and demanded the fulfilment of all of its demands.

The movement has grown principally in the state of Chiapas in the south of Mexico, with different forms of representation at the national level, mainly among indigenous communities. In this chapter we analyse the development of the broader Zapatista movement. We consider the different phases of its interaction with government, its forms of activism and the levels at which these actions have been focused to show how they have promoted a kind of communitarian citizenship through both local and global forms of networking.

To better understand the character and implications of the Zapatista movement, it is necessary to refer to the context in which it has developed. It is particularly useful to refer to the conditions surrounding the rise of the movement – that is, the accelerated integration of Mexican society into the globalization process during the late 1980s and 1990s, and the impact of state-initiated neoliberal policies imposed since the 1980s, a process that has meant the reduction of Mexican state intervention in the economy and the growth of the market as the central regulator of socio-economic life. NAFTA, initiated in 1994, has been pivotal to this process, with an important impact on the Mexican economy as a whole, but particularly on agriculture and on the rural population.

Almost half of the Mexican population are excluded from this economic process by virtue of their socio-economic situation.[8] They are not able to produce for the market, or to be incorporated into the labour market, or to generate an income that allows them to be 'consumers' in the global market. This general situation has been particularly critical in the south of Mexico, where most of the people, particularly rural and indigenous people, live in poverty and have the lowest human development index in the country. Social and economic inequality is characteristic of Mexican society, and this inequality has grown deeper as result of the way in which the Mexican state has encouraged integration into the globalization process, as well as the political strategies implemented to buttress the economic integration process.

The changes to economic policy at national level have affected indigenous people, particularly the youth, making it impossible for them to access agricultural land, while at the same time not providing them with other income-generating or work possibilities. In sum, for a high percentage of people, the globalization process has meant a reduction in the possibility of gaining social and economic rights. Strikingly, this has happened in a society with a long history of struggle in terms of achieving civil and political rights.

Crisis and social movements in Chiapas

The southern Mexican state of Chiapas is the poorest in the country, with the lowest human development index (PNUD 2002). Historically the state has been inhabited by different ethnic groups, and it is has one of the largest percentages of Indian-language speakers in the country.[9] In terms of social structure, the region is defined by the index as having the highest birth rate, the highest levels of poverty, exclusion and discrimination against indigenous people, and a long history of social movements. In recent years, principally since the emergence of the Zapatista movement, a process of emigration to other regions, mainly from the rural areas, has been a feature of the state. Its geography is characterized by great biodiversity, and it is home to some of the most important natural protected areas. Its territory is part of the Mesoamerican Biological Corridor, where international initiatives are geared to protecting biodiversity.

The problem of land access has historically been one of the most significant for indigenous people, as for centuries they have been deprived of their land. In the past, young people had the option of settling in the rainforest and acquiring land in that way, but with the changes in the Mexican constitution in preparation for NAFTA, and with growing international pressure to protect the rainforest, this option was closed. One young woman stated: 'There is not enough land, and new generations will have a lot of problems getting land. The youngest generation is looking to the Zapatistas for the possibility to get access to land.'[10] At the beginning of the 1990s, the economic situation in Chiapas was critical, particularly for young people entering the workforce. Without access to land, with prices for coffee, one of the most important regional products, at an all-time low, and with the exploitation of the rainforest prohibited, thousands of young indigenous people had no chance of getting a job or generating income.

This critical situation occurred in a region with a long history of political movements, a variety of organizational experiences and the significant influence of the liberation theology of the Catholic Church. In 1974 an Indigenous Congress was held through an initiative of the Catholic Church in collaboration with a group of left-wing political activists of various persuasions. This congress became the starting point for a new organizational process that allowed indigenous people to act against the injustice and abuses of which they were victims. The demands of the Indigenous Congress were for land, health, education and commercialization, very similar to the demands presented in the First Declaration of the Lacandon Rainforest, which the Zapatistas had presented when they initiated the rebellion (EZLN 1993). As a result of the Indigenous Congress, a number of organizations created throughout the region, having gained organizational experience, formed the basis for the creation of the Emiliano Zapata National Independent Peasant Alliance (ANCIEZ),[11] the predecessor to the EZLN, which, in January 1994, declared war on the Mexican state and initiated the rebellion in Chiapas. On that date thousands of indigenous people took control of seven municipalities and thousands of hectares of land that had been in the possession of landowners.

During the 1980s and early 1990s, there were important developments involving social organizations in some regions of Chiapas, principally the rainforest. A number of organizations were created around the demand for land and means of production. Some of these organizations were part of national organizations. As a result of the social emergency of the 1990s, and particularly following the Zapatista rebellion, the demand for the fulfilment of social, political and cultural rights had a major impact. The Zapatistas had a different perspective to other social organizations, expressed through their political demands, but also in relation to the government. This included the movement's refusal to accept any resource or programme coming from government that was not linked to its demands for radical political change at the national level. Some affiliated social organizations agree with the Zapatistas' approach but still believe that they have the right to receive 'basic needs' resources from government programmes, such as those relating to health, education and infrastructure (Cortez 2004). The phases of the movement, as well as the differences between the core movement and its allies, are discussed in the next sections.

Phases of the Zapatista movement

Since the inception of the movement, the Zapatista movement has passed through several phases: the first (1994–96), 'from rebellion to negotiation', began with the armed rebellion and included political negotiations with the Mexican government; the second phase (1996–2000) was one of 'resistance' to the military and paramilitary pressure against the movement; the third (2001–06) took the form of 'building autonomy'; and the last, initiated by the Sixth Declaration of the Lacandon Rainforest and including elements of the previous phases, which we will call the 'impulse to communitarian citizenship', clearly defines the movement as part of the globalization of rebellion. We refer broadly to these phases.

From rebellion to negotiation On 1 January 1994, the Zapatistas declared war on the Mexican state, and followed this with an armed attack on some municipalities in Chiapas and demands that included a new national constitution, new elections and profound changes to the situation of indigenous populations. The essence of the rebellion was summed up in the First Declaration of the Lacandon Rainforest, in which the movement explained the causes of the rebellion and that it was part of 500 years of resistance (since the Spanish conquest of independent Mexico). The declaration set out the initial demands made by the movement, which included education, food and housing, as well as autonomy, freedom and dignity for indigenous peoples.

The response of the Mexican government to the movement was initially a military one, but a vigorous national demonstration from civil society required a political response and obliged the government to develop strategies for negotiation with the Zapatistas. Demonstrations demanding a ceasefire were held right from the first days of the rebellion, and different social groups developed forms of solidarity, including visits to communities, missions to monitor the observance of human rights, security belts to protect the Zapatista leaders during negotiations, and the organization of national and international meetings. In a sense the mobilization of civil society reflected the profound political changes that had developed in Mexican society over several decades.[12]

Early in 1996 negotiations ended with the San Andrés Accords (ASA).[13] As a consequence of the Mexican government's failure to meet its obligations set out in the accords, the dialogue was interrupted and it has not been resumed since. One of the central issues relating to the interruption of dialogue is the differences of approach between the government and the movement on territorial rights.

The resistance phase From 1996 until 2000, the principal governmental response to the movement was framed as one of countering civil insurgency. After the Mexican government had undermined the dialogue by its military actions, it developed a 'low-intensity war' against the movement which included the militarization of the region and the creation of paramilitary groups as counter-forces to the Zapatistas. During this period the demands of indigenous peoples were overwhelmed by the militarization of public spaces and by violence against not only the Zapatistas, but all those considered in agreement with their demands. Significant public resources were used to try to gain military and political control of the population.

Some groups, promoted principally by the traditional local powers and condoned by the state government, used violence to try to limit the influence of the Zapatista movement. Mainly during the first phase of the movement, these groups received armaments from the government and used repression to try to control the population and reduce the Zapatista movement's influence. As a result, thousands of indigenous people were displaced from their communities and found refuge in areas where they were relatively safe from paramilitary repression.[14]

In December 1997 the situation turned critical and forty-six defenceless civilians, principally women and children, were killed by a paramilitary group under the protection of several civil servants. The United Nations Commission on Human Rights identified ninety groups linked to the government with direct responsibility for the violence against Zapatista indigenous groups as social actors. The commission continues to demand changes on the part of government in the cultural, political and social arenas.

Building autonomy Pressure on the Mexican government to fulfil the terms of the ASA continued to be the central campaign of the movement. In 2000 changes to the federal and Chiapas governments heralded a more positive phase. With these changes, repression has at least ceased to be the principal response of the government, and aggressive action against the movement has been reduced since then – but has not stopped entirely.

Since 2000 a number of initiatives by the government, and some development programmes, have been launched in the region with the explicit intention, at least in their stated objectives, of responding to the causes of the rebellion. From the Zapatistas' point of view, however, these programmes are aimed at breaking down the movement's resistance and maintaining the government's control over the population. In pursuit of their rights, the social movement decided to resist government authority and reject official programmes and policies as long as the ASA had not been fulfilled. An alternative government was created by the Zapatistas at the local and regional level through new participatory spaces called autonomous rebel Zapatista municipalities (MAREZ)[15] and good govern-ance councils (JBG)[16] consisting of several municipalities.

The MAREZ and the JBG focus on developing health, education and justice systems, achieving the sustainable management of the territory and creating an alternative form of citizenship. Autonomous government is based on participation at local and regional level through consultation and assemblies.[17]

Impulse to communitarian citizenship The Zapatista political perspec-tive has changed over the years, as can be deduced from the various

Declarations of the Lacandon Rainforest, principally the first, third and sixth. These declarations, presented by the Zapatista leadership, express the political perspective of the movement through a cluster of demands that can be defined, from a Western point of view, as calling for collective social, cultural and economic human rights. In the course of 2005, the Sixth Declaration of the Lacandon Rainforest was presented together with a proposal for a new strategy to demand rights through an alliance with other social sectors at the national level to ensure that the objectives of the indigenous struggle were met.[18]

The model developed over the years by the Zapatistas has emphasized participation and collaboration, on the assumption that these are the basis of good government. The MAREZ and the JBG have framed the desire for participation, fundamental both to the development of a political perspective at a personal and collective level for the movement and to the capacity needed to solve some of the most important problems of the population.

A central characteristic of this form of collective participation is summed up in their slogan 'leading by obeying', meaning that the members of the collective autonomous government must define priorities and actions through a participatory process in the assembly; only after consensus is reached may they issue orders as part of, and in obedience to, the collective decision-making process. These elements have been fundamental to the drive towards communitarian citizenship.[19] The political definitions of the last phase are in the Sixth Declaration of the Lacandon Rainforest (EZLN 2005). At the global level it advocates resistance to neoliberalism and the struggle for humanity. At the national level it advocates the advancement of political organization and the struggle for democracy, freedom and justice through a leftist programme, and calls for a new constitution.

Levels of action

One important characteristic of the movement is that since it started it has been active at three different levels – the local and regional, the national and the global – all sharing convergent objectives.

Local and regional At the local and regional level, the movement's efforts have been directed at changing the power structure and developing a territorial model of governance. While the Zapatistas demand political solutions, in parallel the grassroots have developed their own autonomous government organized around the MAREZ and the JBG. These are located in spaces called *caracoles*,[20] where there are various institutions such as cooperatives, schools and health facilities. As the principal objective is the fulfilment of all of the movement's demands, collective efforts are directed at guaranteeing the right to land, health, education and information, among other things.

The autonomous governance process has been built up over the years through strategic actions emphasizing areas such as justice, health, education, production, the participation of women and in particular the development of capacity for the administration of the territory. For the Zapatistas these advances have been possible because they focus on the revival of productive resources such as land, cattle and machinery.

The basis of local and regional transformation is the agrarian changes that the Zapatista movement has realized through appropriating the land that, until 1994, was controlled by big landowners and delivering it to the peasants.[21] It is estimated that the Zapatistas occupied around 60,000 hectares, but during the years that followed, other organizations occupied around 148,000 hectares throughout the state (Villafuerte et al. 1999: 131). The fight for the right to land is one of the central issues of the movement, as set out in the Zapatista Revolutionary Agrarian Law:

All poor-quality land in excess of 100 hectares and all good-quality land in excess of 50 hectares will be subject to the Revolutionary Agrarian Law. ... The lands affected by this agrarian law will be distributed to the landless campesinos and the agricultural laborers ... as collective property for the formation of cooperatives, campesino societies or agricultural production/livestock collectives. (Marcos 2007: 25; English translation from flag.blackened.net/revolt/mexico/ezln/law_agrarian.html)

In the occupied lands some new towns were created with young peasant families that had not had access to land in their original communities. This kind of political arrangement has served to sustain the grass roots of the movement.

Another important basis of transformation has been the changes to local gender relations. Historically indigenous women have suffered tremendous disadvantages. Gender inequalities within their communities are greater than in the rest of society, and exclusion, violence and oppression are common features of their daily life. While their exclusion has social and cultural roots, it is reinforced by legal and political practices. Their subordinate status is manifest in a range of phenomena, from violence in the home – often associated with male alcoholism – to their exclusion from basic services, such as health and education (Cortez 2005).

Indigenous women's struggles for their rights therefore cut across different spheres of life and imply the transformation of power relations at all levels. Various factors have facilitated these struggles, including the shift from subsistence production to market-orientated production, which provides women with an income, increasing participation in organized groups, and, of course, social movements, such as those formed by indigenous women linked to the Zapatista movement. The Zapatista movement has given indigenous women a heightened awareness of their rights and of the possibilities for social and cultural transformations that would allow them to realize both their right to difference as indigenous women and their right to equality as human beings. The basis for this transformation was established by the Zapatista Women's Revolutionary Law, which prompted a discussion of women's rights that had been historically violated. With this as a basis, the growing participation of women has been promoted in a range of activities, opening the way for young people to participate in building this initiative.

The JBG, working in the *caracoles*, are central to the drive towards the achievement of the rights demanded by the movement. There are five autonomous Zapatista regions, each with a JBG working in a *caracol*, where actions for between four and seven different MAREZ are coordinated. The JBG must include women, something that is accomplished at a different level, and there are some JBG where there is more balanced gender participation than in others. For example, at the end of 2007 there was a JBG with twenty-eight members, of whom seven were women (Gama 2007; Muñoz Ramírez 2004).

Autonomous governance has had several effects. One considered very important is that '[c]onflict between communities and between organizations in Zapatista territory has been reduced and the crime rate has fallen ... you can consult the archives, the judges, public ministers, in jails and hospitals ... compare before and after and draw your own conclusions ...' (Marcos 2007).

National level At the national level, the Zapatistas' actions have been directed at creating a movement to encourage state reform down to the level of the indigenous poor. This social movement demands political, cultural and economic rights for the entire population, particularly the historically excluded and those who have been denied their rights. In a sense this perspective demonstrates a characteristic of communitarian citizenship, understood as the right to define rights in a collective form rather than individually.

The Zapatista movement has profoundly changed the focus of the indigenous movement at the national level. It has gone from the need for land to the demand for change in the agrarian structure and for the recognition of indigenous territories; from the requirement that basic needs be met to the demand for social justice; from health and education to the demand for change in unequal power relations at the national level. As a result of the movement's efforts, demands for the rights of indigenous people and social action supporting this have gained momentum within society in recent years. Even though this momentum has not been sufficient to achieve the political, cultural and economic changes demanded at the national level, it is part of the drive towards communitarian citizenship.[22]

The Zapatistas have emphasized cultural rights that include people's right to have their own language and to maintain their traditions and forms of organization, but also the right to bilingual education and to their own communication media, such as radio. These demands refer to the acceptance of indigenous traditions and normative systems but are also related to other social, cultural and political rights. Most of the demands are accepted by the government, but there is strong resistance to recognizing indigenous territorial rights and control of natural resources, even in areas historically inhabited by indigenous people.

The key political demand of the Zapatista movement is constitutional reform to guarantee indigenous cultural and political rights, which was required principally in the context of change in the national government. With this objective the Zapatistas mobilized during 2001 in the national capital, in the aptly named 'March of the Colour of the Earth', to demand the fulfilment of the ASA and constitutional changes to guarantee the cultural rights of indigenous people. It had massive support from millions of people throughout the country. It included a speech by a woman EZLN leader at the National Congress demanding constitutional changes.

The Commission for Concord and Pacification (COCOPA), created by the National Congress in 1994 to negotiate with the Zapatistas, was in agreement with the central themes of the ASA. But the opposition of important interest groups, including the governing party, resulted in a dilution of the constitutional changes to very restricted issues that did not match the agreements signed with the Zapatistas and did not substantively change the situation of indigenous people. The amended constitutional changes did not recognize the right to self-determination and to indigenous territories. The result was that the constitutional changes were rejected, not only by the Zapatistas but by a number of social and political organizations. Indigenous municipalities from all over the country took legal action in the national Supreme Court of Justice against the approved constitutional changes, stating that they essentially violated the cultural rights of the indigenous population. The controversial constitutional dispute was rejected by the Supreme Court, which ruled that the indigenous people's cultural rights had not been violated.

The Zapatista movement questioned the system of representation, from local government at the municipal level to national government, including the character of the National Congress. The electoral process and the party system have been consistently criticized by the Zapatista movement and rejected as serving only the powerful national groups which use it merely to validate the maintenance of the status quo.

Over the years the movement has uncovered evidence of the profound social inequalities that are characteristic of Mexican society and has demonstrated the government's inability to reduce them.[23] The Zapatistas have made a major effort to give impetus to the creation of a political front with a national agenda aimed at redressing this situation. From the call to Mexican society to participate in the Convention of Aguascalientes[24] in 1994, to the 'Other Campaign' promoted in 2006 (a critical reference to the political campaigns for the Mexican presidency in 2004), various initiatives have been promoted to pursue an agenda of change at the national level. The political action has put the emphasis on generating an action plan for struggle from the bottom up. All these initiatives have a common political perspective, oriented to developing awareness in society of the need for profound reforms to the Mexican state.

Global level From its beginning the Zapatista movement has identified with anti-globalization movements around the world. In some senses it could be understood as an 'anti' movement – that is, 'anti-government', 'anti-state' and 'anti-system' – but in other senses it is recognized as a proactive movement, as its demands are clearly for social justice, for the recognition of cultural diversity and for the right to define rights. The proactive elements of the movement may be the key to its success at both the national and the global levels.

Through this process the Zapatista movement has enjoyed the solidarity of a broad range of groups, principally from Europe and the United States, which include anti-globalization networks, municipal governments from Spain and Italy, syndical organizations and non-governmental organizations (NGOs).

The movement's opposition to globalization is both general and in relation to government policies relevant to the Zapatista cause. In this perspective, 'capitalism divests, exploits, represses and discriminates ... [The] production of new merchandise and the liberalization of new markets are achieved with the conquest of territories and social spaces ... big transformations do not begin from above or with monumental facts, but with little movements ... from the organized conscience of groups and collectives ... that construct another politic' (Marcos 2007: 9). This position has been expressed through the various events orchestrated over the years, from the so-called 'Intergalactic Encounter' to the recent 'Encounter of the Zapatista People with the People of the World'. These initiatives have been recognized as part of the origin of the World Social Forum.[25]

From the Zapatista movement to autonomous rebel government: characteristics, success and challenges

The political position taken by the Zapatista movement to achieve its demands has meant a profound change in its relations with the different levels of government, and this has had important implications for communitarian and regional social life and for the movement's relations with other social organizations. As a result of the government's failure to meet the terms of the ASA, the Zapatistas decided to construct their autonomy in practice at the regional level.

The movement has combined profound ideas of change with a new kind of political praxis and the quotidian construction of local power alternatives oriented towards sustainable production, the addressing of cultural issues, the democratization of communication, social justice and fair trade. All this is based on social participation and the assumption of responsibilities and rights, applied in a territory where empowerment is built up from the local to the regional level. The principal characteristics of the Zapatista construction of autonomy at the regional level are the following.

- It is an active position. It can be understood as the expression of communitarian citizenship where the people have to participate and assume different responsibilities. They act as collective agents (Cornwall 2004: 6). This implies having to debate and agree on a very different scale, from the local level, through direct involvement in the solution of problems, up to the municipal and regional level, through a representative process.
- It is directed at achieving different kinds of transformation at the local

and the regional levels. Actions are based principally on the people's own resources and capacities, although they have different forms of support and are oriented towards solving fundamental needs. Actions are viewed in a long-term perspective, within a framework that takes into account social, political and cultural rights.

• It provides the impetus for the people's own view of change. It is based in the control of land taken during the rebellion, but it includes the creation of new settlements and the drawing up of a territorial code of conduct. This implies the capacity to negotiate and agree with other social groups and with government (principally the Chiapas state government) for the solution of common problems (Harvey 2001).

Autonomy implies a space to coordinate and communicate priorities and expectations, a place to express and reproduce resistance, through practice. MAREZ and JBG have brought important advances in the development of capacities for self-government and for the construction of a communitarian citizenship. Each JBG sets out its own agenda related to that population's political, social, cultural, productive and environmental priorities. The responsibilities are very wide-ranging, from establishing medium-term work plans to finding solutions to education and health needs, from the establishment of regulations on the use of natural resources such as forests to the application of traditional laws, and from the solution of communitarian land conflicts to the organization of collective work.

Since 2003, each JBG has had as its central structure the *caracol*, the seat of the autonomous regional government, where the authorities coordinate the work and which includes various institutions such as schools, health facilities and cooperatives. Through the JGB working at the *caracol* level, and based on the Sixth Declaration of the Lacandon Rainforest, the Zapatistas have opened a dialogue with different sectors of civil society, including social organizations, human rights organizations and others that want to collaborate in solving mutual problems at a regional level. One important objective of the JBG is to coordinate the activities or initiatives that come from outside – from NGOs, other organizations in terms of expressions of solidarity, and governments. All these external initiatives must be presented to and accepted for approval by the JBG in the form of projects, groups or even research, but only if the autonomous authorities consider that there is a mutually binding interest. These activities must address the Zapatista priorities: health, education, food, housing and jobs.[26]

One of the characteristics of the JBG is the insistence on accountability in relation to the use of the resources obtained and the purposes for which they are used. Periodically each of the JBG presents information on the resources obtained, which vary among them. An example is the information presented by the Caracol de La Realidad, which, in 2004, received around half a million dollars, while the Caracol de Roberto Barrios received about $150,000 in the same period. In session the JBG presents information on its situation, considering aspects such as relations with the official state and municipal governments and communication strategies to solve shared problems. In collaboration with other social organizations the JBG has also established its own law to protect forest and natural resources through a prohibition on exploiting the forest for commercial purposes and an acceptance that it can be used for community needs only with the permission of the land and territory commission of the autonomous rebel municipality.

One of the important changes is in the application of Zapatista justice. It is argued that this is not in conflict with the state and federal justice system, but rather complements it. In recent years an important discussion has been developing in Mexico on the differences between and complementarity of these different perspectives on justice and the way in which the system works at the local level. As part of a participatory research project with NGOs working on human rights, we analysed experiences of local justice for different kinds of problems (Burguete 2003).

The MAREZ and the JBG have been participatory spaces for education (autonomous schools) and infrastructure (potable water, health clinics) and in developing some local projects (bakeries consumption and production cooperatives, coffee exports, etc.). All these processes rely on the active participation of thousands of young indigenous people who take responsibility for production, health, education, etc. on behalf of their people. An important example is the work on health and the preparation of the young people of the community to work at the communitarian level as part of the local health system (Cortez and Heredia 2007).

In this perspective, the Zapatista MAREZ and JBG spaces are designed to transform relations (technical and productive, cultural and political), to advance the management of social life and to construct a better future from the local level upwards, but they also offer a way of revalorizing the people's own cultural interests and reformulating some cultural means to achieve this. In both instances great work has been done to develop local capacity and leadership.

Practitioners are very important in building capacity. Local communitarian practitioners, most of them young men and women, are nominated by their communities to be trained and to work in the areas considered priorities in each MAREZ and JBG, such as health, education, human rights and agro-ecology.

The participation of women in all the activities of the JBG is becoming more important every day. Even though the traditional situation of women has not changed sufficiently, it is evident that more women are playing an active role in the construction of autonomy. One student at a Zapatista rebel autonomous secondary school (ESRAZ)[27] preparing to be an education communitarian practitioner explained the situation of the women:

> We can talk and decide for ourselves. We can decide how many children we want to have because nobody, not even our husbands, can impose on us how many children to have. It will allow us to participate and to have responsibilities in the organization and in our struggles ... We have a right to a healthy life ... We have the right to study, because a lot of the time this right is neglected ... We demand the accomplishment of this right ... the right to organize ourselves ... [W]e don't want the government to continue oppressing us ... We have rights. Rights are not just for rich people. Indigenous women and men have rights too: a right to justice and democracy, to participate and to organize ourselves in the way we want.[28]

Those nominated to be representatives in the MAREZ or JBG accept that their responsibility is to the community and the people. This role allows them to gain knowledge of the situation in a more general way and to understand that problems are collective and that different kinds of actions are needed to solve them at the technical, organizational or political level. A representative at an autonomous municipal authority describes the situation:

> [Zapatista] authorities have no relations with the official government and they don't accept any kind of help or projects from governmental institutions ... They try to meet their needs with their own resources and with the collaboration of NGOs and activists. They have received help for education and infrastructure and to develop some local projects.[29]

An important form of activism that can help one understand the kind of work that the MAREZ and the JBG do is the development of a health model based on communitarian participation, capacity-building and the requisite infrastructure creation. The communitarian participation method has entailed a process of defining health priorities and developing local capacity to deal with common health problems. The health system works through community clinics, in each of which there is a medical doctor to attend to a population of around thirty communities, usually isolated or with poor communication links. In most of these isolated communities, a health 'house' has been created that is attended by a practitioner who has a stock of basic medicines to provide the primary level of care. When a communitarian health practitioner is not able to resolve a case, it is referred to the regional clinic attended by a doctor, where health promoters can help translate if the sick person does not speak Spanish. These promoters are nominated by the community assembly and receive training in basic healthcare. The infrastructure (clinics and health houses) and the medicines are acquired partly from sympathizers and partly with communitarian resources.

As an example of advances in health, in December 2006 one of the JBG provided the information that in its region there were eighteen practitioners in health houses, 171 communitarian health practitioners with knowledge of basic healthcare, forty-seven fully equipped health houses and forty-four health houses that still did not have the required equipment.

The meaning and implications of this participation in the health system are illustrated by the vaccination campaigns. These involve the participation of health authorities, municipal officers, NGOs, universities and the health structures in the communities. The Zapatista population refuse to be vaccinated at government institutions, where the official health authorities would normally administer the vaccines. Instead the collaborators in the Zapatista health system request the required doses from government health institutions through an NGO, and they coordinate with the local population to ensure that vaccination takes place.

This form of collaboration means that the movement is even able to make an epidemiological commitment, because if there is an outbreak of infectious disease in a village with Zapatista communities engaged in resistance, the health promoters and doctors working at the Zapatista clinics will inform health officials. This happened to a Zapatista community in 2006, for example, when there was an outbreak of whooping cough that the Chiapas Health Secretariat offered to deal with. Since this disease can be fatal to children, a quarantine area was set up to stop it spreading, in coordination with community promoters, nurses and doctors working at the Zapatista clinics. The health secretariat provided vaccinations and medication to contain the outbreak, and it was controlled with the active participation of health promoters from Zapatista communities, who played a key role in this process, from diagnosis to follow-up and maintenance of the emergency plan, with the support of medical personnel. The health authorities at the regional, state and even national level acknowledge the capabilities of the Zapatistas in health issues.

Another important activity for the JBG is education, which includes the training of education promoters. In each region education must take place in Spanish and in the regional language, such as Tzeltal, Tzotzil, Zoque or Chol. Initially external practitioners were brought in to act as education promoters, but this practice has to some extent been revised and now most are local. This does not mean that all the work is done by local practitioners; external practitioners are still used for certain functions, such as the compilation of teaching materials. There are two training centres for communitarian promoters involved in five subjects: mathematics, languages, history, life and environment, and integration. Zapatista educational objectives emphasize the development of new capacities related to indigenous culture and tradition, and older people are seen to have an important role in the education of children. Another emphasis is relating education to projects in other areas, such as health, agro-ecology and communication. For example, in the Benito Juarez MAREZ, children begin taking care of the land through agro-ecological practices. The educational practitioners take them to the mountains and rivers to educate them directly about caring for the environment. They also try to relate agriculture practices to healthcare (Gama 2007).

In relation to the point made above, a significant attempt has been made to develop sustainable production practices. With the collaboration of NGOs there has been a major effort to restore indigenous agro-ecological practices and to develop new capacity in accordance with this approach. The purpose has been to make better use of natural resources, develop local capacity and improve production and produce for the market. In JBG such as La Garrucha, noteworthy efforts have been made to train agro-ecology practitioners in sustainable food production. In an interview, a member of one of the JBG explained that according to their understanding of autonomy, their communities should take care of the land. The importance placed on this issue is underlined by efforts to modify some productive practices through, for example, the substitution of organic raw materials for agrochemicals. The process is seen as not only technical, but an important issue in the development of social organization for resistance and the development of the movement.

Related to all the above issues is the effort the movement has made to create different kinds of cooperatives, from those oriented to the production and commercialization of local produce (coffee, cattle, pork, fruit and honey) to those focusing on handcrafts and light industries (e.g. food, construction, textiles and shoes). These alternatives are aimed at solving some of the most important needs at the regional level: to ensure sustainable production, to generate jobs and income, to eliminate intermediaries in the commercialization of local production (warehouses, transport) and to promote food security.

Conclusion

This chapter has highlighted the success of the Zapatista movement in mobilizing at the local, regional, national and global levels to advance the rights of indigenous peoples. Through self-created governance structures such as the MAREZ and JBG, which parallel local and regional government structures, a long-term perspective has been created in which participation is part of the struggle to be assured of political and socio-economic rights. The Zapatistas' demands have been related to political and civil rights, but give increasing weight to cultural and socio-economic ones as well. The movement poses a profound challenge to the vision that reduces citizenship to the exercising of civil and political rights, with no consideration of socio-economic and cultural rights.

The process of change has been a complex one, with some advances but also many setbacks. Nonetheless there is sufficient evidence in the fieldwork presented here to suggest that the lives of indigenous people are changing, from the community to the autonomous municipalities, from the cooperatives to the demands for women's rights.

Clearly the Zapatista movement has been an important force in giving meaning and expression to a new kind of citizenship for indigenous people. It has created new organizational spaces, and through different forms of participation, indigenous people have struggled to find a voice, generate awareness and construct alternatives in the areas of health, production and education, among others. One of the most interesting contributions of this movement is its capacity to inculcate a notion of active citizenship in its members that strengthens their capacity to act to realize their rights, and to mobilize for the right to define their individual and collective rights. This has given rise to active forms of communitarian citizenship that challenge the state directly and indirectly.

Notes

1 Ejercito Zapatista de Liberación Nacional.

2 There is an extensive bibliography on the historical, political and social causes of the rebellion, and on the principal demands, actions and characteristics of its leaders. Gordillo (2006) provides a good overview of this body of 719 publications, in Spanish, referring to the EZLN.

3 Kabeer (2005: 23) discusses the importance of understanding citizenship in terms of two axes of participation. Horizontal forms of participation refer to the linkages forged between citizens and communities themselves at local, national and global levels. These linkages are not necessarily stable, nor do they necessarily represent a fixed notion of citizen identity on the part of those who participate. Leach et al. (2005: 29) refer to these shifting notions of citizenship and engagement as 'practiced engagements around emergent solidarities'.

4 Fuerzas de Liberación National.

5 The history of the movement is set out by Harvey (2001).

6 Article 39, Political Constitution of the United Mexican States.

7 An interesting analysis of the differences between liberal and communitarian citizenship – including some of the dangers, such as the possibility of lapsing into a kind of essentialism – is developed in Rubio (2007).

8 The Mexican population was around 90 million in 1994, about half of them living in poverty, and in 2008 the population was estimated at 106.7 million. It is believed that around 11.7 million have emigrated to the United States, most of them in recent years. The indigenous population of those who speak one of the sixty-two languages other than Spanish used in Mexico is estimated at around 9 per cent of the national population, most of whom live in extreme poverty (www.inegi.org.mx).

9 The principal indigenous groups of the region are the Tzeltal, Tzotzil, Tojolabal, Chol, Mam, Zoque and Lacandon.

10 An indigenous Tzeltal communitarian teacher from the rainforest region.

11 Alianza Nacional Campesina Independiente Emiliano Zapata.

12 For a specific analysis of the participation of civil society, see Parra (2002).

13 Acuerdos de San Andrés.

14 In 1997 Human Rights Watch released information on the effects of the so-called 'low-intensity war' and demanded an end to violations of human rights in rural areas around the country. López and López (2000) compiled evidence on the relationship between paramilitary groups and governmental help. Ten years later (2007), the Fray Bartolomé de las Casas Centre for Human Rights presented evidence that the judicial system was being used to criminalize the social movement in Chiapas.

15 Municipios Autónomos Rebeldes Zapatistas.

16 Juntas de Buen Gobierno.

17 For evidence of the participatory process in the Zapatista municipalities and how it has evolved, see Cortez (2004), Gama (2007) and Bravo (2008).

18 'A new step forward in the indigenous struggle is only possible if the indigenous join together with workers, campesinos, students, teachers, employees ... the workers of

the city and the countryside' (enlace-zapatista.ezln.org.mx/especiales/2).

19 The experience of communitarian citizenship in a Zapatista municipality is recorded by Gama (2007).

20 The word *caracol* means 'snail' or 'spiral shell'. It is used as a metaphor, reminding one not to forget, and, as explained by one member of a JBG, because the Zapatistas are advancing in their project as slowly as a snail.

21 The name 'Zapatista' refers to Emiliano Zapata, the leader of the Mexican Revolution, who said that 'the land belongs to those whose work it'.

22 Rubio (2007: 77) analyses communitarian citizenship from a theoretical and historical perspective.

23 The Mexican constitution recognizes the multi-ethnic character of the society, and the government has signed most of the international agreements that recognize the rights of indigenous people, but this is not reflected in their actual situation, as the human development indicators show.

24 The 1994 'Convención de Aguascalientes' referred to a stage of the Mexican Revolution in which a new constitution, with important advances in social and political rights, including the right to land for peasants, was realized in the city of Aguascalientes in 1914.

25 '[T]he launching date of the NAFTA, January 1, 1994, was used for the launching also of the Zapatista movement in the severely globalized, marginalized and exploited state of Chiapas ... [T]he Zapatistas rapidly revealed entirely novel characteristics ... [P]articularly two international encounters ... gave rise, or shape, to

a new wave of internationalism ...' (Waterman 1998: 57).

26 Gama (2007) and other researchers have analysed how these requirements are met in the Zapatista municipalities.

27 Escuela Secundaria Rebelde Autonomia Zapatista.

28 Student communitarian education practitioner at an ESRAZ of the Caracol de Oventic, Chiapas.

29 Reflections of a MAREZ representative while painting a communitarian mural for the Caracol de Oventic, Chiapas.

References

Belausteguigoitia, M. (ed.) (2007) 'Rebeliones en la frontera sur: las mujeres y la construcción de ciudadanía en los limites de la nación', in M. Belausteguigoitia and L. Melgar (eds), *Fronteras, violencia, justicia: nuevos discursos*, Mexico City: UNAM.

Bravo, S. (2008) 'La semilla que vamos sembrando: aniversario de las Juntas de Buen Gobierno', *Rebeldia*, 62, November.

Burguete, A. (2003) 'Las juntas de buen gobierno: otras autonomías *de facto* son posibles', *Memoria*, 177, November.

Congreso Nacional Indígena (1996) 'La voz de las mujeres', *Cuadernos Agrarios*, 13.

CONPAZ (1996) *Militarización y violencia en Chiapas*, Coordinación de Organismos no Gubernamentales por la Paz, Centro de Derechos Humanos Fray Bartolomé de las Casas, Convergencia de Organismos Civiles por la Democracia, Mexico City: Producción Editorial SIPRO.

Cornwall, A. (2002) 'Making spaces, changing places: situating participation in development', IDS Working Paper 170, October.

— (2004) 'New democratic spaces? The politics and dynamics of institutionalised participation', *IDS Bulletin*, 35(2).

Cortez, C. (2004) 'Social strategies and public policies in an indigenous zone in Chiapas, Mexico', *IDS Bulletin*, 35(2), April.

— (2005) 'Rights and citizenship of indigenous women in Chiapas: a history of struggles, fears and hopes', in N. Kabeer (ed.), *Inclusive Citizenship*, London: Zed Books.

Cortez, C., and J. Heredia (2007) 'Movimientos sociales y derecho a la salud en Chiapas', in R. Miranda and L. Cortes (eds), *Chiapas: la paz en la guerra*, Mexico City: UNAM and ECOSUR.

Declaración Política de la Sociedad Civil en su Encuentro con el EZLN (1999) *Revista Chiapas*, 7.

EZLN (1993) *Primera Declaración de la Selva Lacandona*, Ejercito Zapatista de Liberación Nacional.

— (2005) *Sexta Declaración de la Selva Lacandona*, Ejercito Zapatista de Liberación Nacional, enlacezapatista.ezln.org.mx/especiales/2?lp_lang_view=es.

Gama, A. (2007) 'Es lo que soñamos que hay que hacer para ser: reconstrucción de la autonomía desde la apropiación en lo cotidiano en un Municipio Autónomo Rebelde Zapatista', Unpublished master's thesis in rural development, Universidad Autónoma Metropolitana – Xochimilco.

Gaventa, J. (2002) 'Introduction: exploring citizenship, participation and accountability', *IDS Bulletin*, 33(2).

Gordillo, O. (2006) *EZLN, una Aproxi-mación Bibliográgica*, Mexico: Ed. Praxis.

Harvey, N. (2001) *La rebelión de Chiapas: la lucha por la tierra y la democracia*, Mexico City: Editorial Era.

INEGI (n.d.) *Sistema Nacional de Información Estadística y Geográfica*, website of the Instituto Nacional de Estadistica, Geografía e Informática, www.inegi.org.mx, accessed 15 March 2008.

Kabeer, N. (2002) *Citizenship and the Boundaries of the Acknowledged Community: Identity, Affiliation and Exclusion*, Brighton: Institute of Development Studies.

— (ed.) (2005) *Inclusive Citizenship: Meanings and Expressions*, London: Zed Books.

Leach, M., I. Scoones and B. Wynne (eds) (2005) *Science and Citizens: Globalisation and the Challenge of Engagement*, London: Zed Books.

López, J. and F. López (2000) *Paramilitares: la serpiente se muerde la cola. La agresión en Tila: grupos paramilitares, bajo el cobijo gubernamental*, www.eco.utexas.edu/~archive/chiapas95/2000.11/msg00495.html.

Marcos (Subcomandante Insurgente) (2007) 'Ni el centro, ni la periferia', Papers presented at the First Internacional Colloquium in memory of Andrés Aubry, Universidad de la Tierra, Chiapas.

Moguel, J. (2001) 'Claroscuros del Plan Puebla Panamá: de cómo se escamotean los derechos indios y se traslada el debate a los presuntos temas del desarrollo', in A. Bartra (ed.), *Mesoamerica, los ríos profundos: alternativas plebeyas al Plan Puebla Panamá*, Mexico City: El Atajo Ediciones.

Muñoz Ramírez, G. (2004) 'Caracol v Roberto Barrios', *Chiapas la*

Resistencia, 20th anniversary special supplement, *La Jornada*, Mexico City, 19 September, www.jornada.unam.mx/2004/09/19/barrios.html.

OACNUDH (2004) *Diagnóstico sobre la situación de los derechos humanos en México*, Oficina del Alto Comisionado de las Naciones Unidas para los Derechos Humanos en México, Mexico City: Mundi-Prensa.

Paré, L., C. Robles and C. Cortéz (2002) 'Participation of indigenous and rural people in the construction of developmental and environmental public policies in Mexico', *IDS Bulletin*, 33(2).

Parra, M. A. (2002) 'Sociedad civil, movimiento zapatista y conflicto en Chiapas', *Informe final del concurso: fragmentación social y crisis política e institucional en América Latina y el Caribe*, Programa Regional de Becas CLACSO, Buenos Aires, bibliotecavirtual.clacso.org.ar/ar/libros/becas/2002/fragmenta/parra.pdf.

Peruzzotti, E. and C. Smulovitz (eds) (2000) *Controlando la politica: ciudadanos y medios en las nuevas democracias latinoamericanas*, Buenos Aires: Editorial Temas.

PNUD (2002) *Informe sobre Desarrollo Humano, México*, Programa de las Naciones Unidas para el Desarrollo, Mexico City: Mundi-Prensa.

Rayner, S. (2003) 'Who's in charge? Worldwide displacement of democratic judgment by expert assessments', *Economic and Political Weekly*, 38(48), November/December.

Rubio, J. (2007) *Teoría crítica de la ciudadanía democrática*, Madrid: Editorial Trotta.

Villafuerte, D., S. Meza, G. Ascencio, M. García, C. Rivera, M. Lisbona and J. Morales (1999) *La tierra en Chiapas: viejos problemas nuevos*, Mexico City: Plaza y Valdés.

Villoro, L. (1997) *El poder y el valor: fundamentos de una ética política*, Mexico City: Coedición de Fondo de Cultura Económica y El Colegio Nacional.

— (1998) *Estado plural, pluralidad de culturas*, Mexico City: UNAM.

Waterman, P. (1998) *Globalisation, Social Movements and the New Internationalisms*, London: Mansell.

THREE | **Mobilization, social movements and inclusive governance**

8 | Participation, inclusion and development under conditions of social mobilization[1]

VERA SCHATTAN COELHO AND
ARILSON FAVARETO

This chapter analyses processes of social mobilization and the dynamics of participatory forums in the Vale do Ribeira, Brazil, discussing the argument that mobilized actors and 'well-designed' institutions enable the inclusion of a broader spectrum of actors in political debates, as well as reducing the asymmetries between them, thereby facilitating the negotiation and agreement of politically and economically viable projects that may help to encourage development in the region.

The Vale do Ribeira Paulista is a poor region, made up of twenty-five municipalities located between two of the richest metropolitan regions in Brazil; 350,000 people live in the area, with a large number of traditional communities, such as indigenous groups, *quilombola* (rural Afro-Brazilian) communities, *caiçaras* (artisanal fishers and smallholders of mainly indigenous descent) and family farmers, many of whom are organized into associations. The region also contains the largest remaining area of Atlantic rainforest, covering two-thirds of the territory. In these circumstances there are inevitable tensions between, on the one hand, a demand for revitalizing the economy, based on the necessity of dealing with poverty, and on the other, the delicate problems of environmental control, due to the urgent need to preserve the native Atlantic rainforest.

This chapter focuses on two participatory forums active in the region and analyses how they have been dealing with these issues. The two cases are the Committee for the Management of Water Resources (CGRH) and the Consortium of Food Safety and Local Development (Consad). The two forums were observed in terms of how they dealt with two polemical regional issues: the proposal to build a big dam (the Tijuco Alto), a process that has been going on for more than a decade, and the definition of a programme of sustainable development capable of reconciling environmental conservation and growth in the local economy.

The literature on social participation, which will be looked at in more depth below, suggests that forums of this type may, in specific situations, open up space where various actors may take up positions concerning these polemical issues and negotiate alternatives. These situations depend on the institutional design, the degree of organization of civil society and the involvement of state actors. Nevertheless, if it is true that the presence, for example, of a 'good institutional design' facilitates inclusion, dialogue and negotiation, then it is also true that there still exists great difficulty in identifying what might be considered a 'good design', or even the conditions that would lead state actors and politicians responsible for the organization of these forums to choose this 'good' design instead of another favouring the reproduction of their own political coalition. This chapter works between these two perspectives, investigating the institutional conditions capable of fostering inclusion and dialogue, be that of the forums or of the political system. Furthermore, it questions the logic and the values that motivate the actors involved in the creation of these forums, a question that the literature is only beginning to broach. From the resulting observations the initial question will be revisited, since, if it is necessary to recognize which procedures are inclusive and democratic, it is equally important to identify the conditions that lead the actors responsible for the forums to adopt such procedures.

The analysis suggests that, during the period of research, the forums analysed re-created in the participatory sphere coalitions that were already present in the regional political scene, thereby acting as an extension of the party political game rather than as arenas where new arrangements of actors could agree on alternative projects. From a theoretical perspective, this result raises again the question of the origin and the evolution of institutions, in that it questions the mechanisms necessary for the creation of institutions explicitly designed to alter the status quo.

The chapter is divided into four main parts. The first section briefly sets out the theoretical debate concerning the relationship between participation and development and presents the questions and the methodology that guided the research. The second section presents a brief history of the Vale do Ribeiro to contextualize the debates about sustainable development, briefly describing the local civil society; highlighting the evolution of two important local organizations, the Movement of Dam-Affected People (MOAB) and the Union of Farming Families of the Vale do Ribeira (Sintravale); and finally presenting the controversy surrounding the dam. The third section deals with the two forums (CGRH and Consad), describing in detail the involvement of MOAB and Sintravale in them. The fourth section analyses the role of the forums in dealing with the two polemical issues mentioned above. The conclusion sets out the principal lessons that can be learnt from the experiences in the

Vale do Ribeira concerning the relationship between participation and development.

About social participation and development

The literature that unites supporters of social participation in public policy is based upon two assumptions. The first is that the local population would be encouraged to participate because of a reduction in the costs involved in the process of political mobilization. This reduction would take place because local participatory bodies would be authorized by the public authorities to make substantive decisions about policy, and also because of the expectation that the citizen would participate using his or her own experience of the issues being discussed, therefore enabling resources to be used more efficiently. Problems of asymmetry, which might inhibit the inclusion of actors who have fewer resources, be they communicative, material or technical, would be successfully dealt with by good institutional engineering (Fung and Wright 2003; Fung 2004). The second argument is that providing the opportunity for the various actors involved to set out more explicitly their demands would allow those demands to become clearer and more understandable for the state actors, thereby highlighting local specificities that would encourage changes in the distribution of public funds, the way policies are implemented and the way regional agreements are reached; which in turn could contribute to the successful implementation of private initiatives, as well as public policies and programmes (Cunnil 1997; Abers 2001; World Bank 2001; UNDP 2002). The implicit causal mechanism consists in giving a voice to groups who have traditionally been marginalized, encouraging participation, negotiation and cooperation between various social segments, thereby increasing the trust and coordination between them, which in turn contributes to the promotion of development projects that coincide with their needs and interests (Avritzer 2003; Gaventa 2004).

Various texts question the viability of putting these mechanisms into action, pointing out the asymmetries that shape the relationships between the actors, as well as the excessive power of state actors in the participatory forums. Furthermore, they point out that special interest groups and party political groups can capture these forums. Some studies highlight a sort of 'dark side' of these forms of social assembly (Ray 2000, 2002): in general the selection of projects and the mechanisms for competition between territories, regions and social groups have the tendency to reinforce the positions of those who already have the best technical and political conditions, and thus are in a better position to obtain the available resources. In Brazil the work of Veiga (2005) and Abramovay (2005) also presents evidence that there is no automatic link between the existence of participatory forums and development. Pritchett and Woolcock (2004) and Manzuri and Rao (2004) go farther, arguing that there are intrinsic faults in making this link, since the interests of the actors involved in the forums are not always the same as those who implement the policies and public services discussed by such forums. The authors even suggest that complex ideas such as participation, social capital and empowerment are being naively applied.

Other authors argue that, under specific conditions, it is possible to achieve relevant results in terms of inclusion as well as distribution through participation (Abers 2001; Marquetti 2003; Coelho and Nobre 2004). One of these conditions is the existence of an organized civil society, above all in the form of associations and social movements that meet the social demands concerning the policies under debate in the participatory forums, and also that provide legitimacy to the public initiatives, thereby increasing social support for them. Another condition is the quality of institutional design: the key variable concerns the rules of these spaces and their ability to provide incentives that influence the actions of the actors in a way that fosters particular desired features of the policy in question, as well as their capacity to alter the balance of forces between the participants, favouring the expression of demands by those who have fewer resources. Finally, a third condition involves the commitment and openness of the managers to the organization of and the decisions taken by these forums, which is a crucial element in guaranteeing their functioning and the permeability of the institutional environment to the demands made by the forums.

This literature, briefly set out above, enables us to construct different assumptions concerning the possible contribution of the participatory institutions in dealing with the two polemical regional issues analysed in this chapter. For those who do not believe in this path, these forums will either simply reproduce the asymmetries between the actors without moving beyond them, or be at the mercy of the executive power, or even be captured by party political groups. For those who do believe in participation, however, it will be possible to move towards a negotiated solution, and the debates conducted by the CGRH and Consad, the two forums analysed in this chapter, will play a role in this process as long as they can establish incentives capable of bringing together and merging the expectations and the investments of the agents involved.

This study engages with this debate, aiming to set out more clearly the conditions for running the forums that favour the inclusion and negotiation of alternatives to resolve the polemical regional issues. In the following sections, and in the following presentation, we address empirically the validity of certain assumptions underlying different arguments that would derive from these distinct analytical positions. The first two of these arguments derive from the institutionalist position and the third from the literature on participation and development.

The first argument relates the design of the forums to their performance. The assumption being assessed is that the more equitable the distribution of seats between civil society and public officials, and the more open and transparent the process of selecting the councillors, the more inclusive the forum. Our aim here is to explore the impact of the rules and recruitment procedures of councillors on the inclusiveness of the forums.

The second argument predicts that groups with fewer communicative, material and technical resources will have increased participation as a result of using discussion techniques that aim to promote the capacity for expression of these same groups. The assumption we assess here is that the discussion and decision-making processes resulting from the use of such techniques give more clarity to the demands made by less-favoured groups and as a result enable such demands to be linked to more general debates and the interests of other social groups.

The third argument is that the greater the inclusiveness of these forums, judged by the profile of the participants and the opportunities for participation, the greater the contribution towards the resolution of the conflict about the Tijuco Alto dam and the debates about regional development. The implicit supposition of this argument – and thus the assumption that we address – is that the more participatory a forum, the greater its capacity to encourage the formulation of viable economical and political proposals.

Research involved three principal phases:

- analysis of secondary data, a survey involving 103 of the 192 councillors of the studied forums, and interviews with their leaderships;
- observing *in loco* the daily routines of the selected social movements, together with interviews with the leaders of both, with a view to understanding how they organized their participation in the forums, and the repercussions that this had on the way they perceived and modified their position with respect to the dam and to sustainable development; and

- discussion of results in meetings with the managers and local leaders previously interviewed.

History, social mobilization and conflicts in the Vale do Ribeira

The history of the Vale do Ribeira enables us to understand some of the reasons for its current situation, marked by its poor economic and social indicators, as well as the significance of the social conflict concerning the Tijuco Alto dam and the local support for the rhetoric of sustainable development.

The rise of the rhetoric of sustainable development The period from the colonization of the sixteenth century until the beginning of the twentieth century was marked by economic cycles, principally involving mining and the cultivation of rice, during which the region attained moments of prosperity, to be later interrupted by decline in these activities. The subsequent arrival of Japanese immigrants in the first half of the last century established certain practices that continue through to the present: agriculture with a reasonable degree of mechanization and commercialization, with the native population becoming labourers or withdrawing into subsistence farming. The 'traditional communities' in the Vale do Ribeira practise family and rudimentary farming and are structurally dependent on the Ribeira river and its margins to maintain their subsistence. A large proportion of the native population are family farmers, but they are faced with problems such as gaining access to larger regional markets since middlemen ('dealers') end up being the principal agents responsible for buying these family products at very low prices. The combination of these characteristics with poor access and the precarious nature of the transport links contributed to the relative isolation of the region – in comparison with the rest of São Paulo – during the twentieth century.

The final part of the last century marked the start of a distinct phase of development, with a series of government initiatives aimed at breaking the situation of economic stagnation and poverty. This period coincided with the growing importance of environmental issues, which prompted the creation of various conservation units. The public initiatives that have come about since then seem to have contributed towards the containment of deforestation, which had been making significant inroads into the remaining Atlantic rainforest. They have also prompted numerous conflicts with the traditional populations, however, together with the discourse, espoused mainly by municipal authorities, that conservationist policies would damage the local economy since they restrict potential industrial development and the expansion of agricultural activities (Resende 2002). By studying the development of the economy and of the social structures of the Vale do Ribeira over the last decade, it is possible to see signs of change and a movement towards heterogeneity: the rural exodus no longer seems to be a general trend; farming is no longer the principal activity, ceding space to growth in other areas, especially services; and while different development indices continue to be relatively low, health and education in eight municipalities have improved, there was economic growth in almost all the region, and forest cover declined in only eight municipalities (Chabaribery et al. 2004; Favareto and Brancher 2005). In this scenario it is possible to say that the image of a poor region, economically stagnant and dependent on agriculture, is giving way to one of a region characterized by increasing internal differentiation, the result of a various factors, largely unrecognized by the local actors themselves.

It is at this moment in the region's history that the rhetoric of sustainable development emerged as an attempt to balance environmental conservation with the expectations of economic development utilizing the potential energy and the biodiversity of the local landscape. Nevertheless, sustainability is perceived in different ways by different groups. Traditional communities' discourses on sustainability emphasize the recognition of their rights to the use of the land and the forests. For farmers and their organizations, sustainable development is synonymous with giving priority to 'the small' as opposed to big investments, while local government views it as an opportunity to take advantage of the local natural resources, but in a way that requires 'the environmental legislation to be more flexible'. For other councils it represents the possibility of receiving large external investment so as to take advantage of tourism or the potential biodiversity. Finally, federal government projects aim to encourage private investment and profitable exploration of natural resources, such as the recent project to support the production of bio-diesel.

Diversity and social mobilization in regional civil society These changes also appear in the sphere of civil society. One survey identified 211 active organizations in the region, for the most part business associations, workers' unions, environmental organizations and residents' associations. With respect to owners' organizations there are some traditional groups, such as the trade and industry associations and the associations of banana growers, as well as newer organizations, such as the Association

193

of Flower Growers. In turn popular organization has its origins in the 1980s. Various organizations have been formed since then, and many have their roots in residents' associations promoted by left-wing Catholics whose presence was felt through the pastoral agents (Pastoral Commission of the Earth). Some of these organizations remained as residents' associations, while some evolved to represent more specific interests, for example the Guapiruvu Residents' Association, which today is an important example of an economic organization for traditional groups.

This was also the case for the *quilombola* communities, whose origins can be traced back to the expansion of mining activities in the eighteenth century, which brought a large number of slaves to the region. The subsequent decline of these activities and escape of slaves gave rise to the formation of various rural communities of Afro-Brazilian people, known in Brazil as *quilombos*. It is estimated that in Vale do Ribeira there are twenty remaining *quilombola* communities. These communities occupy remote areas and are difficult to reach. The creation of environmental conservation areas (UCAs) in ownerless areas (*areas devolutas*) had a direct impact on the *quilombos'* everyday agricultural and political life, in that the majority of their land was transformed into areas of environmental conservation. Between 1959 and 1995, twelve UCAs were created throughout the valley, with six of them in particular superimposed on the land originally inhabited by the Afro-Brazilian communities of Eldorado and Iporanga.

In order to understand the context in which the mobilization of the rural Afro-Brazilian communities of the Vale do Ribeira emerged, the legal apparatus established by the 1988 constitution to attend to ethnic claims must be analysed. The special rights guaranteed by the new constitution for *quilombola* territories – considered collective and non-transferable properties – transformed these territories into an important basis of *quilombola* identity and power. The mobilization against the construction of the dams in the Vale do Ribeira began in the same period. The threat of eviction presented by the possible flooding of their territories served to bring communities together, first because it helped mobilize older inhabitants of the Afro-Brazilian communities and second because it stimulated the younger members to identify with a common struggle (Carril 1995: 176). Furthermore, under the flags of 'sustainable development' and 'socio-environmentalism', an important coalition was formed between Afro-Brazilian communities and environmental groups such as the Socio-environmental Institute (ISA), the Serrana Institute Environmental Association (ASA) and the Institute for Sustainable Development and Citizenship in the Vale do Ribeira (IDESC), which have all historically positioned themselves against the construction of hydroelectric plants on the Ribeira river.

In summary, then, the political mobilization of the Afro-Brazilian communities of Vale do Ribeira and the constitution of MOAB occurred through the alignment of three parallel struggles – the struggle for land, the struggle for *quilombola* identity and the struggle against dams. This history provided the *quilombos* with a repertoire of confrontational strategies that, as we shall see in the analysis of the forums, shaped their positioning with respect to the CGRH.

A parallel process resulted in the creation of the workers' unions, such as Sintravale. Sintravale is a union whose origins date back to the mid-1980s, and it is connected to conflicts involving the inhabitants of the areas that were converted into national parks and conservation areas. These conflicts were motivated by the traditional populations' lack of title to the land they occupied, which meant that they were simply ignored in the demarcation of these areas. Furthermore they were prohibited from building houses, felling trees and removing vegetation. There were several cases of violence involving land racketeers (*grileiros*), settlers, traditional populations and the forest police. The problems experienced by the inhabitants of these protected areas attracted the attention of various organizations, neighbourhood associations, environmental non-governmental organizations (NGOs), unionists connected to the CUT, members of the Workers' Party (PT) and groups from the Catholic Church that became involved in supporting the occupants of these areas. This network of alliances came about in part as the result of two changes that took place in the institutional arena of environmental politics and development in rural Brazil in the 1990s. First was the growth of the rhetoric of sustainable development, which brought the need to think about how to balance conservation with the social use of natural resources (CEDI 1991). Second was the creation of the National Programme for Strengthening Family Agriculture (Pronaf), a successful policy aimed at supporting small farmers (Abramovay and Veiga 1999; Schneider et al. 2004).

It was in this context that, at the end of the 1990s, Sintravale was officially established. It soon began to voice family farmer demands for credit and business opportunities, as well as to compete with agro-business for resources and policies. It also began establishing links with NGOs, with the aim of formulating projects that could combine income generation with environmental conservation. This historical background helps us to understand Sintravale's willingness, as will be seen in the analysis of

195

the forums, to participate in Consad, an institution responsible for the distribution of resources to help family farming.

This brief presentation of the origins and the positions of these social movements makes it possible to better understand how the characteristics of social conflicts coupled with particular forms of state intervention can translate into different forms of activism. In the case of Sintravale, participation in the forums is a prerequisite to gaining access to particular resources and public policies, while for MOAB the same is not true. Now that these themes have been highlighted, the following section aims to illustrate how the trajectories of social mobilization in the region mark the controversy surrounding the construction of the dams on the Ribeira river.

The controversy surrounding Tijuco Alto The project to build a dam in Tijuco Alto dates back to the 1950s, but it took on its current form at the beginning of the 1980s when the CBA (Brazilian Aluminum Company), a company belonging to one of the largest Brazilian conglomerates, asked the then DNAEE (National Department of Water and Electrical Energy) for permission to use part of the river basin of the Ribeira to construct a hydroelectric dam. Permission was given in 1989, and preliminary studies of the environmental impact were carried out, as required by law. According to the Water Resources Management Plan, it was to be the first in a series of four dams that, apart from generating electricity, would solve the problem of flooding which blighted the region. A third of these dams would affect land occupied by traditional communities, remnants of *quilombos*. Environmental groups and the threatened communities reacted with a series of protests which changed this decision.

From the 1980s onwards Brazil saw the development of an important national movement of communities affected by the building of dams. They were strongly influenced by left-wing Catholic groups and formed alliances with important international NGOs. At the same time, the democratic transition that followed the military regime inaugurated new legislation and regulatory instruments that facilitated opposition to, and the positioning of civil society in relation to, these projects. As a result, years later, these movements managed to reverse the previous decision authorizing the construction of the dam. The judges heeded the environmental arguments and opposed the permission, asserting that, since the project involved two states of the federation, São Paulo and Paraná, it needed to be licensed by a federal authority. In 2004, the National Institute for the Environment (IBAMA) argued that the planning permission was outdated, cancelled the original application and ordered that a new application be made. Consequently the whole process was started again, and this is the present situation: new reports are being written and new public meetings are to be called to present the proposal for discussion.

The positions concerning the controversy about the Tijuco Alto and the three other dams planned for construction reflect reasonably well the mosaic of the local social organizations and their differences. Politicians responsible for the local councils, business leaders and business associations see the dam as a means to encourage economic growth, thus providing investment, jobs and flood control. Conversely, the *quilombos*, the grassroots religious movements, the Green Party, the Communist Party of Brazil and environmental NGOs, as well as many academics, see the project as incompatible with a model of development that values environmental and cultural heritage. It is worth pointing out that while various sectors of government, especially mayors and state managers connected to the management of water resources, agree on the construction of the dam, there are other departments within the government, such as SEPPIR (Special Secretariat of Policies for the Promotion of Racial Equality) in the federal government and the São Paulo Land Institute (ITESP) in the state of São Paulo, that strongly support the *quilombola* communities from the Vale do Ribeira and are radically opposed to the dams. This conflict reproduces in an exemplary way the range of possibilities and the system of positions and oppositions that guide the actions of the agents in the region.

To summarize, it is worth highlighting three themes. First, this is a region with enormous comparative advantages (being situated near to the most dynamic economic centre in Brazil and enjoying great natural beauty and biodiversity), which do not transform themselves into competitive advantages. This shifts the problem from the terrain of natural resources to that of the institutions that would be able to make use of them. Second, the recent tendency towards economic diversification has resulted in a certain division of interests between traditional agents and those connected to expanding activities (such as the increased value of the service sector). Third, the polysemic nature of the discourse of sustainable development makes it difficult to translate the idea into a project capable of bringing together a broad coalition between agents and organizations.

This prompts us to question how the participatory forums work and to what extent, given the intentions of civil society actors in the region, it is reasonable to expect that they will enable the creation of broader coalitions that are capable of negotiating issues such as that of the dam, or reaching agreements about desirable forms of regional development.

The participatory forums

CGRH and Consad are currently the two most important regional participatory forums in the Vale do Ribeira, covering twenty-three and twenty-five municipalities respectively. They discuss local development plans, follow the implementation of the respective public policies with which they are connected and allocate financial resources, varying from US$65,000 to US$850,000, to projects that are considered a priority and in line with development and conservation plans. Interviews held with the local leaders leave no doubt that these forums play a role in the everyday life of the region. Furthermore, given the intense party political competition that exists in the region – between the PT, which controls the federal government and three councils in the region, the PSDB, which controls the state government and eight councils in the region, and the PMBD, a traditional party that controls seven local councils – leaders of these different groups place great importance on securing space in these forums.

Procedures In order to analyse the capacity of these forums to encourage negotiation and organization between various social groups, it was necessary to find out who in fact participated in the forums. This section presents and discusses the information on this as well as on how rules and procedures are defined in each forum, thereby helping to explain the differences between the two forums.

The first differences can be found in terms of the length of time they have been constituted and the social forces that were behind their constitution. The CGRH was formed in the 1990s as a result of Brazilian legislation dealing with water resources, which called for the formation of such committees in each river basin. Consad was set up more recently during the first months of the Lula government, in 2003, based upon the Zero Hunger Programme, which was intended to be his most important social policy. In the CGRH, civil society occupies a third of the seats, public officials of the state of São Paulo another third and members of the twenty-three municipal authorities of the region the final third. Therefore two-thirds of the members belong to the public sector. The forum is composed of fourteen members representing the state, fourteen representing the local councils and fourteen representatives of civil society. The committee is coordinated by a president, a vice-president and an executive secretary. The president is a representative of the municipal government, the vice-president is a representative of civil society and the executive secretary is a representative of the state government.

In Consad the weighting is inverted. Civil society occupies two-thirds of the seats, the public sector the remaining third. In this forum each of the twenty-five municipalities elects six representatives (four from civil society and two from the public sector) and each of the forum's 150 members has equal standing in debating the issues raised, as well as electing the president of the forum and the members of the fiscal and thematic commissions.

As a result, there is a more technocratic and governmental form of operation in the CGRH, while the Consad system has more a civil society form. This has led to many complaints by the civil society representatives in CGRH, who feel that sometimes the debates are difficult to follow. The more pro-civil-society operating style of Consad presents another problem: as a result of the politicians' lack of control over the decisions of this forum, it tends to be considered less relevant by the municipal authorities as well as principally by the state authorities.

In each case participation is open only to representatives of organizations; an autonomous citizen is not permitted to run for the position of councillor. To deal with the problem of mobilizing councillors spread over twenty-five municipalities in both rural and urban areas, both forums rotate the location of the meetings. Furthermore, they try to guarantee transport and sometimes accommodation for the councillors. In order to guarantee that the process of selecting the councillors is publicized, the CGRH and Consad use different strategies. In the CGRH, the councils and state organizations connected to the management of water resources have reserved seats, whereas civil society is informed through a list of organizations that act in the twenty-three municipalities organized by the executive secretary of the CGRH. These organizations are informed of the selection process, and it is up to them to mobilize their members and choose their candidates. In the case of Consad, the selection process is organized in each of the twenty-five municipalities. The managers together with the municipal officials organize meetings explaining what Consad and Agenda 21[2] are, and where the councillors are presented and voted for. In both forums all the seats are occupied, but there is not much competition for them. The biggest differences appear at the time when the posts that direct the forums are chosen.

With these design features in mind, we can now consider the first argument we aimed to address: namely, how far a more equitable distribution of seats between civil society and public managers, together with a more transparent selection process for councillors, has led to a greater capacity for inclusion, and what repercussions these rules and procedures have had for the capacity of these forums to represent local society. There are at least two ways of answering this question. One consists of comparing the organizations present in the forums and the existing social actors in the region. The other is to contrast the general profile of the members of the forums with the socio-economic characteristics of the population of the Vale do Ribeira.

With respect to the social actors who participate in the forums, these rules have contributed towards reinforcing the exclusion of both the poorest segments of the local population, such as those who live by subsistence farming in isolated regions, *and* the most dynamic sectors, such as those connected to the service sector. This is because neither group is organized in associations, making their representation impossible. Furthermore, comparison between the two forums shows how the recruitment process is dependent on the managers. While in the CGRH the presence of business associations is guaranteed by invitations formalized by the managers, in Consad they are almost non-existent, owing to the fact, according to the managers of the latter, that they were not invited.

In comparison with the profile of the general population, both forums fail to represent the principal characteristics of the local society. Both in the CGRH and in Consad, the participants earn more and have a better education than the average in the region. In both cases the number of Afro-Brazilian representatives is lower than the proportion of this group in the local population. Likewise, the percentage of women is lower than the regional average. The same survey also shows that in Consad there is somewhat less divergence, which almost certainly is due to the greater weight given to civil society. While a social distance exists between the population and the organizations and active members, it is not as wide as that in relation to governmental organizations and state bureaucracy.

It was clearly observed that the difference in the number of government and civil society representatives contributed to maintaining a more popular profile in the case of Consad and a more technocratic one in the case of the CGRH. The system of recruitment was seen to be expensive and heavily dependent on previously established relationships between the managers of the forums and local actors, particularly those from party organizations and civil society, which are already mobilized, a feature that does not help to foster the inclusion of new actors. This can be partly attributed to the complexity and high cost involved in publicizing the selection processes more widely, highlighting the practical difficulties of organizing a recruitment process that follows the prescriptions of inclusiveness present in the literature.

Participation In order to explore the second assumption that this study addresses – namely, that groups with less communicative, material and technical resources will participate more when discussion methods that aim to promote their ability to express themselves are used – we observed specifically the involvement of two social groups that, as pointed out above, represent traditionally marginalized and poor sectors. The two groups are Sintravale, which includes small-scale rubber tappers, palm-heart collectors and *caiçaras*, and MOAB, which brings together groups who are against the dam in the region, especially the *quilombola* communities. The aim was to analyse how the participatory dynamic set up by the forums has influenced the performance of these organizations and to what extent they have enabled their demands to connect with the more general debates and with the interests of other social groups.

The first aspect to be noted is the way in which the debates are organized. In the CGRH there is a clear tendency to give priority to technical knowledge and speed up the discussions through majority voting. This fact contributes to a feeling expressed by the members of civil society that the issues dealt with are too technical, making it difficult for them to understand or participate in the discussions, and furthermore making it difficult for them to make applications for funding from Fehidro (the investment fund generated by the forum). In the case of Consad, the immediate issues and concerns of the social movements have been prioritized, and on the whole it has aimed to reach decisions by consensus rather than by majority decision.

With respect to the dam, the CBA, which is proposing the project, initiated preparation of a new application for planning permission, without having started the phase of public meetings. The last meeting of the CGRH in 2005 testifies to how the issue is being dealt with in this forum: the presentation of the new report, made by technical staff contracted by the company, was followed by a long sequence of interventions by the councillors, whose tone, on the whole, reaffirmed their position for or against the construction of the dam, with little reference to the technical information presented by the invited specialists. In general the discussions stressed the political positions involved in the dispute, reaffirming the idea that this space is important for obtaining information and making alliances, but not for negotiating and influencing the definition of policies (Martins 2005). In this sense, the various actors simply reinforced their positions without opening up space for debate, be that between these actors, or between them and new actors bringing less crystallized positions that could have opened up new spaces and themes for deliberation. In the period during which this study was conducted, discussion of this issue simply did not take place in Consad.

Nonetheless, the question of sustainable development did appear in these forums, above all in connection with discussion of the projects to be financed by the CGRH and Consad. In this case it was possible to identify a clear difference in perspective between the two forums. The CGRH determined in its first years of operation that it would allocate funds only to state entities concentrating funding on more technical activities, thereby excluding civil society for several years. Over the last few years, however, environmental organizations have successfully applied pressure to make this rule more flexible, promoting activities related to, for example, environmental education or reforestation by traditional communities. In contrast, from the beginning Consad set out to transfer funds to non-state organizations, especially those connected to the workers' unions.

The fact that Consad provides a space for organizations like Sintravale has direct repercussions for its members' perceptions of the forum. Interviews with the leaders of this union showed that Consad was seen as an important space, and participation in this forum was prioritized. It is not merely the rhetoric of the leaders which testifies to the fact that it is a space where resources and policies can be disputed – the investments allocated by the forum also attest to its importance. During the selection of representatives, Sintravale mobilizes itself to ensure that its leaders and activists are among those chosen by local civil society. The other regional forum, the CGRH, does not receive the same attention from the union. According to its leaders it gives more weight to the public authorities, thereby restricting any scope that workers' organizations have to influence its decisions.

Interviews with representatives of MOAB suggest that, while the organization participates in the CGRH, it does not recognize it as a strategic and legitimate forum where it can negotiate issues with respect to the Tijuco Alto dam. The committee is seen purely as a way of obtaining information about the issue and a place where the movement can present itself, together with the environmentalists who develop projects in the region, as a united front against the construction of the dam. Participation takes place not to discuss and negotiate ways of contemplating the positions of all the parties involved in the conflict, but to make clear their radical opposition to the project. Instead of having faith in these forums, the movement has opted to form other spaces, such as the Forum of Entities against the Dam, which brings together various organizations opposed to the dam. The special status of *quilombola* communities does not give the movement any greater faith in their ability to use these forums as vehicles for influencing projects or public investment.

While both groups use these forums to seek alliances and obtain information, their experience of participation is quite different: Consad provides a space for the negotiation of projects and policies for Sintravale, while the CGRH is an arena for dispute and contestation for the *quilombolas*. This difference should be understood as an extension of both the participatory dynamic of each of the forums and the evolution of these movements. That MOAB participates more by disputing than negotiating constitutes a reaction to the CGRH's strategy of guaranteeing their formal representation without making any effort to promote methods that would favour more participatory and inclusive processes of negotiation and decision-making; it also reflects the extent to which MOAB is making use of a repertoire of confrontational strategies that were acquired through their struggles for land, for the recognition of their ethnic identity and against the building of the dams.

In the case of Consad, which has the strong support of Sintravale and where the marginalized sectors actively participate, no effort is made to provide a space for positions supported by business associations in the region, as was mentioned previously; these groups are simply not represented in this forum. It could also be inferred that this position is a result of the evolution of Sintravale, which, interested in guaranteeing its associates the resources distributed by these forums, has developed strategies to limit the access of other groups, be they more organized or more marginalized.

This scenario reinforces the institutionalist hypothesis that the dynamics of discussion and decision-making to a large extent determine who participates and how. It also illustrates that there is a long way to go in the use of participatory techniques – given that they are used in only an incipient form by Consad and are totally absent in the CGRH – before it will be possible to test in a consistent and systematic way the second assumption set out in this chapter. Furthermore, and equally importantly, this scenario suggests that to understand the real dynamics of these forums and their capacity to succeed, it is vital to bear in mind the styles of activism and negotiation that characterized both civil society and state actors even prior to their involvement in these forums.

Participation, dams and development

In this section we discuss the argument, present in the literature on participatory democracy, that claims that broader social inclusion in policy processes will lead to the elaboration of proposals that are economically and politically more viable. From this perspective the third assumption presented in the first section would suggest that the more inclusive the forum, the greater its ability to set in motion solutions to the two polemical regional issues around which the local debate is currently polarized: the construction of the Tijuco Alto dam and the implementation of the rhetoric of sustainable development.

In the case of sustainable development, it was noted that while the notion is present in both forums, there is still very little agreement as to the way in which to translate the idea into a concrete framework for defining projects and allocating resources. There are also divisions that have frustrated the drawing up of the Sustainable Territorial Development Plan. This was meant to be finished by the end of 2006 as a means of orienting Consad's activities and carrying forward the Agenda 21 process in the region. As this is an initiative of a forum that is linked to federal government policy, however, and thus to the PT political party, it has not received support from the state government (linked to the PSDB party), limiting from the outset the range of actors and resources that this plan could mobilize and articulate in a coherent fashion. Yet such federal–state coordination is vital for the successful implementation of a regional project, since the recognition of land titles, which is one of the principal obstacles to investment in the region, is a function of a state body, ITESP, while funding for investment in family farming comes from a federal government programme, Pronaf. Furthermore, the recognition of *quilombola* land is a federal function, while the overall management of conservation areas, where some of them are situated, is a state responsibility.

The results of the survey undertaken to establish the position of the members of the forums with respect to the dam illustrate a further important point. While in the CGRH four in every ten members support the dam, in Consad this figure is only two in every ten. There is no clear relationship between the level of education and income of the interviewees and their position with respect to the dam. The variable with the strongest connection to their position in relation to the issue is their link to, or sympathy or support for, the left-wing parties: the supporters of the Green Party and the PT tended to be against the dam.

These positions seem to have been influenced very little by the forums. Indeed, on the rare occasions on which the issue was discussed, as in the meeting of the CGRH when the new Tijuco dam project was presented, discussion involved open and sometimes hostile confrontation between the participants. This scenario seems to have little in common with the theoretical descriptions of deliberative democracy in which debates are organized according to procedures which ensure that arguments both for and against particular decisions are heard, and that participants, once given the chance to reflect upon these arguments, are able to make their own decision (Dryzek 2001).

Both cases also suggest that the forums made only a modest contribution to the negotiation of alternatives between those who supported short-term projects, capable of favouring the less fortunate segments of the region, and those arguing for medium- and long-term investment in infrastructure to guarantee the continuation of initiatives aimed at promoting economic growth. In Consad the social movements prioritized alternative initiatives rather than grand projects, seeking to balance development with the conservation of natural resources, while the specialists in the CGRH tended to promote investments in infrastructure projects.

If negotiation within these forums is constrained, there is also limited coordination between them. Not only is there no institutional dialogue, there is also open dispute between the different levels of government. Furthermore, the rules that define the parameters for distributing grants and evaluating results themselves hinder any pooling of knowledge or any contact between different state agencies and sectors of society.

Bearing these elements in mind, let us revisit the third assumption, which links the inclusiveness of these forums with their ability to find solutions to the conflict surrounding the dam and debates about regional development. From this perspective, the CGRH's approach, emphasizing the importance of medium- and long-term investments, while compatible with its more 'technical' vision linked to the bureaucracy responsible for the management of the water resources, is very different from that supported by Consad, which emphasizes the importance of investing in short-term projects, a strategy compatible with the vision of the social movements, which call for a rapid improvement in the living conditions of the poorest segments.

It can be argued that both forums open up channels of communication between managers and civil society, and as such help make explicit the divisions that exist around both dams and sustainable development strategies. This merely took place within pre-existing coalitions, however, each with already well-defined positions with respect to these issues. Furthermore, those responsible for the organization of the forums appeared to have little interest in encouraging inclusion and debate between different parties. This dynamic reveals much more about the efforts that organizers of each of the forums make in order to maintain the space for their own positions in regional politics than it does about any attempt to open up space for the inclusion of conflicting perspectives. The dynamic of these forums responds less to any normative ideal of inclusiveness and more to what Amable and Palombarini (2005) recognize as an intrinsic characteristic of institutions: rather than being spaces where interests can be aligned, they are the expression of particular configurations of interests.

Conclusion

This chapter has discussed the presumed relationship between participation, inclusion and development under conditions of social mobilization around the relationships between environment, territory and economy. One branch of the literature on participation suggests that, in the presence of a mobilized civil society, of managers committed to the project of social participation, and of 'well-designed' institutions, it would be possible to find forums capable of encouraging coordination between agents, thereby facilitating the resolution of the conflict over the Tijuco Alto dam, as well as the formulation of a project of sustainable development for the region. Conversely, another branch suggests that this contribution would practically be nil: the forums would tend towards the re-creation of already existing asymmetries, thereby limiting the possibilities of negotiation between the actors, be at the mercy of decisions made by state actors, or be captured by political parties or special interest groups.

The situation in the Vale do Ribeira brings together various factors that the literature suggests ought to favour the emergence of effective participatory governance institutions. There is an active process of social mobilization in the region, managers are committed to the organization of the forums, and there is a reasonable amount of variation in the designs being used (which ought to help learning and adaptation). The research set out in this chapter illustrates the importance of the rules that organize the processes of inclusion and discussion in two very different forums: the CGRH and Consad. As previously seen, however, these rules have functioned in a very different way to that anticipated by authors such as Fung (2004) and Avritzer (2003), who predict that such rules ought to lead to the construction of a new and broad coalition between different actors. In the cases studied here, these rules appear to have served more to reproduce the coalitions that support the organizers of these forums. It is interesting to note that, had the research concentrated solely on the CGRH, there would have been a tendency to conclude that these forums achieve little more than legitimizing the decisions made by the executive body. Alternatively, if it had concentrated only on Consad and the central role played by the PT and Sintravale in this forum, then the tendency would have been to endorse the idea of capture by political parties. The comparison has allowed us to come to a different conclusion, which is that forum dynamics can be understood as a replication of the party political game in the participatory sphere.

To a certain extent this is a predictable result when we take into account that it is the state actors and politicians who have the incentive to fight for space in the participatory sphere and the resources to organize these forums. Yet this same result also suggests that the participatory sphere is more heterogeneous than is supposed by much of the literature, which tends to focus on only one or another actor – for example, the progressive coalitions or the corporate interest groups – as its principal artifice. Our research shows that the nature of this sphere is to a large extent determined by the efforts of politicians and managers connected to different coalitions to guarantee that these participatory spaces will facilitate their own political reproduction. This suggests that future studies of such participatory governance mechanisms must consider three points in order that their analyses are less idealized and normative than has been the case to date.

The first concerns the relationships between design, inclusiveness and the democratization of the political process, since the latter may not occur in the ways suggested by the literature. This is because these participatory forums, rather than being spaces for the convergence of different interests, may themselves be an expression of specific coalitions.

The second point is that participatory governance processes actually conceive the role of marginalized actors as that of co-producers of public policies and co-generators of innovative development alternatives, principally at a local level. Beyond any normative judgement as to whether this is desirable or not, this possibility presents an analytical challenge which has not been explored in depth by the literature; that of understanding the conditions under which actors who are traditionally mobilized to criticize and make demands move towards dialogue and cooperation – if, indeed, that is what happens.

The third point concerns the relationship between 'democraticness' and 'effectiveness'. The democratization of the political process, a desirable feature in itself, is not a sufficient criterion to guarantee its efficacy. After all, participation can be increased without the political process becoming more effective. For example, poor economic growth can be the result of counterproductive economic policies, which accurately reflect popular choices. In this sense we are working with two notions of the quality of democratic processes: one in terms of degrees of democratization and the other in terms of the efficacy of decisions that ensue from these processes. If it is the case – and surely it is – that the popular majority can be as mistaken about policy options as can insulated technocrats, then a perfect responsiveness of the government to popular decisions could lead to disastrous policies. In short, there is an inevitable tension between democracy and effectiveness that needs to be considered with care (Plattner 2004).

Our efforts here have been to understand analytically under what conditions the association between participation and development occurs in a concrete situation and the theoretical implications thereof. Inversely, we could now think in terms of what the normative implications are for those involved in such an experience: social movements, policy-makers, advocacy groups and expert advisory groups. First, it would be necessary to find ways to avoid the risks of the capturing of the forums or other participatory instruments by more organized and influential groups. This could be achieved by publicizing the activities more, or even by searching for ways to involve the less organized. Second, it would be fundamental to try to diminish the asymmetry between the more and the less influential by adopting, for example, methodologies oriented to that end more than to facilitating dialogue. Third, it is also necessary to overcome the fragmentation between institutions, participatory spaces or policies, enhancing convergence and complementarity. Lastly, it is important to adopt these measures in a way that may generate more learning about participatory and development linkages.

Altogether, these findings point to the fact that the rules of the game, expressed in formal institutions, can be understood only as part of the social context within which they are embedded. Just as there are rules of the game as highlighted in the institutionalist assumptions, there is also a game of rules. The dynamic of the participatory sphere is the result of these two dimensions: of its laws and its own internal dynamic, and its relationship with other spheres of the social world. Knowledge of each of these two dimensions – that internal to the participatory sphere and that which inheres in its relationship with other spheres – is still in its early stages. A great deal of research, especially in terms of comparative analysis, will need to be carried out in order to evaluate with more confidence the conditions under which it is possible to hope for a successful association between participation and development. This will require approaches that build links between apparently competing approaches in the literature, some of which are more optimistic and normative, others of which are more pessimistic. Only on the basis of such work will it be possible to preserve the principles underlying the political discourse of participatory democracy and overcome the naivety that often surrounds it.

Notes

1 This chapter is a modified version of a paper published in *World Development* in 2008. The study is part of a research programme coordinated by Rimisp (Latin American Centre for Rural Development, Santiago de Chile) and was financed by the International Development Research Centre, Canada.

2 The international environmental agreement reached at the United Nations Summit on the Environment and Development held in Rio de Janeiro in 1992.

References

Abers, R. (2001) *Inventing Local Democracy: Grassroots Politics in Brazil*, Boulder, CO: Westview Press.

Abramovay, R. (2005) 'Representatividade e inovação', Paper presented at Seminário Nacional de Desenvolvimento Rural Sustentável, IICA-SDT/MDA, Brasilia, August.

Abramovay, R. and J. E. Veiga (1999) 'Novas instituições para o desenvolvimento rural: o caso do Programa Nacional de Fortalecimento da Agricultura Familiar (Pronaf)', *Texto para Discussão*, 641, Ipea, Brasilia, April.

Amable, B. and S. Palombarini (2005) *L'Économie n'est pas une science morale*, Paris: Raisons d'Agir.

Avritzer, L. (2003) *Democracy and the Public Space in Latin America*, Princeton, NJ: Princeton University Press.

Carril, L. F. (1995) 'Terras de negros no Vale do Ribeira: territorialidade e resistência', Master's thesis, FFLCH/USP, São Paulo.

CEDI (1991) *Sindicalismo no campo: avaliação, perspectivas e desafios – balanços e controvérsias*, Rio de Janeiro.

Chabaribery, D. et al. (2004) 'Desenvolvimento sustentável na Bacia do Ribeira de Iguape: diagnóstico das condições sócio-econômicas e tipificação dos municípios', *Informações Econômicas*, 34(9), São Paulo, September.

Coelho, V. S. and M. Nobre (2004) *Participação e Deliberação: Teoria democrática e experiências institucionais no Brasil contemporâneo*, São Paulo: 34 Letras.

Participation, inclusion and development

Coelho, V. S. et al. (2007) 'Foros participativos y desarrollo territorial en el Valle de Ribeira (Brasil)', in J. Bengoa (ed.), *Territorios rurales: movimientos sociales y desarrollo territorial rural en América Latina*, Santiago de Chile: Catalonia.

Cunnil, N. (1997) *Repensando lo público a través de la sociedad*, CLAD, Caracas: Editorial Nueva Sociedad.

Dagnino, E. (2002) *Sociedade civil e espaços públicos no Brasil*, Rio de Janeiro: Paz e Terra.

Dryzek, J. S. (2001) 'Legitimacy and economy in deliberative democracy', *Political Theory*, October, pp. 651–69.

Favareto, A. and P. Brancher (2005) *O Desenvolvimento Territorial no Vale do Ribeira e os Projetos do Pronaf-infraestrutura: análise e recomendações*, Relatório de Pesquisa, IICA-SDT/MDA.

Fung, A. (2004) 'Survey article: recipes for public spheres: eight institutional design choices and their consequences', *Journal of Political Philosophy*, 11.

Fung, A. A. and E. O. Wright (2003) *Deepening Democracy: Institutional Innovation in Empowered Participatory Governance*, London: Verso.

Gaventa, J. (2004) 'Towards participatory governance: assessing the transformative possibilities', in S. Hickey and G. Mohan (eds), *From Tyranny to Transformation*, London: Zed Books.

IGBE (2001) *Census 2000*, Brazilian Institute of Geography and Statistics.

Manzuri, G. and V. Rao (2004) 'Community-based and driven development: a critical review', World Bank Policy Research Working Paper 3209.

Marquetti, A. (2003) 'Participação e redistribuição: o orçamento participativo em Porto Alegre', in L. Avritzer and Z. Navarro (eds), *A Inovação Democrática no Brasil*, São Paulo: Cortez.

Martins, S. (2005) 'Decentralisation and participation: the dynamics of the Committee of Basin in Vale do Ribeira; the case of the hydroelectric project in Tijuco Alto', MPhil research paper, IDS, Brighton.

Plattner, M. F. (2004) 'The quality of democracy: a sceptical afterword', *Journal of Democracy*, 15(4), October.

PNUD (2005) *Atlas do desenvolvimento humano*, United Nations Development Programme, www.pnud.org. br/atlas.

Pritchett, L. and M. Woolcock (2004) 'Solutions when the solution is the problem: arraying the disarray in development', *World Development*, 32(2): 191–212.

Ray, C. (2000) 'The EU Leader Programme: rural development laboratory?', *Sociologia Ruralis*, 40(2), April.

— (2002) 'A mode of production for fragile rural economies: the territorial accumulation of forms of capital', Guest editorial, *Journal of Rural Studies*, 18: 225–31.

Resende, R. U. (2002) *As Regras do Jogo: Legislação Florestal e Desenvolvimento Sustentável no Vale do Ribeira*, São Paulo: Annablume.

Schneider, S., L. Mattei and A. Casella (2004) *Políticas Públicas e Participação Social no Brasil Rural*, Porto Alegre: Ed. UFRGS.

UNDP (2002) *Human Development Report: Deepening Democracy in*

a Fragmented World, New York:
UNDP.

Veiga, J. E. (2005) 'Articulações inter-
municipais para o desenvolvimento', Paper presented at Seminário
Nacional de Desenvolvimento

Rural Sustentável, IICA-SDT/MDA,
Brasilia, August.

World Bank (2001) *World Development Report 2000/2001: Attacking
Poverty*, New York: Oxford University Press.

9 | Popular mobilization, party dominance and participatory governance in South Africa

LAURENCE PIPER AND LUBNA NADVI

This chapter seeks to explore the character of popular mobilization in South Africa, mostly at the local level. This is done through exploring the interaction of two independent processes. The first concerns the relative empowerment of political parties and the disempowerment of civil society (especially social movements) by the democratization process in South Africa. The second concerns the introduction of new institutions of public participation in local governance. Hence, while the latter are portrayed as 'invited spaces' in which communities can engage the local state constructively, the poor design of these spaces, a lack of genuine will on the part of elites and the relative power of key social actors mean that, in practice, they are either meaningless processes or simply co-opted by political parties. Notably, civil society has tended either to disengage from the local state and focus on provincial and national levels, or to resort to forms of popular protest to be heard by local government – the non-governmental organization (NGO) sector usually favouring the first approach and social movements the second.

This 'disengaged–enraged' dichotomy reflects clearly the failure of the formal invited spaces for public participation in local governance. Furthermore, it is hard to see how this dynamic will change, even with better-designed invited spaces, until the balance of social forces is restored with the revivification of civil society, and especially social movements. Reasons for optimism include the growing popular disgruntlement at poor delivery of public goods by local government – which is arguably exacerbated by the introduction of meaningless forms of public participation – and evidence of a new crop of local and organic community-based organizations which could form the basis of future social movements. In short, popular mobilization at the local level in South Africa remains dominated by political parties, despite new participatory institutions, although we are witnessing the creation of conditions for new and powerful forms of popular mobilization into the future.

In making this argument, the chapter begins with theoretical literature on state–society relations, and the character of and relationship between 'invented' and 'invited' spaces. It then moves to the received views in the literature on popular mobilization in recent South African history, and the nature and purpose of new forms of 'participatory governance' at local government level. The relationship between these 'invented' and 'invited' spaces is then explored through case studies of two municipalities, with special focus on the consequences for popular mobilization. The chapter concludes by analysing the causes of demobilization that result from participatory governance, identifying the consequent tendency of civil society to 'disengage' from or become 'enraged' at local government, and pointing to the necessity of oppositional-movement revival to change state–society relations in a more democratic fashion.

Theorizing state–society relations through invented and invited spaces

In recent years almost every democratic country in the world, regardless of economic development or democratic robustness, has witnessed attempts to enhance public participation in governance, especially local governance. The reasons for this are many and complex, and can be traced to new theories and practices of development (World Bank 1996); new theories and practices of democracy (Cohen 2002; Habermas 2002) and democratization (Mattes 2002); and at the intersection of all of these, new theories and practices of citizenship (Cornwall 2002). Following Cornwall (ibid.: 17), these new participatory institutions and practices can be termed the 'invited spaces' of participatory local governance. These invited spaces would include Hendricks's (2006: 486) 'micro deliberative structures' and Fung and Wright's (2001: 5) 'empowered deliberative democratic structures'. Examples are the participatory city budgeting in Porto Alegre, Brazil; functionally specific neighbourhood councils in Chicago, USA; village governance in Kerala, India; and citizens' juries in the United Kingdom.

Initiated by the local state, invited spaces typically look to draw local communities into processes of consultation, deliberation and sometimes joint decision-making on key local issues. Perhaps just as important in understanding emergent local state–society relations is popular mobilization led 'from below' by civil society or local communities. Hence Cornwall (2002: 17) contrasts the 'invited spaces' created 'from above' by the state with 'organic spaces' created 'from below' by those outside the state. The latter include spaces created from popular mobilization, as well as spaces in which 'like-minded people join together in common pursuits'. Holston and Appadurai (1999) describe the emergence of a rights-based citizenship among the urban poor, marginalized by neoliberal governance and mobilized through social movements, which looks to transform social relations from the ground up. Miraftab (2006) paints a picture of 'invented' spaces opposing 'invited' spaces in South Africa, but also elsewhere in the world, for the same reason, the globalization of neoliberal economic policy.

Importantly, as Cornwall and Coelho (forthcoming: 1) indicate, the conceptualization of local state–society relations is not exhausted by a binary opposition between top-down, state-driven, invited spaces and bottom-up, social-movement-driven, invented spaces. Hence they talk of a 'participatory sphere' that lies at the interface of the public sphere and the state, composed of hybrid institutions, some of which are extensions of the state and some of which are claimed from the state. The critical point is that the relationship of these institutions with the state and the general public is partial: 'its institutions have a semi-autonomous existence, outside and apart from the institutions of formal politics and everyday associational life … They are spaces of contestation, but also of collaboration and co-operation …'. Lastly, but most importantly, Gaventa (2007: 2) points out that international experience shows that a functioning participatory sphere or meaningful public participation in local governance requires three things: good institutional design, political will to make it happen and a strong civil society.

These theoretical reflections matter to the South African case precisely because the last ten years have witnessed a process of institutional reform of local governance in the name of greater public participation on issues related to the delivery of key social goods. Hence there are very specific and identifiable 'invited spaces' that have the potential, in theory, to both engender more constructive and democratic state–society relations and enhance the delivery of social goods. At the same time, there is a particular history of social mobilization in South Africa around the liberation struggle which has empowered political parties at the expense of civil society and especially social movements. It is this particular dialogue between 'invented' and 'invited' which we wish to explore and characterize. In the following section we outline this history of popular mobilization, and then move to outline the democratic reforms of local governance.

Invented spaces: the changing patterns of popular mobilization in South Africa

With the formal deracialization and democratization of South Africa in the early 1990s, the fundamental shape of inclusion and exclusion in the political system began to change. Beyond the changes in the formal institutions of rule were parallel shifts in the patterns of popular mobilization in the country. During the struggle period, and especially the 1980s, popular mobilization was channelled into explicitly political anti-apartheid activities. Hence grassroots organizations that emerged mostly in urban centres to secure basic public goods like education, healthcare and housing united under an explicitly political formation, the United Democratic Front (UDF), which identified clearly with the ideology and organization of the banned and exiled African National Congress (ANC). Closely associated with the ANC-aligned Congress of South African Trade Unions (COSATU), the two organizations captured most popular mobilization behind the political project of national liberation. In effect, then, grassroots and issue-based mobilization was quickly united and generalized in national and political terms. In a sense, the ANC was the social movement of the 1980s.

While there can be no doubt that this popular mobilization of the 1980s was tremendously effective and important in hastening the end of apartheid, many have pointed out the demobilizing effect that democratization had on social movements in South Africa (Ballard et al. 2006: 14–17). With the unbanning of the ANC in 1990, the UDF effectively collapsed into the ANC as the latter reconstituted itself as an open organization in the country. After the 1994 elections the movements that mobilized people were absorbed into the ANC government or into partnership with government, and most held the view that government would deliver to the poor (Heller 2001: 134). Further, the remaining NGO sector came under pressure to 'professionalize' and withdraw from advocacy to a more limited role in service delivery (Greenstein 2003).

Notably, this demobilization paralleled shifts in donor funding too, such that most foreign aid money was channelled into and through the new democratic state to build its capacity to meet the many challenges of proper administration and the delivery of social goods eschewed by the apartheid state on racist grounds. Perhaps not surprisingly, the delivery of water, electricity, housing, healthcare and education by the democratic state to poor and working people has not met popular expectations. Clear evidence of the mounting frustration at what is often seen as government incompetence and corruption is found in many popular demonstrations about poor service delivery. Hence, in the year preceding the 2006 local government elections, there were 5,085 protests against local government nationwide (Daily News 2005).

Indeed, according to Ballard et al., these protests are representative of a broader shift in state–society relations. More specifically, they hold that from the late 1990s there has been a rebirth in oppositional civil society, although only some of this is framed in terms contrary to the 'emerging pro-growth consensus' of Thabo Mbeki's governance, while much is framed in broader rights-based opposition (Ballard et al. 2006: 400). In addition, foreign donors are now spending more money on civil society, but mostly on projects that emphasize practical delivery rather than advocacy or challenge. Notably, while there is no neat division between those movements which will engage the state and those which will not, the counter-hegemonic movements' engagements 'tend to create crises, which more rights-based campaigns can capitalise on to influence policy and government practice' (ibid.: 404). Critically, however, oppositional civil society is not tremendously strong, and hence Beall et al. (2005: 681) argue that emergent state–society relations exist in a kind of 'fragile stability' that is likely to continue into the medium term until new social actors emerge to change this equilibrium.

In sum, then, South African state–society relations are in a state of transition, recovering from the vacuum of mobilization left by the social movements of the anti-apartheid era becoming the party in government or its allies. While enduring real-world problems mean that the conditions remain for popular mobilization around social goods, and there is evidence of the growth of more organic and local community-based organizations, civil society in all forms, and especially oppositional social movements, is not particularly strong. Notably, parallel to these developments in state–society relations, the post-apartheid state has also looked to meet the challenge of better service delivery through reforming local governance to operate in more democratic ways. By creating 'invited spaces' for communities to input into key municipal processes such as budgeting and development planning, conditions are created for a new and more constructive engagement between state and society. But what are these new 'spaces' and how well do they work? The next two sections explore these questions.

Invited spaces: 'participatory governance' and local government reform

Post-apartheid local government reform has been an intricate and prolonged affair, beginning in the early 1990s and continuing until 2000. Central to the functioning of new-look local government is the requirement for it to operate in a more democratic manner. Thus Section 152(1) of the constitution includes among the objects of local government 'to provide democratic and accountable government for local communities' and 'to encourage the involvement of communities and community organizations in the matters of local government'. In terms of the Local Government: Municipal Systems Act 32 of 2000, municipalities are required to complement their formal structures of representative government with a system of 'participatory governance'.

Participatory governance Notably, 'participatory governance' is not representative democracy, understood as the regular election of councillors, but refers to the manner in which municipalities govern *between* elections. As argued by Barichievy et al. (2005), there are three substantive aspects to the innovation of 'participatory governance': the redefinition of the municipality, requirements for public participation and ward committees. As outlined in Section 2(b) of the Municipal Systems Act, the local community is included alongside councillors and administrators in the legal definition of a municipality, a move of great symbolic significance.

The second innovation is really a set of requirements for public involvement in various decision-making processes. Especially important here are the imperatives regarding public consultation on the annual budget, the integrated development programme (IDP) review process, the performance management system, service delivery contracting and all by-laws, among others. These bring community participation to the foundational activities of local governance. Notably, the practical mechanism through which most of this consultation occurs is the mayoral *imbizo*: a public meeting convened by the mayor on one or more of the above issues, usually the IDP and the budget.

Last are ward committees, first mentioned in the 1998 White Paper on Local Government, but outlined in some detail in the Local Government: Municipal Structures Act. This act provides for ward committees to be established in each ward of a category A or category B municipality (i.e. cities and towns) if the municipality so chooses. Chaired by the ward councillor, ward committees are intended to consist of up to ten people representing 'a diversity of interests' in the ward, with women 'equitably represented'. In respect of their role, ward committees are mostly advisory bodies for ward councillors but may enjoy greater powers if the council sees fit. Notably, the *Guidelines for the Establishment and Operation of Municipal Ward Committees* (Government Gazette 2005) specified that the 'duties and powers' delegated to ward committees may *not* include executive powers (Section 5(3)(d)), and instead emphasized their role in communication and mobilization.

While the democratic reform of local government is a worldwide trend, especially in the developing world, where the ideas of decentralization and democratization have World Bank and donor backing, there is little doubt that in South Africa the poor performance of local government is an additional reason for participatory governance. As already noted, there were 5,085 protests against poor service delivery and corruption in local government in 2005. The question naturally arises: did the reforms work? To answer this question we conducted two case studies, outlined in the following section.

Popular mobilization and 'participatory governance' in Msunduzi and eThekwini

Msunduzi and eThekwini are two municipalities in the province of KwaZulu-Natal. They are different municipalities in many ways. They are different categories of municipality, B (town) and A (metropolitan) respectively, and thus have a significantly different scale of responsibilities and resources. Msunduzi covers an area of approximately 649 square kilometres with a population in excess of 500,000, whereas eThekwini covers an area of approximately 2,297 square kilometres with a population estimated to be 3.5 million. In addition, the annual budget of Msunduzi is in the region of R1.9 billion, whereas eThekwini's annual budget is seven times bigger, at R15 billion. Where Msunduzi spends just less than R40 million on salaries, eThekwini spends roughly R559 million on staff.

Msunduzi 2001–06: the sleepy hollow

In recent years the Msunduzi municipality has worked quite hard to counter the small-town image that the city has enjoyed for some time. The city is regularly bombarded with advertisements pronouncing the transformation of 'sleepy hollow' into 'vibrant valley', and the official town motto is 'the city of choice'. Yet if one looks at local governance in Msunduzi through the lens of public participation, the view is very much one of laid-back, if party-captured, municipal governance intersecting with limited community initiative. To sum up in spatial terms, public participation in Msunduzi between 2001 and 2006 was mostly a 'sleepy hollow'.

Invited spaces: between benign administration and party capture
POLICY It is notable that the Msunduzi municipality did not finalize a public participation policy during the five years from 2001 to 2006. It did manage to generate a draft in 2005, which is still reported to be in the consultative phase (Jackson-Plaatjies 2007). Notably, the draft policy

is very brief, at less than five pages in fourteen-point font, and makes no reference to civil society whatsoever. Instead emphasis is placed on ward committees, *izimbizo* and various forms of communication between communities and councillors. Reference to public participation is also to be found in other policies, notably the 2006 *Msunduzi Municipality Spatial Development Framework Review – Proposed Communication Strategy and Plan*.

Of these documents, only the latter deals with public participation in general terms, and it is notable in identifying civil society organizations as development stakeholders with rights to participate (and related responsibilities) in the project process. Clearly, then, it took some time for policy on public participation to make it on to the agenda of the Msunduzi municipality, and this despite the fact that Msunduzi implemented ward committees as early as 2001. Further, there seems to be no coherent or common conception of public participation, as evident in the inconsistencies between the various documents as to who the public are (communities and/or civil society) and how they ought to participate (ward committees, *izimbizo*, stakeholder forums or all three). In short, it seems that public participation has not been taken seriously as a policy priority by the Msunduzi municipality, an insight confirmed by the poor implementation of the ward committee system and the public consultation processes outlined below.

WARD COMMITTEES Ward committees in Msunduzi operated poorly in the period studied for three sets of reasons. First, ward committees depend on their ward councillors to operate effectively. Hence, the ward councillor is responsible for how often the ward committee meets, what it discusses, what information ward committee members acquire and what information the council obtains from ward committees. In the Msunduzi case there was evidence that a significant minority of ward councillors were simply not up to these tasks, because they were either incompetent, ignorant of their responsibilities in respect of ward committees, or constrained by party political or local power contests (Gardner 2005; Mngadi 2006). Thus less than 50 per cent of ward committees met regularly, and even among those that met regularly, the frequency varied widely, from weekly, monthly or bimonthly to annually. In addition, the speaker reported that 40 per cent of the ward committees were nonfunctional. Conversely, just eight (roughly 25 per cent) were described as 'very functional'. Further, the internal operation of ward committees was also dictated by the preferences of the ward councillor, with some reporting an inclusive deliberative style and equal voting rights, and others reserving the decision moment for themselves.

In addition to the functioning of ward committees, the Msunduzi case also illustrates the centrality of ward councillors to the constitution and composition of ward committees. Thus while consultants were meant to institute ward committees, they did not do this in all cases. Several ward councillors, many from the Democratic Alliance (DA), reported setting up their own structures. Research indicated that as many as eight of the original ward committees were later re-established or reformulated. Further, the way ward committee members were 'elected' varied tremendously. Some ward councillors reported having sectoral representation with meetings in localized areas, some had one mass meeting, and others co-opted people from existing organizations. Notably, many ward councillors reported co-opting new members as ward committee members left or stopped participating. Second, ward committees struggled to function effectively owing to a lack of support from the municipality. More specifically, the municipality needed to ensure the correct constitution of ward committees, train ward councillors and ward committee members, resource committees and, perhaps most importantly, clearly define the role of ward committees in council processes. In Msunduzi's case, none of these was done to any satisfactory degree.

Third, and perhaps most importantly for us, ward committees were largely captured by local parties or were defined as sites of local political competition. Hence, it appeared that all the Inkatha Freedom Party (IFP) ward committees, many ANC ward committees and some DA ward committees were subject to control by their respective local party branch. Not only was the perception of the party politicization of ward committees widely shared (Steele 2006; Pillay 2006; Nkosi 2005; Thompson 2006; Gardner 2005), but the official in charge of public participation stated that the 'politicization' of ward committees was especially a problem in historically black areas (Mngadi 2005, 2006). The politicization took the form of overt party control, such that no other parties were tolerated on the ward committees (typical of IFP and some ANC wards); intra-party competition, such that people in the wrong factions were marginalized (Mbeki–Zuma factionalism in the ANC); and policy competition, in that DA-led ward committees often refused to cooperate with the ANC-led council's vision of ward committee operation.

Notably, the implications of partisan ward committees extend beyond just undermining their independent role, but also directly impact on the health of civil society, undermining its ability to engage the local council. This is because the establishment of ward committees has affected other organizations and structures already in existence in Msunduzi. In formerly advantaged white and Indian areas, ratepayers' associations had tended to carry out some of the functions now allocated to ward committees. One ward committee (W25) was effectively composed of members of the previous ratepayers' associations in the area; another (W27) was either replaced or supplanted by the existing ratepayers' association; and others (W34 and 37) were said to be less effective than, or to duplicate, previously existing community structures. One ratepayers' association in a formerly disadvantaged area, the Edendale Landowners and Ratepayers Association, continues to exist in a close but ambiguous relationship with both the local ANC branch and the ward committee. As the former association chair, Mr L. E. M. Nkosi (2005), put it, a close relationship between the ANC branch and the ward committee is 'inevitable', given the very strong influence of the ANC.

Ward committees thus appear to draw on local organizational legacies, either ratepayers' associations in historically white and, to a lesser extent, Indian areas, and political parties in historically black or African areas. On one level, this is simply a matter of ward committees drawing on existing social capital (social networks and relations of trust) to populate themselves, but on another level, ward committees seem to assume much of the functions of ratepayers' associations, or come into the ambit of some form of party agenda-setting. Thus, to the extent that ward committees supplant other civil society formations and these same ward committees remain colonized by party agendas, we see the effective extension of party authority over local areas.

PUBLIC CONSULTATION OVER BUDGET, IDP, ETC. From 2001 until the present, the Msunduzi municipality has undergone four separate public consultation processes over the budget and IDP. The first process concerned the adoption of the first IDP in 2002. This was a process run from the municipal manager's office, as required by the Municipal Systems Act, by a team of five people. Notably at this time there was no IDP manager as such. Following the standard IDP process of the time, the first IDP was drawn up in roughly a year. There was consultation conducted during the analysis and strategy phases of the project, but it was restricted largely to various stakeholder groups rather than the local community. Thus Holmes (2006) notes that although they had hoped to use ward committees as part of this initial IDP process, ward committees were not functional enough to fulfil this role in 2002.

In addition to the emphasis on stakeholders, rather than the general public or local communities, in the public participation of the first IDP, several stakeholders such as the chamber of commerce and some NGOs complained that public consultation was inadequate. Indeed, Holmes (ibid.) conceded that while they made a sincere first effort at public participation in the IDP process, it was inadequate. That the lopsided nature of public participation mattered was reflected in the fact that most feedback from stakeholder meetings came from organizations rooted in more advantaged communities, such as the chamber of commerce, the Scottsville Residents Association and the DA.

The second round of public participation concerned the annual review of the IDP and budget in 2004. This round saw the introduction of two practices that have become standard since then. The first is the integration of the annual IDP and budget review into one process in terms of statutorily required public participation. Second has been the introduction of a series of at least five public meetings or mayoral *izimbizo* located in the five service areas of the Msunduzi municipality. A survey of the minutes from these meetings in May 2004 revealed a similar format which has endured until today. Following presentations on the IDP and budget, the audience asked a number of questions which were then answered by the various officials on the stage. Meetings took between three and four hours. Unfortunately it is not clear from the minutes how many people attended the meetings and whether entertainment and food were provided for the community. In this regard Madeline Jackson-Plaatjies (2007) reports that at this time entertainment and food were provided only at some venues, but 'since then it has now become a standard practice that we provide refreshments at all venues. In terms of the entertainment, this is still at selected venues as performances are voluntarily conducted by these groups.'

A survey of the issues raised reflected a significant variety of concerns, often particular to the local areas. Hence in the mostly Indian area of Northdale concern over indigent policy was high, whereas in the African township of Imbali and the rural area of Vulindlela more emphasis was placed on service delivery, especially relating to water and housing. A common concern across all meetings was the discrepancy between a 2 per cent increase in rates and a 6 per cent decrease in the electricity tariff. Another notable claim related to *izimbizo* in that, apparently, many of the people who attended did not know their ward councillors (Gwala 2006). The third round of public participation was a series of eleven public meetings in November 2004 that served as the formal basis of the IDP review of

2004/05. Again the pattern is one of great local variety, with an enormous number of often very parochial issues being raised. Nevertheless, overall it is clear that service delivery was the most important concern (22 per cent) closely followed by social issues (including unemployment, HIV/AIDS and crime) at 21 per cent and then billing in third place at 13 per cent. Housing was fourth at 11 per cent.

OTHER EXPERIMENTS IN PUBLIC PARTICIPATION Two further developments in respect of participatory governance during this time are worth noting. The first concerns experiments in ward-level budgeting. The initiative of the former municipal manager, Bheki Nene, the Shoshaloza campaigns were implemented in 2003/04 and 2004/05, using money from a national grant. In Shoshaloza One, all thirty-seven wards got R250,000, whereas in Shoshaloza Two, just twenty-four of the more needy wards got R250,000. In the first round the officials and politicians travelled to an area and met the community and talked about their needs, and then the councillor would decide on which projects to establish in the area. In the second round, councillors drove the process using various combinations of ward committees and public meetings to identify projects. While the processes were far from uniform or always participatory, many nevertheless reported more enthusiasm and participation in both ward committees and *izimbizo* dealing with this issue (Raja 2006; Davids 2006). This suggests that empowering public participatory structures may well improve participation in them. It is worth noting that the Shoshaloza campaign is now also a subject of the ongoing investigation by the Scorpions (the special intelligence unit of South African government, since disbanded) into corruption in the municipality, and that the official in charge of administering the campaigns refused either to provide documentation he had previously promised us or to talk to us further.

Last but not least, many respondents noted a reasonably transparent and inclusive culture of governance during Mayor Hloni Zondi's tenure. As shown below, many key civil society organizations had a reasonable working relationship with the city, and the council was remarkably accessible to the public as regards meetings. Hence members of the public were not just entitled to attend every council meeting, but could attend committee meetings too, and could speak for up to three minutes on any issue. Further to facilitate participation, public contributions were taken at the start of the meeting rather than the end. In the words of current Msunduzi municipal manager and long-time city councillor Rob Haswell, community participation in committee life was 'vigorous'. There were moments of political crisis when the executive used its right to hold meetings 'in committee' (i.e. behind closed doors) to exclude the press and public, but these were the exception rather than the rule.

Invented spaces: disengagement from below

CIVIL SOCIETY: THE NGO SECTOR While not as manifold or as powerful as in eThekwini, the NGO sector in Msunduzi is significant in size and role. Bear in mind we are referring to that section of civil society which is reasonably 'professionalized' nowadays, and usually has a management board and outside funding. We do not include in this category the many more local community-based organizations which Ballard et al. (2006: 17) see as underwriting emergent social movements around the country. Owing to time and resource constraints we decided to focus on one sector in the NGO pantheon, and identified the welfare sector for two reasons. First, it is a relatively well-developed, well-run and accessible sector in Msunduzi, and second, it tends to work quite closely with the state. In many ways, then, it promised to be a good candidate for exploring local state–society relations in general and civil society's engagement with participatory governance in particular. To this end we collected a range of documentation and interviewed thirteen activists in the welfare NGO community, including from the Children in Distress Network (CINDI), Pietermaritzburg Child and Family Welfare, and the Msunduzi Hospice and Thandanani Children's Foundation. We also interviewed probably the biggest NGO network in Msunduzi, the Pietermaritzburg Chamber of Business.

In terms of engaging the state, respondents were divided between those who work quite closely with government, especially provincial government, such as Pietermaritzburg Child and Family Welfare, which essentially does government work; those who work periodically with government around specific projects, such as CINDI and the Msunduzi HIV/AIDS projects; and those who work independently of government, such as the Thandanani Children's Foundation. Most respondents who did engage government had relationships with provincial government rather than local, either exclusively (hospice) or predominantly (Pietermaritzburg Child and Family Welfare, AFRA) given the location of welfare resources in this sphere rather than the local. This is an important consideration, especially when contrasting Msunduzi and eThekwini, with its much more extensive resources. The reality is that for many NGOs there is little reason to engage the local state rather than the province.

Despite these different relationships with government, all respondents were unhappy with the nature of state–society relations. All complained of the slow and narrow vision of government bureaucracy (Molefe 2007; Andrew 2007), and many pointed to incompetence and unreliability on the part of government in supporting projects (Spain 2007; Layman 2007). The key variable here was whether there was a champion in government committed to a project who could remain in office long enough to see it through. Perhaps most important, though, almost all felt that government tended to treat them like service delivery providers rather than equal partners, an attitude that was clearly deeply resented (Mfeka and Brisbane 2007). Indeed, one organization had decided not to engage government despite the potential for fruitful partnership precisely because of government's 'dismissing and patronizing' attitude. They had found advocacy 'meaningless' as 'decisions were already taken, and it was a waste of time' (anonymous interviewee). Another respondent reported that 'the term public participation is just a token ... our inputs are always ignored. It is like a vacuum' (Todd 2007).

For those who worked closely with local government in the period from 2001 to 2006, the feeling was perhaps a little more positive. Hence CINDI was part of an (initially) successful HIV/AIDS partnership with the Msunduzi municipality, and the Chamber of Business reported a 'cooperative' relationship with the Hloni Zondi administration. Notably, though, both respondents reported a deterioration in relations when key individuals in government changed, scuppering the HIV/AIDs partnership for over a year in one case and setting back council–chamber relations substantially in the other (Spain 2007; Layman 2007). This very personal character of local state–society relations, plus the comparative insignificance of local government resources compared to other spheres, meant that on the whole relations with local government were quite limited.

In this context it perhaps comes as no surprise that while respondents were aware of ward committees and municipal *izimbizo* to review the budget and IDP, almost none had participated in any of these processes. The reason given was simple and consistent across organizations: it was a waste of valuable time. On closer inspection, though, it was revealed that this was not only because these structures or processes were perceived as making little difference, but because they did not deal with issues of direct concern to the welfare sector. To put the point differently, welfare organizations did not feel that the municipal budget or development planning were that important to them.

Notably, despite the widespread disillusionment with the current nature of state–society relations, almost all respondents expressed a desire for more constructive engagement with the state, including local government. Doubt was expressed about the possibility of this, given past experience, but most noted the synergies in development agendas between the post-apartheid government and the NGO sector. The divide, it seems, was much more about how good policies should be implemented rather than the nature of the policies themselves. To put the issue another way, the current problems are more practice-based than ideology-based. This is not necessarily the case with social movements, however.

SOCIAL MOVEMENTS The kind of militant social movement 'direct action' experienced in eThekwini is largely absent in Msunduzi. This is despite the existence of a small social movement forum comprising a few left-wing academics, and some community activists. It seems that the main organizational ingredient in this forum is the Eastwood Community Forum (ECF), which has had a series of conflicts with the local ward councillor, including over the failure to instal traffic calming in the area (Makhatini 2006). According to the leader of the ECF, Fred Wagner (2005), the ECF was formed because the local councillor 'was useless' in dealing with the local issues of water, housing evictions and rates, hence the community's turning to direct action:

> The only time the council listens is when we toyi-toyi [protest]. Government only listens when you take to the streets. You send letters and so on and nothing happens. Paperwork they throw ... in the bin. They don't come to the people with public meetings. It's only now that it's going to elections that they start to do stuff.

Notably, one respondent (Homeboy 2007) accused Wagner of a similarly exclusive style of operation, with few public meetings and little debate at those meetings. 'Mostly Fred just gives report-backs and handles issues on an individual basis with his close allies. He is effectively a paternalistic Godfather figure.' There have also been periodic local protests against various social issues in poor communities: for example, a community march in Edendale against a taxi fare increase was tear-gassed by police, but as far as we can tell these events have not spawned community-based organizations nor been sustained over time.

eThekwini 2001–06: the neoliberal battleground

The differences between Msunduzi and eThekwini are not just of quantity, but of quality too. This is especially the case in respect of the administration of the two cities. Whereas in recent years Msunduzi has had a succession of municipal managers who have left in their wake a somewhat dubious set of managerial practices, eThekwini has been under the clear guidance of city manager Mike Sutcliffe (who, it is worth noting, is senior in the ANC to eThekwini mayor Obed Mlaba). Under Sutcliffe's close attention, eThekwini governance has evolved in a more efficient, if centralized, direction best characterized as 'managerialism'. This orientation has influenced the implementation of participatory governance, and not always in a beneficial way. At the same time – and, some would argue, as a direct result of managerialism – eThekwini has experienced much more radical direct action, especially in terms of housing and rent evictions, of the 'counter-hegemonic' sort typical of social movements. Hence, where the space of state–society relations in Msunduzi constitutes something of a 'sleepy hollow', in eThekwini it is much more of a contest between a 'managerial' centre and the 'militant' margins: it is a neoliberal battleground.

Invited spaces: public participation as managerialism

POLICY In contrast to Msunduzi, eThekwini has a 2006 public participation policy entitled *Citizen Participation Policy: Framework for eThekwini Municipality* (CPP 2006). The document emerged from an earlier project, the 2004 *eThekwini Municipality Community Participation and Action Support Strategy* (COMPASS 2004), which consulted communities and stakeholders in the five management areas of the south Durban basin. From this consultation emerged a critique of the failure of community participation due to the dominance of public spaces by political parties, the lack of city investment in participation between elections, dependence on the ward councillor, poorly developed community stakeholder structures, the limited impact on community policing forums and the general unresponsiveness of local government.

The document advises establishing 'credible, democratically elected and functional civil society and business stakeholder consultation forums' that are not ad hoc like the Big Mama workshops (ibid.: 28).[1] Notably, among other things, the document recommends establishing such a body in each ward, called a ward community forum (WCF). Similar in role to ward committees, the WCF is a body inclusive of all other civil society forums, NGOs, political parties, school governing bodies and so on, and is 'the highest decision-making body in the ward' (ibid.: 32). It elects an executive committee which represents the ward in the IDP process. Other participation 'strategies' listed include regional customer service centres, the area-based management system, more accessible ward councillors, an integrated community information gathering system and more accountable ward councillors (ibid.: 20–24).

In many ways the COMPASS document is an impressive attempt to deal seriously with a felt need for more meaningful community participation in eThekwini. Instead of adopting and implementing the (many) recommendations of COMPASS, however, the municipality decided to draft a distinct public participation policy. The outcome was a document much more oriented towards public participation in theory, and with much less by way of practicable mechanisms or instruments to enhance public participation (CPP 2006). No mention is made of WCFs or, for that matter, ward committees. Instead there is a long list of 'tools' that includes newsletters, citizens' meetings with councillors, talk shows or interviews, public hearings, city festivals, public surveys, local partnerships and an NGO charter (or other enforceable by-law) and rules for co-financing civic initiatives (ibid.: 54–6).

There can be little doubt that, in real terms of empowering citizens, the official public participation policy of eThekwini is a step backwards from the COMPASS document. Further, if one reviews the performance assessment account of the head of the Community Participation and Action Support Unit (CPASU) for 2004/05, it is noteworthy that many key performance objectives are really forms of service provision. For example, CPASU assisted in setting up soup kitchens in poor areas, facilitated youth business training, lent support to gender policy programmes, organized Masakhane road shows (government-initiated participatory public meetings where local and national political leaders listened to issues relating to service delivery at community level) and held live broadcasts for key government events, such as the state-of-the-nation address. In respect of actual public participation, the CPASU drew up a draft policy, encouraged members of the public to attend council meetings, participated in ward-based IDP workshops, helped organized Big Mama 5 and organized thirteen decentralized budget hearings. Given the role of the IDP organizers, the CPU, in driving the Big Mama and IDP process, it seems the CPASU did not do very much by way of facilitating meaningful public participation.

WARD COMMITTEES Perhaps the most noteworthy feature of ward committees in eThekwini between 2001 and 2006 was that there were none. According to city Manager Mike Sutcliffe (2006), the reasons for this were twofold. First, when the IFP controlled the provincial government, the party decided to implement sub-councils instead of ward committees.

Second, when the ANC came to power in KwaZulu-Natal in 2004, the city decided to go the ward committee route, and approached the province to apply in terms of the Municipal Structures Act and publish a Section 12 notice formally constituting eThekwini as 'a municipality with a collective executive system combined with a ward participatory system'. The provincial local government department under Mike Mabuyakhulu 'dropped the ball', however, and this was never done.

In the interim, though, the city proceeded with ward committee elections on the assumption that the legal niceties had been completed. A large number of ward committees were elected. According to Sutcliffe (ibid.), in this process the ANC 'out-mobilized the DA' with regard to the ward committees in about four DA wards, by dominating ward committee election meetings although they had lost the ward. This meant that while the ward councillor belonged to the DA, the majority of the ten members of the ward committee belonged to the ANC. In response to this the DA took the matter to court, objecting to the whole ward committee process in terms of the failure by province to publish the required Section 12 notice. The court upheld the objection and ward committee elections were shelved until the next term of local government in 2006. Once again, we see party interests undermining the operation of ward committees.

PUBLIC CONSULTATION IN BUDGET, IDP, ETC. eThekwini made an impressive start to public consultation over the budget and IDP with the first draft IDP in 2001 and 2002. First, it integrated the two, such that instead of the traditional approach of allocating resources to departments, resources were allocated to priorities as defined by the IDP. Second, it used these priorities to establish the key performance areas and indicators central to the performance assessment of senior officials. Third, the process of drawing up the IDP was both participatory and needs-driven – that is, it also drew on community-based planning methodologies. As part of this there were a series of five 'Big Mama' workshops which constituted the main public input into the process.

These workshops drew together some 450 participants from all sectors of civil society and spatial areas of the city, spheres of government, unions and traditional leadership. The first such workshop reflected on eThekwini's draft Long Term Development Framework, which envisaged the city in 2020. Next were a series of a hundred community workshops across the city to assess local needs, followed by a strategic budgeting exercise culminating in Big Mama 2 on 4 May 2002 (CPU 2004: 20–26).

The needs list obtained through the community process was related to sets of existing data and the planning teams proposed various technical interventions which were considered at Big Mama 2. Based on this, and after engagements with other spheres of government, the municipality launched its 2002/03 people's budget (Big Mama 3) at Kings Park on 29 June 2002. In February 2003 another Big Mama was called to reflect on and revise the budget.

While there is much to admire about the Big Mama process, what has happened since 2003 is also important. Not only has there been a clear downturn in regular and effective public participation in city planning, but a significant amount of time and effort has been invested in the development of technical systems in the municipality. The main reason for this appears to be the challenge of coming to terms with various new statutory and policy requirements from national government, for example the Local Government: Municipal Finance Management Act (MFMA) of 2003. In part, though, it also has to do with the growth of a culture of professionalism, and the particular commandeerist style of the city manager, Mike Sutcliffe. Hence tremendous energy has been invested in developing performance management systems for top officials and implementing a new system of area-based management to integrate planning spatially within the city. At the same time the city has found itself drawn increasingly into international networks of management and funding, and it seems clear that the top leadership have global ambitions for the city of eThekwini.

All these trends suggest a growing managerialism among the city elite, an attitude reflected in the indifference towards public participation of late. In the words of city manager Mike Sutcliffe (2006), 'we know what people's needs are. Indeed, for the next hundred years the needs will remain the same, although the rank order might well change.' By implication, public participation can contribute in this regard. He further expressed the view that the IDP and budget processes were too complex for ordinary people and that meaningful public participation was a long-term strategy:

> communities will spend their money on things that do not do anything. Communities spend their money on things that have no lasting impact on their lives. All that happens is that the public feels better about developing their area. Interest groups play a more significant role in public participation as they are useful in having more practical goals for the municipality.

Invented spaces: public participation as radicalism If the implementation of participatory governance 'from above' has been uneven, and undermined by party conflict and managerialism, the engagement with the new institutions 'from below' has been quite vigorous. Not only has community participation in the IDP process been enthusiastic, but direct action outside of these limited participatory governance mechanisms has been significant, with several communities engaged in militant protest against a perceived council lack of both delivery and policy. Unfortunately time and money have prevented us from working in the NGO sector to fill out this picture with responses from a sector historically more amenable to partnership with government.

SOCIAL MOVEMENTS eThekwini is famous for its radical social movements. Communities in eThekwini, especially in Chatsworth, were beginning to mobilize around issues relating to poverty, social delivery and housing as early as 1997, just a few years into the new democracy. In eThekwini, the Concerned Citizens Group (CCG), which eventually evolved into the Concerned Citizens Forum (CCF), is considered one of the earliest documented community-based social movement formations, mobilizing around the plight of poor and indigent communities in KwaZulu-Natal. The origins of the CCF are located in a series of political engagements arising out of attempts by well-known sociologist Professor Fatima Meer to campaign on behalf of the ANC in the Indian township of Chatsworth in 1999 (Dwyer 2006: 93). She discovered, however, a reluctance by the community to vote for the ANC, given the high levels of poverty and pending evictions faced by residents. Eventually, mobilization led to a situation where the cases of several families facing eviction were taken up by the CCG. This mobilization also led to the revival of 'flat residents associations' in various parts of Chatsworth.

What is arguably significant about these early mobilizations is that they began within the context of a refusal by poor residents to participate in local government processes, or a frustration with the lack of responsiveness from local councillors and the city. As long as these structures of local government, and in particular the municipality, were seen as the cause of the social problems faced by these residents, they were not going to 'legitimize' these structures by participating in them. Arguably this political stance came to define and shape much of the social movement formation and history that followed.

Between 1999 and 2003, a series of protest activities took place in the eThekwini metro under various organizational banners, including

231

the CCF, and some under the auspices of a variety of coalitions such as the anti-war coalition, the Palestine Support Committee and People Against War. In 2003 a group of eThekwini-based activists and academics came together to form a social movement group called the eThekwini Social Forum, which eventually evolved into the People's Social Movement (PSM). The broader space of the PSM then affiliated to the KwaZulu-Natal branch of the nationally based Social Movements Indaba (SMI), which was formally launched in 2005/06, with a variety of eThekwini-based civic groups such as the South Durban Community Environmental Alliance, the Bayview Flat Residents Association and the Wentworth Development Forum being part of this broader collective. Since 2006, the KwaZulu-Natal SMI, together with its affiliate bodies, has been one of the most active spaces for protests against state forces in eThekwini and the province of KwaZulu-Natal, on issues such as housing, service delivery, subsistence livelihoods and the environment.

In 2005 a series of frustrations concerning living conditions felt by people residing in the various shack settlements in and around the Sydenham and Clare Estate area of eThekwini spilt over into a sustained day-long protest, which resulted in the residents blockading major roads in the city and burning tyres. This protest activity was the start of a number of ongoing protest actions organized by a coalition of shack dwellers, who eventually came to call themselves Abahlali baseMjondolo (ABM) or the Shackdwellers Movement. The ABM has become very popular in the social movement landscape, both provincially and nationally. It is regarded as one of the largest mass-based movements in the country and attracts a considerable amount of financial support from a variety of donors.

The ABM has also become well known for its popular campaign slogan, 'No Land, No House, No Vote', reflecting once again a clear refusal to participate in local governance processes if their very basic social demands are not addressed first. This social movement perhaps stands out from the SMI of KwaZulu-Natal in that it represents primarily informal shack residents and has a very specific agenda, focusing on improving housing rights for its members. While the ABM started out in KwaZulu-Natal, it has also established satellite branches in other provinces.

Social movement protest in eThekwini tends to be very fluid and dynamic, and is usually in response to various ongoing initiatives by the city government to bring about major changes that will impact on city residents in a substantive manner. What has become far more evident within social movement activity in this municipality since 2006 is a growing resentment by particularly low-income communities at the way in which their lives are being disrupted by proposed citywide changes that are being carried out by the city authorities in preparation for the 2010 FIFA World Cup. This is most evident in the increased levels of protest activity that are being undertaken by groups such as the KwaZulu-Natal Subsistence Fishermen's Coalition, the street traders, the residents' associations of South Durban (most of whom are affiliated to the KwaZulu-Natal SMI) and various groups representing informal settlements throughout the city, which are all in some way affected by actions taken by the city authorities in an attempt to create, according to its IDP, 'Africa's most caring and liveable city', having factored into their plans the changes that must be made to the city in order to host the soccer World Cup (Nadvi 2007).

Conclusion

Our examination of the cases of Msunduzi and eThekwini confirms much in the broader literature on the centrality of political parties to popular mobilization in South Africa. This is clear in the way political parties manage to dominate the formal local governance landscape, including the supposedly neutral and inclusive institutions of 'participatory governance'. There is also evidence, however, of significant civil society and social movement mobilization, even if the latter is somewhat uneven across the case studies. Furthermore, and perhaps most importantly, there is evidence to support the claim of growing disenchantment with service delivery failure, and the incapacity of the new institutions of participatory governance to change this. Indeed, it seems safe to conclude that the failure of 'participatory governance' can only exacerbate dissatisfaction, and so the pressure for change can only grow.

Importantly, though, there is also reason to assert that such change is best led by oppositional movements rather than ruling political parties. One obvious critique of participatory governance is that the new institutions are largely disempowered, through explicit design in limiting the powers and resources of ward committees and public consultation processes, but also through less than optimal practices by politicians and officials. Where politicians are quick to hijack ward committees – and, to some extent, *izimbizo* – to their own more particular ends, officials have approached public participation issues with either indifference or a technocratic gaze. In different ways, both actors have undermined the limited potential dividend offered by the new 'invited' spaces.

While the technocratic approach of officials may be ascribable in part to the elitist managerialism of the Mbeki regime (which effectively centralized local government financial practices through the MFMA and procurement policies), the behaviour of politicians cannot. Notably the political capture of ward committees is not simply an ANC problem, and therefore is not fully explicable, as Heller (2001: 154) suggests, in terms of the 'dominant party syndrome'. Rather, the reason political parties tend to capture ward committees has to do with a design that places ward councillors at the heart of ward committees. It is in the interests of every politician to minimize risk and maximize power, and hence political capture is incentivized. Importantly, this capture is less obvious in relation to processes of public consultation, precisely because these are tied less closely to institutions of local party power.

What this means is that even empowering the structures and processes of 'participatory governance' is not the entire solution in seeking more inclusive and constructive state–society relations. They need to be better designed, especially ward committees, so that power can be shared between officials and politicians on the one hand and civil society and communities on the other. As Gaventa (2007) notes, however, empowered institutions of local power-sharing are not enough. Politicians and officials have to want to make them work, and civil society must be strong enough to take the opportunities new spaces provide. To our mind, the second of these criteria is the larger challenge. As regards political will, it is important to note that, contrary to what Heller (2001) says, the ANC is the party with the greatest commitment to public participation in South Africa. Hence there is a 'people's democracy' strain in the ANC rooted in the 'people's power' style of politics opposing apartheid of the 1980s (Friedman 2005). Of particular importance here was the experience of participation in civic and other community-based organizations in historically black areas, which directly influenced the drawing up of the Municipal Systems Act of 2000 (Carrim 2006). Further, with the leadership change in the ANC, forces more sympathetic to the discourse of popular democracy have a greater status.

Of more concern, then, is the relative weakness of civil society and especially social movements as regards political parties in South Africa. Consequently, the vivification of state–society relations requires the rebirth of oppositional movements strong enough to make ruling parties pay attention and take communities seriously. At the moment it is only really the labour unions which have the potential to do this, but they are very closely tied to the ruling party, especially the incoming faction of the ANC. Hence, until there is a shift in the broader patterns of social mobilization for the poor and marginalized, and at the expense of ruling political parties, invited spaces will remain meaningless or co-opted spaces. The good news for oppositional movements is that it is precisely by excluding the poor and marginalized that 'invited spaces' help to create the conditions for the emergence of the movements needed to transform local power.

Note

Big Mama workshops include all sectors (youth women etc.), areas (wards) and actors (civil society, officials, politicians) in eThekweni around development planning and budgeting.

References

ABM (2006) *A Short History of Abahlali baseMjondolo, the Durban Shack Dwellers' Movement*, www.abahlali. org/node/16, accessed 11 November 2007.

Andrew, D. (2007) Interview with Duncan Andrew, Thandanani Children's Foundation, 22 August.

Anonymous (2007) Interview, 22 August 2007.

Ballard, R., A. Habib and I. Valodia (eds) (2006) *Voices of Protest: Social Movements in Post-Apartheid South Africa*, Pietermaritzburg: UKZN Press.

Barichievy, K., L. Piper and B. Parker (2005) 'Assessing "participatory governance" in local government: a case-study of two South African cities', *Politeia*, 24(3).

Beall, J., S. Gelb and S. Hassim (2005) 'Fragile stability: state and society in democratic South Africa', *Journal of Southern African Studies*, 31(4).

Bryan, F. M. (2004) *Real Democracy: The New England Town Meeting and How It Works*, Chicago, IL: University of Chicago Press.

Carrim, Y. (2001) 'Bridging the gap between the ideas and practice: challenges of the new local government system', *Umrabulo*, 10, May.

— (2006) ANC MP and former chair of the Parliamentary Portfolio Committee on Local Government, interviewed 26 October.

Cohen, J. (2002) 'Deliberation and democratic legitimacy', in D. Estlund (ed.), *Democracy*, Maldon and Oxford: Blackwell.

COMPASS (2004) *eThekwini Municipality Community Participation and Action Support Strategy*, Unpublished policy document.

Cornwall, A. (2002) 'Making spaces, changing places: situating participation in development', IDS Working Paper 170, CDRC, Brighton: IDS.

Cornwall, A. and V. S. Coelho (forthcoming) 'Spaces for change? The politics of participation in new democratic arenas'.

CPASU (2005) *Performance Assessment, Head: Community Participation and Action Support Unit*, Community Participation and Action Support Unit, period 2004/05.

CPP (2006) *Citizen Participation Policy: Framework for eThekwini Municipality*, Unpublished policy document.

CPU (2004) *Making City Strategy Come Alive: Experiences from eThekwini Municipality, Durban, South Africa*, Corporate Policy Unit.

Daily News (2005) 14 October.

Davids, N. (2006) Area Based Management, Msunduzi Municipality, interviewed 9 October.

Nine

Dlamini, T. M. (2005) Ward councillor, Ward 13, interviewed 19 September.

Dwyer, P. (2006) 'The concerned citizen's forum: a fight within a fight', in R. Ballard, A. Habib and I. Valodia (eds), *Voices of Protest: Social Movements in Post-Apartheid South Africa*, Pietermaritzburg: UKZN Press.

ESF (2003) *Ethekwini Social Forum Declaration*, Unpublished document.

eThekwini Municipality (2006) *Rules Regulating the Establishment and Operation of Ward Committees*.

Friedman, S. (2005) 'On whose terms: participatory governance and citizen action in post-apartheid South Africa', Paper presented at the International Institute of Labour Studies Workshop 'Participatory Governance: A New Regulatory Framework?', Geneva, 9/10 December.

Fung, A. and E. O. Wright (2001) 'Deepening democracy: innovations in empowered participatory governance', *Politics and Society*, 29(1).

Gardner, G. (2005) Speaker, Msunduzi Local Council, interviewed 11 August.

Gaventa, J. (2007) 'How do local governments support citizen engagement?', Background note for the International Workshop for Champions of Participation in Local Government, Institute of Development Studies, University of Sussex, Brighton, 29 May– 4 June.

Gibson, N. C. (ed.) (2006) *Challenging Hegemony: Social Movements and the Quest for a New Humanism in Post-Apartheid South Africa*, Trenton: Africa World Press.

Government Gazette (2003) *Draft Guidelines for the Establishment and Operation of Municipal Ward Committees*, Notice 2649 of 2003, 24 October.

— (2005) *Guidelines for the Establishment and Operation of Municipal Ward Committees*, Notice 965 of 2005, 24 June.

Greenstein, R. (2003) 'State, civil society and the reconfiguration of power in post-apartheid South Africa', Research Report no. 8, Centre for Civil Society, University of KwaZulu-Natal, Durban.

Gwala, S. (2006) Municipal Budget Manager, Msunduzi Municipality, interviewed 27 June.

Habermas, J. (2002) 'Deliberative politics', in D. Estlund (ed.), *Democracy*, Maldon and Oxford: Blackwell.

Haswell, R. (2007) Msunduzi Municipal Manager, interviewed 28 September.

Heller, P. (2001) 'Moving the state: the politics of democratic decentralisation in Kerala, South Africa and Porto Alegre', *Politics and Society*, 29(1).

Hendricks, C. M. (2006) 'Integrated deliberation: reconciling civil society's dual role in deliberative democracy', *Political Studies*, 54.

Holmes, G. (2006) Town planner, Msunduzi Municipality, interviewed 24 October.

— (2007). Town planner, Msunduzi Municipality, email correspondence, 12 September.

Holston, J. and A. Appadurai (1999) 'Cities and citizenship', in J. Holston (ed.), *Cities and Citizenship*, Durham, NC: Duke University Press.

Homeboy (2007) Eastwood resident, interviewed 4 July 2007.

Jackson-Plaatjies, M. (2007) Manager, Strategic Analysis and Research, Msunduzi Municipality, interviewed 5 June.

Kaiser, E. (2007) Interview in *Kenosis*, 11 September.

Krone, A. (2007) Interview in *SaveAct*, 3 September 2007.

Lambert, B. (2005) Ward councillor, Ward 25, interviewed 18 August.

Layman, A. (2007) Pietermaritzburg Chamber of Business, interviewed 8 August.

Local Government: Municipal Finance Management Act (Act No. 56 of 2003), www.capegateway.gov.za/Text/2004/8/mfma.pdf.

Local Government: Municipal Structures Act (Act No. 117 of 1998), www.info.gov.za/gazette/acts/1998/a117-98.pdf.

Local Government: Municipal Systems Act (Act No. 32 of 2000), www.info.gov.za/gazette/acts/2000/a32-00.pdf.

MacPherson, R. (2006) DA Ward councillor, Ward 35, interviewed 19 July.

Makhatini, M. (2006) 'Eastwood fights for humps', *The Mirror*, 9 August.

Mattes, R. (2002) 'Democracy without the people: economics, governance, and representation in South Africa', *Journal of Democracy*, 13(1), February.

Mbeki, T. (2005) Media briefing by President Thabo Mbeki on Cabinet Lekgotla, 24 July, www.info.gov.za/speeches/2005/05072509551001.htm, accessed 11 November 2007.

Mfeka, K. and C. Brisbane (2007) Built Environmental Support Group, interviewed 2 October.

Miraftab, F. (2006) 'Feminist praxis, citizenship and informal politics: reflections on South Africa's Anti-Eviction Campaign', *International Feminist Journal of Politics*, 8(2), June.

Mngadi, S. (2005) Official in the Speaker's Office in charge of public participation, Msunduzi Local Council, interviewed 11 August.

— (2006) Official in the Speaker's Office in charge of public participation, Msunduzi Local Council, interviewed 7 March.

Molefe, M. (2007) Interview in *Sinani*, 27 August.

Moodley, S. (2007) Senior Planner, Corporate Policy Unit, eThekwini Municipality, interviewed 7 June.

Mothlabane, B. (2007) Senior Manager of Regional Services, CPASU, eThekwini Municipality, interviewed 9 March.

Msengana-Ndlela, L. (2006) Speech by Ms Lindiwe Msengana-Ndlela, Director-General of the Department of Provincial and Local Government (DPLG) to the Conference of the Development Bank of Southern Africa, Vulindlela Academy, Midrand, Johannesburg, 13 March, www.dplg.gov.za/speeches/13Mar2006DGv1.doc, accessed 11 November 2007.

Myeza, D. (2007) Manager in Speaker's Office, eThekwini Municipality, interviewed 26 February.

Nadvi, L. (2007) 'The ugly side of the beautiful game: the socio-economic impact of the 2010 FIFA World Cup on the city of eThekwini and its "poors"', *World Journal of Managing Events*, 2(1).

Naidoo, N. (2007) Political reporter for *The Witness* newspaper, interviewed 28 August.

Naidoo, S. N. (2005) Ward councillor, Ward 28, interviewed 24 August.

Nkosi, L. E. M. (2005) Chairperson, Edendale Land Owners and Ratepayers' Association, interviewed 17 October.

Noyce, G. (2007) DA Ward councillor, Ward 9, interviewed 27 February.

Nussbaum, M. and A. Sen (1993) *The Quality of Life*, Oxford: Clarendon Press.

Pillay, M. (2006) ACDP councillor, Msunduzi Local Council, interviewed 20 February.

Piper, L. and L. Nadvi (2007) 'Assessing public participation in local governance in South Africa: eThekwini and Msunduzi municipalities 2001–2006', Final Research Report for the 'Middle Spaces' Project, November.

Raja, R. (2006) Shoshaloza Campaign project manager, Msunduzi Municipality 2003–05, interviewed 23 November.

Spain, Y. (2007) CINDI, interviewed 13 August.

Spence, C. (2007) Msunduzi Hospice, interviewed 21 August.

Steele, M. (2006), DA proportional representation councillor, Msunduzi Local Council, interviewed 20 February.

Sutcliffe, M. (2006) eThekwini city manager, interviewed 16 October.

Thompson, P. (2006) Acting Secretary, Scottsville Residents' Association, and ward committee member, Ward 36, interviewed 3 March.

Todd, J. (2007) Pietermaritzburg Child and Family Welfare, interviewed 21 August.

Wagner, F. (2005) Chairperson, Eastwood Community Forum, interviewed 30 October.

World Bank (1996) *The World Bank Participation Sourcebook*, Washington, DC: World Bank.

10 | Contesting development, reinventing democracy: grassroots social movements in India[1]

RANJITA MOHANTY

It is more than four decades since grassroots-based social movements in India began contesting development[2] by critiquing its ecological and economic consequences for poor people surviving on the natural resources of land, water and forest, the resources that development wants to divert into industrial and commercial use.[3] Transcending a limited critique of specific development projects, these movements critique 'development', with its attendant rationale of technocratic growth, its binary construct of the world into poor and rich, its faith in the linear progress of people and countries from poor, backward and undeveloped to rich, progressive and developed, and the unquestioned desirability of this progress.[4] The movements instead urge that the ecology and economy of the poor, with their knowledge and culture, constitute the basis for the reorganization of society, economy and culture (Escobar 1995; Esteva and Prakash 1999; Shiva 1989). Under neoliberalism, the ruthlessness with which economic growth is pursued has led the movements to intensify their protest. People whose interests the movements articulate and represent include the rural poor – small and marginal peasants, landless labourers, people engaged in off-farm activities such as fishermen, and those who earn their livelihood by providing their services to the village, such as carpenters, artisans and weavers. In terms of their social composition, the movements' members include low castes, women and tribal communities inhabiting forests.[5]

The history of these grassroots movements reveals their power to shape the discourse of development to make it democratic in its form, practice and outcome. In this sense 'development' questions become questions about democracy. I argue in this chapter that the contestations over development are also contestations over democratic politics, for they raise the questions of equity, equality and inclusion. The movements have brought the old questions of democratic distribution of the material benefits of development back to the surface, but also infuse them with new meanings by emphasizing the democratic principles and practices that development has undermined. The movements have filled the spaces left vacant in a formal democracy where neither the local governance spaces created by the state for participation nor the political parties have represented the interests of the poor and the marginalized. The movements have thus both rejected the spaces and emerged as depoliticized sites of alternative grassroots democratic politics. As such, the resistance movements can be looked upon as acts of deepening democracy.

In this chapter I examine the potential of grassroots movements to expand and deepen the democratic ethos of inclusion, equity and equality. I do so by examining what I call the 'deepening democracy tasks' the movements have come to perform in recent times. Five such tasks are:

- The movements replace the exclusionary narrative of state-led development with a counter-narrative of inclusion.
- The movements expand the non-party political spaces for social action.
- Public space is constantly being democratized by the movements.
- The movements renegotiate poor people's relationship with the state.
- The movements are sites of reconstruction of modernity through the discourse of citizenship and rights.

Before I elaborate on all this, let me give a brief account of development and dominance to put the movements in context.

Development and dominance: birth of a people's movement

When India embarked upon its path of development soon after independence in 1947, the national leadership under the first prime minister, Jawaharlal Nehru, painstakingly tried to combine the agenda of development with the agenda of democracy. The leaders, most of whom had been part of the nationalist struggle against colonialism, saw three critical tasks they had to perform: build democracy in a society long ruled by authoritarian colonial oppression; address the economic well-being of the vast majority of its people reeling under poverty; and protect the sovereignty of a country that had just emerged from a long colonial subjugation. Development in the form of economic growth was considered the answer that would secure material prosperity for people and also protect national sovereignty. The development agenda, however, was not seen as independent of the agenda of democracy-building, but rather thought of as a part of it that would contribute to building a society based on the values of egalitarianism and social justice. A socialist element was built into the democratic agenda that development was intended to fulfil (GOI 1951).

Indian developmental planning, in the form of successive five-year plans, put the emphasis on industrialization as the chief vehicle of economic growth. Economic growth was termed 'national growth' and 'a public good', which the state was to pursue for the well-being of its populace. There were many streams of industrial development. One stream generated raw material for industrial use – mining and steel industries, for example. The power projects were designed to generate power for industrial, agriculture and domestic consumption – dams and thermal power plants were in this category. Another stream used technology to harness natural resources such as marine resources and fisheries for export promotion. And yet another stream captured the natural resources, primarily forests, for commercial use, such as paper and textile industries. Industrialization thus used nature as its primary raw material to generate material wealth. The public sector controlled industrial development, with a peripheral role assigned to the private sector in light consumer goods.

Economic growth through industrialization and commodity production thus became the core of the Indian economy, and industry, mining and giant irrigation projects took shape in quick succession to change the economic and social landscape. The developmental path of the democratic state was ideally designed to benefit the disadvantaged and promote equity and social justice. Ironically, though, the democratic developmental agenda of the state was subverted by the dominant forces as they appropriated the benefits of development, much to the disadvantage of the marginalized groups of the poor, the landless, low castes and tribal communities that had suffered social and economic vulnerability in the past and to whom the development projects were designed to bring benefit (Kothari 1986; Bardhan 1984, 1988; Kohli 1987, 1988; Dhanagre 1987). Not only did developmental projects not benefit them, but they added new dimensions of disadvantage to their already disadvantaged position. As the technocentric economic growth took off and huge irrigation, hydroelectric projects and heavy industries took shape, thousands of people were displaced from their original habitat, and in the absence of a comprehensive resettlement and rehabilitation policy, displacement became the inevitable outcome of development.

For almost two decades industrialization was accepted as a strategy of national growth, but during the 1970s voices began to be raised against it. The resistance movements articulated three issues: national growth and the public good had turned into a private good, benefiting only a section of the population – that is, the elites in a position to negotiate with the state; the natural resources of land, river and forest on which rural communities depended for survival were being taken away for development without an alternative means of survival being provided; and decision-making about development had been centralized, denying poor people the chance to voice their opinion. The democratic agenda of development was in crisis.

The Chipko Movement, which heralded people's resistance to the loss of forests, was a movement of the local people, particularly women, in the hills of Garhwal in the western Himalayas to save their forest from commercial felling. It was initiated in the early 1970s, a period significant for the United Nations Conference on the Human Environment, held in Stockholm. Chipko brought home the truth that environmental degradation and social inequalities are intrinsically linked (Guha 1991; Bhatt 1991). The success of Chipko was followed by resistance in many parts of India against big dams (Narmada, Tehri, Koel-Karo), mines (iron-ore mining in Chhattisgarh, bauxite and aluminium mining in Orissa), commercial fisheries and forestry (Kerala, Tamilnadu, Orissa, Uttarnchal), and industrial pollution (the National Thermal Power Corporation in Andhra Pradesh, chemical industries in Maharshtra).

The crisis deepened with neoliberal economic growth. Several changes began taking place during the early 1990s. The liberalization reforms facilitated the entry and growth of foreign capital. This resulted in rapid economic growth, in which industry and special economic zones (SEZs) featured prominently.[6] The new environment gave rise to competition among provinces to behave in an 'investment-friendly' way and increased their zeal to allow private industries entry uncritically.

With the growth of private and global capital, the role of the state shrank. This is not to say that the state had performed its role earlier, but under neoliberalism it no longer seems accountable to its citizens. The retreat of the state under neoliberalism and its changing role to that of mere facilitator also means that the state, while still playing midwife to industrial growth, has lost much of its power to deliver to its citizens. This involves not merely redistributing the benefits of industrialization, but also the normative role the state is expected to play in protecting the rights of its citizens. Under neoliberalism both have suffered. The citizens find that the state either does not respond to them, or else responds rather brutally.

On 16 December 2006, three people were killed by police fire in Maikanch village, Kashipur, Orissa, when the police resorted to extreme violence in suppressing local resistance to Utkal Alumina International Limited (UAIL).[7] On 2 January 2006, the police fired at people protesting against the Tata Steel SEZ in Kalinganagar, Orissa, killing twelve tribal people. On 14 March 2007, the state retaliated to protests against the proposed SEZ chemical hub for the Salim Group in Nandigram in West Bengal, and thirteen people were killed by the police. Since then Nandigram has turned into a site of the worst kind of violence, where the Left Front state administration planned and launched an operation in which its cadre-based men and police stormed the Nandigram villages to capture them by force.[8] The terror that the state has perpetrated in recent times, as exemplified by the brutal killings of poor people in Kashipur, Kalinganagar and Nandigram, reveals not only the ugly side of development under neoliberalism, but also the lengths to which the state can go to pursue it, even if that means curtailing the most fundamental of people's rights, the right to life.[9] Development as a public good not only remains long-forgotten rhetoric, but the situation has worsened for the poor, who cannot interrogate the state and industry primarily because, for far too long, they have remained isolated from the benefits of the economy (Mohanty 2007).

This chapter will not enter deeper into the now well-known school of new social movements to examine in detail whether the movements discussed here indeed represent the new social movements that emerged in Europe, where a new post-industrial political consciousness (as opposed to the old class-based struggles of industrial society) helped shape new identities and new concerns for ecology, peace, feminism and civil rights (Touraine 1985; Offe 1985; Melucci 1995). A brief theoretical positioning here, however, would, I think, help situate the movements in India and in other developing countries.

When the grassroots movements in India began protesting against state-led development in the early 1970s, there was considerable debate about whether the movements were indeed new forms of protest or were a continuation of the old struggles of poor people for equity, albeit in a new form. Both academic and popular writing claimed that while the movements reflected a new consciousness regarding ecology, they were also fundamentally old struggles by the poor for control over ecology-based livelihood resources (Guha 1989, 1991; Agarwal 1985). Old struggles in this context did not always signify quintessential class-based struggles in an industrial society; instead, the movements covered a wide range, from protest movements of the colonial period waged against the kings and the British rulers to agrarian movements in independent India that pitched the peasants against the landowners. In fact, the articulation of contemporary movements as struggles against poverty and inequality emanating from the commercial use of the ecological resources on which poor people subsist helped establish the link between poverty and the ecological consequences of development in the developing countries, thus giving a wider and new connotation to such movements.

This new perspective of the movements also expanded the framework of 'identity' politics of European new social movements, whose membership cut across class and profession in registering protest against ecological degradation. The movements in India have illustrated that the identities that movements mobilize to contest development comprise both old identities of caste, class and gender and new identities, such as dam-displaced or project-affected. Since it is invariably the poor, low castes, tribal people and women who become victims of large-scale development projects, the movements construct identities that often cut across a number of particular identities and provide a mix of old and new.

Seen in the context of earlier movements, however, the movements that have animated the terrain of grassroots protest since the 1970s appear new in three significant ways: the movements have linked ecology-based livelihood struggles with the large-scale development the state pursues; the movements have targeted 'development' and the state, and not any particular group of dominant people; and the movements have kept away from party-political affiliation and have emerged as apolitical sites to represent the interests of poor people.

The deepening democracy tasks the movements perform

In this context of the appropriation of poor people's subsistence resources by development, and of the benefits of development for the resourceful and dominant, questions of democratic values and the practice of equity, equality and inclusion become an essential part of movements' discourse. The movements therefore perform the following 'deepening democracy tasks' as they continue their acts of resistance to development.

Replacing the exclusionary narratives of development with a counter-narrative of inclusion In their acts of contestation over development, movement actors attach three sets of meanings to the consequences of development: a material meaning that relates to the loss of livelihood resources and consequent impoverishment of the poor; a social meaning that relates to the disruption of the community relationships of those displaced by development; and a political meaning that relates to the non-consultative, top-down, imposed nature of decision-making around development. Running through the three sets of meanings is the feeling of exclusion: exclusion from the material benefits of development, exclusion from social and cultural connections, and exclusion from political decision-making. The counter-narrative the movement gives rise to, therefore, is *inclusion* of the marginalized sections – the poor, low castes, women and tribal people – both in the *processes* and in the *outcomes* of development.

As large-scale development takes away the sustenance resources of land, water and forest from the communities that have been subsisting on them, the concerns of livelihood and resultant poverty loom as questions that are at once about equity and about ecology. Chipko was the first such movement to draw the connection between livelihood, equity of resource distribution and consideration for the ecological resources of the poor. Gradually other aspects of livelihood became more visible and began to be articulated by the movements that rose up against mining, dams, chemical industries and commercial fisheries. Large-scale displacement of people by dams, mines and industries became synonymous with development – and, without any adequate policy to resettle the displaced population, the loss of livelihood and habitat, migration to cities and the consequent transformation of peasants into wage labour in the cities, where they finally ended up living as illegal inhabitants in the slums, became the ugly face of development. Even in those instances where the industries did not displace people, the pollution of agricultural land and water resources caused by mines, fishery and chemical industries meant a loss of livelihood for people.

The material aspects of displacement, loss of livelihood and migration are intricately connected with the disruption of sociocultural contexts and communitarian relations. Not only did displaced people lose old relationships, but also the resentment of the host communities they were subjected to in the new settings intensified their feeling of alienation. The competition for scarce resources of drinking water, agricultural land, village commonage, etc., became a source of conflict. Even in instances where a project tried to resettle a few families, the transition from one place to the other generated a feeling of loss. The temporary shelters that were built for the resettled people, the uncertainty about the possession of the land allotted to them, the patronizing attitudes and harassment they faced in the government offices dealing with the resettlement, and finally the aggression shown by the old inhabitants where the new resettlement colonies were built all meant the loss of the certainty and comfort of their social relationships built over generations.

At the heart of material and social exclusion lies exclusion from political decision-making. Industrial development under the rubric of the national and public good never allowed poor people to voice their opinion regarding the design and implementation of projects. Often people came to know about a project only when government officials came to take their land. The Land Acquisition Act of 1894, a piece of colonial legislation which is still used, vests immense power in the hands of the state to acquire land for what is euphemistically called the 'national interest' and 'public good'. This Act has been used unsparingly to facilitate industrial enterprise and the usurpation of large chunks of land in different parts of the country, including farmland, for industrial development.

The three dimensions of exclusion resulting from development are articulated by the movement actors as the dominant narrative of development, which is about the lack of distributive logic of the material benefits of development, its cultural insensitivity and its centralization of decision-making. The contestation of exclusionary narratives of development with a counter-narrative of inclusion of the marginalized groups therefore entails not only democratization of the outcomes of development, but, equally important, democratization of the processes of development. The powerlessness and exclusion that people experience from not being able to counter or tame development on their own terms are doubly dispossessing owing to the aspirations people derive from a democratic polity of which they are a part. The mobilizations contesting development, therefore, are an articulation of interests that resonate with the democratic ethos of inclusion and equality.

The movements do not only see an insertion of principles of inclusion into the existing framework of development as their goal, however; they envision a new framework whose foundation is laid on the principles of inclusion and whose outcomes are measured on the basis of equality, equity and social justice. This, the movements argue, demands not only an alternative to development, but an alternative democratic politics as articulated by the poor people through their acts of protest.

Expanding non-party political space for social action The 1970s were the period when, for the first time in Indian history since independence, acts of resistance began reflecting disenchantment with the political parties as representatives of the interests of marginalized groups. Until then the Indian National Congress, as the main vehicle of nationalist struggle and subsequently as the ruling party, enjoyed unquestioning faith as the agent to fulfil the aspirations of the people. But after two decades of rule, the

Congress was seen as the party of the elites and of dominant interests: the rural and industrial bourgeoisie and the upper castes. The left then became the vanguard of workers and peasant movements. The voices of dissent from students, women, peasants and labour soon discarded the party affiliations, however, and, instead of targeting the class enemy in the quintessential manner of the left, began directing their protest against the state for their failed aspirations, demanding a response.

This was a period when development began to be resisted in a very different manner. Chipko was a continuation of the old peasant struggle, but it added a new dimension by raising the issues of survival, dependence and people's control over their resources and by directing the struggle not against any class per se but against the state (Guha 1991). Jayaprakash Narayan, with his *sampoorna kranti* or 'total revolution' to restructure the entire economy, polity and society, captured the national imagination in a way that was second only to the nationalist movement. Kothari (1984) calls these protests without political party affiliations 'non-party political formations', which declared the autonomy of social actions from political parties.

A series of events unfolded on the political landscape which demonstrated the limited ability of the political parties to articulate ordinary people's interests in a meaningful way. The imposition of a national emergency by the Congress under Indira Gandhi in 1975 to suppress the voices of dissent, the electoral loss of the Congress when the emergency was lifted, the victory of the Janata Party and the subsequent crisis in the party over the post of prime minister, leading eventually to the Congress's return to power, were some of the key events of the 1970s. They signalled a crisis in the power of representative democracy to articulate the interests of the poor and marginalized, and gave rise to autonomous social actors who carved out a space for action uncontaminated by formal politics where they could raise their voices and interests.

The crisis of representative democracy has deepened under neoliberalism. Because neoliberalism offers 'development' as a new source of political legitimacy, both the ruling and opposition parties in India have clung to it to create their constituencies. If the ruling parties have clung to 'development' to invite foreign investment and create an 'investor-friendly' image for themselves, with the long-term aim of staying in power by catering to the interests of industry and global capital, the opposition has clung to it to create a pro-poor anti-development image.

In a historical irony, on 14 March 2007 the left-led government of West Bengal opened fire on people who had assembled at Nandigram to protest against the acquisition of their land for the SEZ. In the events that unfolded in Nandigram during October and November 2007, the Left Front workers together with police captured the site of protest and kept the movement's sympathizers and the press out. When tribal people were killed by the police in Kashipur in December 2006 and Kalinganagar in January 2006, the ruling government in Orissa was led by Biju Janata Dal in alliance with the right-wing Bharatiya Janata Party. The Congress, as the opposition party in the Orissa government, rushed to sympathize with the protesters. But that act was highly suspicious, because the Congress, as the ruling party at the national level, is at the helm in terms of facilitating neoliberal reforms, economic policy and planning. In the same state in the early 1990s, the Congress, which was in power at the time, sanctioned an intensive prawn cultivation project by the Tatas, not caring about the livelihood of the poor fishermen (Mohanty 2003).

In such contexts, the movements, being non-party political formations, help create autonomy for social actors protesting against development without any party allegiance. The movements also help extend the civil society space, which is vital for democracy and which remained subsumed under the state during the first two decades of independence. If, as Mouffe (2000) says, democracy itself is constituted of interests that it cannot rise above, but can at best manage and balance, then we have to seek that counterbalancing force in civil society. It has to stay separable from the state, remain visible and articulate the interests of those whom the state, even a democratic one, neglects in many instances. It is not the capture of the state power, but curbing that power and making the state respond to its neglected citizenry, which movements see as their goal. In the absence of civil society, the state can be pervasive, and even if it demonstrates its capacity for development, it can curtail people's freedom to choose development on their own terms. This space is significant for inspiring what Habermas (1989) calls the 'political public' to engage in 'politics' without a political party affiliation.

Democratizing public space As representatives of the public good, movements are acts of creation of public spaces that are democratic in nature and content. Besides creating autonomous public spaces that are non-political in nature, movements also work towards democratizing the public spaces by saving them from being hijacked and invaded by vested powers. The expansion of public spaces based on the principles of equality, rights and citizenship is what Melucci (1989) calls a process of 'post-industrial democratisation'. The public spaces enable movements to articulate the demands of civil society and to render the power relations of complex societies more visible. Given that power in these systems tends to conceal itself behind a veil of allegedly neutral or technical decision-making procedures, this critical function of public space is indispensable and probably of primary importance in the present period. (ibid.: 230)

The idea of the public sphere gained currency in the work of Habermas, who sees it as a site for deliberation and communicative action. Arguments and reason, not status, are what Habermas demarcates as the defining principles of the public sphere. As sites for equality and freedom, public spaces are sites for empowerment and political modernity (Habermas 1989). The public sphere, which is not pervaded by the state and where individuals can deliberate to create a rational public will, is thus vital for democracy and citizen participation. Writing in the context of western Europe, Habermas was quite aware that the public sphere could be a bourgeois sphere governed by possession of property and education, and in that sense antithetical to the democratic ideas of equality. Hence he contends that the public sphere has to accommodate common people, their will and universal possibilities. As he puts it: 'The public sphere of civil society stood or fell with the principle of universal access. A public sphere from which specific groups would be *eo ipso* excluded was less than merely incomplete; it was not a public sphere at all' (ibid.: 85).

Despite its being conceptualized as 'public', however, there is nothing inherent in public space which prevents it from getting captured and co-opted by dominant interests, official discourses or manipulative truths. In a hierarchical society such as India's, divided along multiple lines, public spaces can be hijacked by powerful interests. Writing about the public consultation processes of the National Thermal Power Corporation, a public sector enterprise located in Andhra Pradesh, on the issues of resettlement, Newell (2006) remarks that the industry often manipulates the practice in a way that keeps the actual stakeholders outside the public hearing. The industry is required to publish the date and place of consultation in a newspaper prior to the meeting, so that people are informed about the process and can join it. It often puts the information in English newspapers and not in vernacular ones, however, and does so only a few days prior to the event, so that either people do not read about the meeting or, even if a few do get to know about it, the time is too short for them to attend. Public spaces are also susceptible to being invaded by the powerful. As the Nandigram incident mentioned earlier showed, public spaces can be invaded to silence the voice of protest. When the government invaded Nandigram and the police fired at the protesters, Budhadeb Bhattacharya, the chief minister of West Bengal, referred to his retaliation against the Bhumi Uchhed Pratirodh Samiti, the organization spearheading the protest, as 'paying back in the same coin' (Mahapatra 2007).

Hence efforts to expand the public space to accommodate the opinions and interests of the powerless, to keep it open to debates and deliberations that are not contaminated by political and official interests, and to safeguard public spaces so as not to let them be captured by the powerful, are critical for deepening democracy. Movements perform this critical task of expanding and safeguarding public spaces as sites of alternative democratic politics that are different from the state and other vested interests.

Renegotiating the relationship with the state The movements embody the conceptualizations and practices of deprived groups focused on re-formulating their relationship with the state. In India, development, as pointed out earlier, was intended to operate within the democratic framework. Development gradually became the overarching domain, however, eclipsing democratic practices. The first two decades after independence saw absolute faith in the state and its agenda of 'nation-building' – that is, reconstruction of a post-colonial society. Nation-building legitimized both development and the state as its designer and executor. Faith in the rationality and neutrality of both development and the state was absolute, unquestioning and without suspicion. As Chandhoke (1998: 32) puts it,

> development was considered to be a value-free social process and a desirable end. That it could breed its own pattern of social oppression was neither recognized nor appreciated. ... Narrowly conceived in an econometric fashion, development portrayed the state as an impersonal vehicle of social change. It not only ejected the power relations of the state from its discourse, it also excluded the power relations implicit in the model of development itself. The underlying assumption was that the state could develop its people and hence should be the repository of untrammelled power.

Ironically, while power was kept out of the rhetoric of development, development not only became the space for strengthening old forms of division and inequality based on class, ethnicity and gender, but also created new forms of inequality as large numbers of people displaced by industrial development became impoverished, migrated to other places as labourers or ended up as unskilled workers in urban industrial towns. In this the state, as the chief force propelling development, was seen as an authoritarian agency of power and imposition to which people could not relate. It is little surprise, then, that development was seized on by the powerless groups to contest inequalities, and that the state was kept at the centre of this rebellion and reform. The movements do not aim to abrogate state power or to achieve a stateless utopia; they aim to reformulate the relationship between the state and its neglected citizenry within a democratic ethos, however contentious that may appear.

The agenda of this reformulation of the relationship with the state is not straightforward; it is fraught with complexities. For one, the state, as several incidents have demonstrated, uses force to silence the voices of dissent. This is particularly evident during rallies and demonstrations, which are seen as publicly challenging the state. The Narmada movement against the Sardar Sarovar Project, the Chilika movement against the prawn cultivation project of the corporate house of Tata, the movement against the Subarnrekha dam, the movement against the UAIL project and, in recent times, movements against SEZs have all witnessed police atrocities.

Second, the state has shown its preference for a certain kind of relationship with the groups working for the marginalized sections. Agragamee, the organization that once spearheaded the movement against aluminium mining by multinationals in the Kashipur region in Orissa, having enjoyed a good relationship with the state after its pioneering work on food security, is now blacklisted by the Orissa government for what the government calls 'anti-government' activities. In other words, as long as the organization worked for the livelihood of the poor tribal communities without questioning the state, it was not seen as a threat; in fact it was seen as 'behaving like the state' in taking care of needy people. These acts indicate that the state still retains the upper hand in shaping the state–society relationship.

There is also evidence to the contrary, however, of the state succumbing to people's demands,[10] though such instances are rare. In recent times the judiciary, unlike the legislative and executive arms of the state, has shown sympathy with the movements. The repeated stay orders from the Supreme Court on the construction of the Narmada dam are an example. These small victories against the state are indication that the state can be tamed, though the process can be arduous.

Even when the state recedes into the background under neoliberalism, it still looms large in the perception of the poor. Recent studies have shown that in many contexts resourceless people continue to look up to the state to intervene and solve their problems (Commonwealth Foundation 2001; Chandhoke 2005). The desire to reform the state, despite the experience of oppression at its hands, or its lack of power under neoliberalism, comes from what Hansen and Stepputat describe as 'paradoxes of inadequacy and indispensability', for, as they put it, 'the state, or institutionalised sovereign government, remains pivotal in our very imagination of *what a society is*' (2001: 2). To understand this paradox, and the willingness of the people to reform the state and reformulate their relationships, it is important to understand the nature of the post-colonial state and the depth of people's relationships of dependence and patronage with it. It is important to capture how the state features in the imagination of people since it is their perception of the state, ranging from disillusionment and despair to seeing it as a patron and a benefit, which is reflected in their relationship with it. As Chandhoke puts it, 'political preferences for the state over other actors are the outcome of historical processes ... that preference formation takes place in a historical context, that of specific institutions or systems of rules. These shape interest, fix responsibility and guide the formation of expectations' (2005: 1037).

The movements as attempts to democratize the relationship between the state and millions of its poor are therefore not to be seen as alternative ideologies of statelessness, but as ideologies of reform. This agenda of reform, however, should not be reduced to or conflated with the neoliberal reforms of 'good governance' spearheaded by the Bretton Woods institutions, the World Bank and the International Monetary Fund, which see the state as an ahistorical and apolitical agency and emphasize its administrative efficiency. The social movements, on the contrary, want to bring 'politics' back to the state and infuse its formulation of development with a strategy for the negotiation of power and resources by deprived groups. Writing about contemporary movements, Melucci says, 'The public spaces which are beginning to develop in complex societies are points of connection between political institutions and collective demands, between the functions of government and the representatives of conflict' (1988: 259).

Reconstructing modernity through the discourses of citizenship and rights In their resistance to development, the movements have sought to counter modernity, which informs development, and reinvent it in their interests by speaking through the language of citizenship and rights – that

252

is, through the language of democracy. The contestation of modernity takes place at the global level; it also takes place within the boundaries of the nation-state. Global modernity becomes more pervasive under neoliberalism.

There are two ways in which global modernity works. First, the basic foundation of modernity – which speaks about the universal agenda of economic growth and the rationality of the linear progression of human societies based on the dualism of progress from rural to urban, backward to progressive, traditional to modern and poor to rich – is reinvented to create a global economy through the invasion of economies of poor countries by the rich and powerful. Second, with neoliberalism, the nation-states are brought into the world system in a manner unprecedented in history. Development in many of its aspects, therefore, has now acquired a global connotation, and seems to have slipped out of the grasp of the nation-states, which earlier had the authority to decide the nature of development within their boundaries.

Hence the movements have to contest global modernity, and the coalescing of movements in the global sphere, most prominently in the form of the World Social Forum, is an indication of the contestation over global modernity. The discourses of global governance and global citizenship that have emerged in recent times owe their origin to global modernity. The movements also contest a micro- or localized version of modernity, however, within the boundaries of the nation-state. The micro-modernity is drawn from macro-modernity but, as the Indian experience suggests, is shaped by yet another form of modernity, which is liberal democracy. As Oommen (2004) writes,

> The very act of framing of development with a democratic discourse,
> and the state strategies of distributive justice, equality, freedom, all have
> given rise to expectations from modernity, the failed promises of which
> have crystallised the construction of the movements.

Rather than denying modernity altogether, however, the movements have tried to reinvent it through the very modern language of citizenship and rights, which talks both to development and to its democracy-building agenda. It is as if, to take revenge on modernity and its agents – the state, the market and their joint product, development – the movements have claimed the language of citizenship and rights to counter modernity on its own terms. By speaking a language that is intelligible to modernity, the movements have invented a weapon with which to contest and reconstruct it.

The movement discourse challenges the liberal notions of universal citizenship located in the constitutional guarantees of rights. The disadvantaged location of the poor, and their subjective experiences of oppression and powerlessness, have led to the re-emergence of the questions of 'particular' identities, experiences and meanings associated with citizenship (Mohanty and Tandon 2006). As a practice of democracy, these questions, on the one hand, make visible the tenuous assumptions of equality in a liberal democracy and, on the other, make claims of equity and equality for those who have remained at the margins of citizenship.

As mentioned, the identities that movements mobilize to contest development comprise both the old identities of caste, class and gender and new identities, such as dam-displaced and project-affected. Since invariably the poor, low castes, tribal people and women become victims of large-scale development projects, the movements often construct identities that cut across a number of particular identities. For instance, 'fishermen' became an identity for mobilization against the struggle in Chilika opposing the Tata industrial house. The 'fishermen' identity symbolically combined the twin identities of class/occupation and caste. Since fishermen belong to the low caste, are poor and depend on fishing for their livelihood, invoking the identity of fishermen conveyed the message that this was a struggle for the assertion of low-class or low-caste identities. Similarly, in the Narmada movement the identities invoked are *adivasi*, *kisan*, *mazdoor* (tribal person, farmer, labourer). These combine the class identity with tribal identity. Both old and new identities are thus mobilized for claiming citizenship. The old identity shows the continuation of old forms of exploitation; the new identity shows the new contexts of exclusion.

The second aspect that the movements have highlighted through the language of citizenship is the agency of people in shaping the developmental agenda. The state-invented term 'beneficiary' subjects people to the patronage and dominance of the state, and the market-invented term 'client' embraces a limited range of people who can be part of the market's ever-expanding profit-seeking agenda, thus leaving a large number of poor people outside its periphery. But poor people are not beneficiaries or clients; they are autonomous actors whose agency has to be recognized in shaping the society, economy and polity in which they live. Hence citizens as 'actors' in the scheme of development and governance are what the movements emphasize.

The language of rights is used by the movement actors to counter the might of the state. If the notion of national and public good gave the state the power to acquire land, forest and river, the communities subsisting on these resources are now claiming their ownership and control over them, giving a different meaning to 'public good'. It is at the very moment of their interface with the state that illiterate communities learn the potential of 'rights' to make their claim. And the claim for rights over subsistence resources has drawn people's attention to many other rights that were given by the state in the form of various pieces of legislation, but never actualized. The tribal people in Kashipur in Rayagada district, Orissa, in their opposition to UAIL, are not only invoking the rights of protection of tribal land; they are simultaneously invoking the rights to be free from bonded labour and from moneylenders, thus articulating the conditions desirable for a dignified life. In the context of police repression by the state, the claiming of rights has highlighted the right to life and the right to freedom of speech and expression, which constitute inalienable fundamental rights guaranteed to citizens under the constitution of India.

The movements are not merely invoking the state-given rights; they are also expanding the scope of the rights by articulating those which are new, which are not given in the constitution, but have grown from the lived experiences of being marginalized and from the struggles waged to address that marginalization: for example, rights over survival resources of land, water and forests, and rights for self-determination in development. As Dagnino (2005: 155) writes,

> In this sense, the very determination of the meaning of rights, and the assertion of something as a right, are themselves objects of political struggle. ... Moreover, this redefinition comes to include not only the right to *equality*, but also the right to *difference*, which deepens and broadens the right to equality.

Conclusion

I have argued in this chapter that acts of resistance to development are also to be understood as acts of deepening democratic politics as conceptualized by the poor. This is critical in a country like India, where the development planning by the state began by associating the democratic outcomes of equity and equality with development. While that goal of development was soon forgotten by the state, it lingered in people's imagination and thus shaped their expectations. Hence the questions of development at once become questions of democracy. The movements thus perform critical democracy-deepening tasks as they question development, its attendant rationality and its consequences for the poor, and as they organize people to resist development and its undemocratic enactors – the state and industry, and their modernization project.

Notes

1 This paper was written with the help of a Fulbright grant I received during 2006 and 2007. I am grateful to Arturo Escobar for commenting on an earlier draft. The original paper was presented in the North Carolina South Asian Studies Consortium. I am especially grateful to Sandria Freitag, Matthew Hull, Matthew Cook, Lauren Minsky and David Gilmartin of the Consortium for their valuable comments. I thank Rajesh Tandon for sharing his comments on the paper. A special word of thanks to the editors of this volume, Lisa Thompson and Chris Tapscott, for commenting on the paper and sharing their critical insights on social mobilizations in the South.

2 'Development' (which grassroots movements contest) in this paper refers to state-led development. Soon after independence in 1947, the Indian state conceptualized its modernizing project of economic growth with a heavy emphasis on industrialization, which includes dams, mining, thermal power industries, commercial fishery and forestry. This model of development requires an intensive technology-based use of natural resources on which a large number of rural poor are dependent for their livelihood. The neoliberal projects of economic growth currently pursued by the state have further intensified this process.

3 This chapter deals with a particular type of social movement that addresses the issues of ecology-based resource distribution for the poor in the context of large-scale developmental interventions – such as mining, industry and dams – by the Indian state. There are other kinds of social movements that also raise issues of resource distribution. Some of them have become separatist, claiming resource distribution in terms of the 'sons of the soil' argument (the Assam movement, for example), and some have turned violent (such as the Naxalite movement, which began as a move for land distribution to the poor). The resource distribution claims of the movements I am talking about in this chapter have been grounded on a critique of the modernization and development drives of the Indian state and the ecological and economic consequences that result. These aspects of the movements are well documented (Agarwal 1985; Baviskar 1995; Bhatt 1991; Fernandes 1991; Gadgil and Guha 1994; Guha 1989, 1991; Mohanty 2003; Omvedt 1993; Pathak 1994).

4 In other words, the movements no longer believe in finding different or better ways of 'doing development'; they critique and reject the entire paradigm of development. This has led to the shift from 'alternative development' to 'alternative *to* development' (Escobar 1995).

5 When common resources such as rivers, lakes and forests are threatened by development, we find affluent people (affluent peasants

in the case of the Narmada dam, which threatens to submerge the agricultural land and habitat of hundreds of villages, and affluent fishermen in the case of the commercial prawn cultivation project in the Chilika lake, which threatened the interests of fishermen, rich and poor alike) becoming part of the same movement. This has confronted the movements with the critical question of whose interests they represent. A subaltern approach to movement politics (Guha 1982), I suggest, will help understand this. That is, while the affluent and locally dominant people may be part of the movement for their self-interest, as long as they subscribe to and take part in the core politics of the movement, which represents the interests of the poor and marginalized, they are part of the same social action, and their membership of the movement is no reason to discredit the discourse of the movement.

6 The creation of SEZs for export promotion, industry set-up and infrastructure development is facilitated by the Special Economic Zones Act of 2005, under which goods for the development, operation and maintenance of SEZ units can be imported or domestically procured duty-free. There is also an income tax exemption on export income for SEZ units of 100 per cent for the first five years and 50 per cent for the next five years. The Ministry of Commerce and Industry web portal on SEZs (sezindia.nic.in) sets out the rationale for SEZs and the incentives given to them. SEZs in many parts of India, however, have given rise to conflicts between industry and government on one side and the local populace on the other owing to the forcible acqui-

sition of productive agricultural land from farmers (Bunsha et al. 2006).

7 UAIL was a consortium of industries. Its partners, the Tata group and Alcan, withdrew following local resistance to UAIL's mining ventures. It is now owned by the Aditya Birla group of industries.

8 The citizens' report on Nandigram gives a vivid account of the brutal events that took place in the Nandigram villages during October and November 2007 (sanhati.com/news/519/).

9 In keeping with Gandhian tradition, the movements have been largely peaceful in response to state-led violence and oppression.

10 One example is the success of the movement against the commercial export-oriented prawn cultivation project – the Integrated Shrimp Farm Project of the Tata business house – which threatened the livelihood of fishermen subsisting on the Chilika lake in the province of Orissa. See Mohanty (2003).

References

Agarwal, A. (1985) 'Ecological destruction and the emerging patterns of poverty and people's protest in rural India', *Social Action*, 35.

Bardhan, P. (1984) *The Political Economy of Development in India*, Delhi: Oxford University Press.

— (1988) 'Dominant proprietary classes and India's democracy', in A. Kohli (ed.), *India's Democracy: An Analysis of Changing State–Society Relations*, Princeton, NJ: Princeton University Press.

Baviskar, A. (1995) *In the Belly of the River: Tribal Conflicts over Development in the Narmada Valley*, Delhi: Oxford University Press.

Bhatt, C. P. (1991) 'Chipko Movement: the hug that saves', Survey of the Environment, *The Hindu*, Madras.

Bunsha, D., S. S. Chattopadhyay, P. Das, P. Manoj, M. Raghuram and T. K. Rajalakshmi (2006) 'Rural resistance', *Frontline*, 23(20), 7–20 October.

Chandhoke, N. (1995) *State and Civil Society: Explorations in Political Theory*, New Delhi: Sage.

— (1998) 'The assertion of civil society against the state: the case of the post-colonial world', in M. Mohanty, P. M. Mukherji and O. Tornquist (eds), *People's Rights: Social Movements and the State in the Third World*, New Delhi: Sage.

— (2005) '"Seeing" the state in India', *Economic and Political Weekly*, 40(11), 12–18 March.

Commonwealth Foundation (2001) *Citizens and Governance*, London: Commonwealth Foundation.

Dagnino, E. (2005) '"We all have rights, but ..." Contesting concepts of citizenship in Brazil', in N. Kabeer (ed.), *Inclusive Citizenship*, London: Zed Books.

Dhanagre, D. N. (1987) 'Green revolution and social inequalities in rural India', *Economic and Political Weekly*, 22.

Escobar, A. (1995) *Encountering Development: The Making and Unmaking of the Third World*, Princeton, NJ: Princeton University Press.

Esteva, G. and M. S. Prakash (1999) *Grassroots Postmodernism*, London: Zed Books.

Fernandes, W. (1991) 'Power and powerlessness: development projects and displacement of tribals', *Social Action*, 41(3), July–September.

Gadgil, M. and R. Guha (1994) 'Ecological conflicts and the environmental movement in India', *Development and Change*, 25(1).

GOI (1951) *First Five Year Plan*, New Delhi: Planning Commission, Government of India.

Guha, R. (1982) 'On some aspects of the historiography of colonial India', in R. Guha (ed.), *Subaltern Studies I : Writings on South Asian History and Society*, Delhi: Oxford University Press.

— (1989) 'New social movements: the problem', *Seminar*, 355, March.

— (1991) *The Unquiet Woods: Ecological Change and Peasant Resistance in the Himalaya*, Delhi: Oxford University Press.

Habermas, J. (1989) *The Structure of the Public Sphere*, Cambridge: Polity Press.

Hansen, T. B. and F. Stepputat (eds) (2001) *States of Imagination: Ethnographic Explorations of the Post-Colonial State*, Durham, NC: Duke University Press.

Kohli, A. (1987) *The State and Poverty in India: The Politics of Reform*, Cambridge: Cambridge University Press.

— (ed.) (1988) *India's Democracy: An Analysis of Changing State–Society Relations*, Princeton, NJ: Princeton University Press, Princeton.

Kothari, R. (1984) 'The non-party political process', *Economic and Political Weekly*, 19(5).

— (1986) 'Masses, classes and the state', *Economic and Political Weekly*, 21.

— (1987) 'On humane governance', *Alternatives*, 22.

— (1988) *State against Democracy: In Search of Humane Governance*, Delhi: Ajanta Publications.

Mahapatra, D. (2007) 'Right to life

throttled in Nandigram', *Times of India*, 19 November.

Melucci, A. (1988) 'Social movements and the democratisation of everyday life', in J. Keane (ed.), *Civil Society and the State*, London: Verso.

— (1989) *Nomads of the Present: Social Movements and Individual Needs in Contemporary Times*, Philadelphia, PA: Temple University Press.

— (1995) 'The new social movements revisited: reflections on a sociological misunderstanding', in L. Malhue (ed.), *Social Movements and Social Classes: The Future of Collective Action*, London: Sage.

Mohanty, R. (2003) 'Save the Chilika Movement: civil society interrogating the state and the market', in R. Tandon and R. Mohanty (eds), *Does Civil Society Matter? Governance in Contemporary India*, New Delhi: Sage.

— (2007) 'Rights, citizenship and state accountability: contentious claims of industry over tribal land', in R. Tandon and M. Kak (eds), *Citizen Participation and Democratic Governance*, Delhi: Concept Publishers.

Mohanty, R. and R. Tandon (eds) (2006) *Participatory Citizenship: Identity, Exclusion, Inclusion*, New Delhi: Sage.

Mouffe, C. (2000) *The Democratic Paradox*, London: Verso.

Newell, P. (2006) 'Corporate accountability and citizen action: companies and communities in India', in R. Mohanty and R. Tandon (eds), *Participatory Citizenship: Identity, Exclusion, Inclusion*, New Delhi: Sage.

Offe, C. (1985) 'New social movements: challenging the boundaries of institutional politics,' *Social Research*, 52(4).

Omvedt, G. (1993) *Reinventing Revolution: New Social Movements and the Socialist Tradition in India*, New York: M. E. Sharpe.

Oommen, T. K. (2004) *Nation, Civil Society and Social Movements: Essays in Political Sociology*, New Delhi: Sage.

Pathak, A. (1994) *Contested Domains: The State, Peasants and Forests in Contemporary India*, New Delhi: Sage.

Patkar, M., A. Talwar, D. Dutt, S. Tripathi and B. Chanda (n.d.) *November in Nandigram: A Citizen Report*, sanhati.comnews/519/.

Shiva, V. (1989) *Staying Alive: Women, Ecology and Development*, London: Zed Books.

Touraine, A. (1985) 'An introduction to the study of new social movements', *Social Research*, 52(4).

11 | Social mobilization in Cape Town: a tale of two communities

CHRIS TAPSCOTT

Political opportunity theorists (Tilly 1978; McAdam 1982; and Tarrow 1989, among others) have pointed to the fact that the strategies adopted by social movements are contextual and that they are to a considerable extent determined by the prevailing political system and by the opportunities that present themselves for social mobilization. According to Meyer, 'the organisation of the polity and the positioning of various actors within it makes some strategies of influence more attractive and potentially efficacious than others. The wisdom, creativity, and outcomes of activists' choices – their agency – can only be understood and evaluated by looking at the political context and the rules of the game in which those choices are made – that is structure' (Meyer 2004: 129). At the same time, resource mobilization approaches have pointed out that while agency is central to the success of social movements, so too are the material, organizational and intellectual resources at their disposal (McCarthy and Zald 1977). Evidence of this reality is to be found in the burgeoning social mobilization under way in post-apartheid South Africa. As will be seen, however, what differentiates this type of collective action, common in some states in the South, is the fact that it has, for many poor and disadvantaged communities, become a normalized mode of engagement with the state over basic socio-economic rights rather than, as is more often the case in the North, the practice of specific interest groups. What the case studies that follow amply illustrate is the fact that the prevailing political opportunity structures in South Africa are such that resource-deprived communities have little option but to take to the streets in their struggle to achieve their rights as citizens.

The upsurge in social protest activity in South Africa during the second decade of its new democracy is reflective of the extent to which formal institutional channels for citizen engagement with the state have failed. Indicative of the scale of this trend, some six thousand protests were officially recorded during the 2004/05 financial year and an estimated fifteen protests were being held *per day* somewhere in South Africa during 2007 (Delaney 2007). The reasons for this failure are extensive and have been discussed elsewhere at length and from a variety of different theoretical perspectives (Bond 2000; Terreblanche 2002; Daniel et al. 2005; Ballard et al. 2006; Tapscott 2008; and Piper and Deacon 2008, among others). Most authors concur that while frustration with the slow pace of service delivery and job creation are the proximate stimuli for this protest action, an ensemble of mutually reinforcing factors has given rise to this state of affairs and serves to inhibit the substantive participation of the poor in democratic institutions and processes. Despite the fact that the 1996 constitution and a plethora of policies emanating from that founding document have created an enabling framework for participation, the institutions and processes set in place to engage citizens in this process, the 'invited spaces', have not yielded returns in the form of service delivery (houses, water, electricity, etc.) or job creation. In large part this is due to the fact that the state has set the parameters for engagement in these forums, and has arrogated to itself the right to determine when, how and to whom services are allocated.

While most states presume the right to determine what constitutes the public good, in more consolidated democracies this practice is mediated, to a greater or lesser extent, by the interventions of civil society in the form of opposition parties, the media and other interest groups. In developing states, where civil society is weak, the dominance of the state tends to be aggravated by the political character of the ruling elites. In that respect, a feature of the process of democratic consolidation that has taken place in South Africa since 1994 has been the uneven mutation of the ruling African National Congress (ANC) from a liberation movement to a more formal political power in office. Having swept into office on the tide of popular resistance, the incoming ANC government effectively brought the notion of participation into the political and theoretical mainstream and raised it to a first principle of government policy. It is evident, however, that politically the ANC still perceives itself to be the vanguard of popular struggles and, in so doing, it crowds out attempts by other social movements to represent popular aspirations. In this context, the independent mobilization of citizens on even the most mundane of matters is perceived to be a threat to the status of elected officials and a direct challenge to the party as a whole.

Faced with the reality that the state is generally unresponsive to demands raised through formal institutional channels, disaffected citizens and the organizations that represent them have increasingly sought alternative means to express their grievances. The channels chosen have varied from community to community, according to their social, economic and political contexts, and they have differed in their effectiveness in extracting concessions from the state. In essence, nevertheless, these social movements are challenging the hegemony of the state exercised through formally designated sites of participation (including ward committees, public meetings – *imbizos* – and local elections) and are insisting that their concerns be addressed directly and as a matter of urgency. In eschewing formal channels, furthermore, the options that present themselves for redress are several: to embark on protest action (peaceful, violent or a combination of both) or alternatively to pursue their rights through the courts.

While the resort to violent protest holds the potential to evolve over time into a revolutionary movement with the further potential to overthrow the state, it is evident that this is not the intention of most social movements in South Africa.[1] Furthermore, while a significant number of service delivery protests have turned violent, there is little evidence to suggest, at the level of individual communities at least, that this form of engagement with the state has yielded any particular gains. Typically, the state has responded with force and has portrayed these struggles as the work of thugs and criminals, thus delegitimizing them in the public eye. This response is typified in a statement by the premier of the Western Cape province following protest action in one of Cape Town's informal settlements.

> I am warning that in no way should our sympathy for grievances around housing, services and amenities be interpreted as condoning illegal actions. The police will have no option but to restore order and only then can government enter into discussions around the problems of housing, services and amenities. ... [W]e will not be held hostage to burning barricades and illegal marches. I appeal to those at the forefront of these actions to much rather use the legitimate democratic institutions such as the many Imbizos, the ward committees, the structures for social dialogue and the offices of local councillors and MPs to present their case. If they choose not to do so, then they must face the consequences of a government determined to protect the interests of all its citizens. (Rasool 2005)

For most citizens, therefore, formal political structures, peaceful demonstrations and a recourse to litigation remain the only channels open for the attainment of rights.

The constitution and the legal framework to which it gave rise, however, are based on normative Western ideals of citizenship. Thus the constitution prescribes 'a common South African citizenship' and asserts that all citizens are 'equally entitled to the rights, privileges and benefits of citizenship' (RSA 1996: para. 3). In this context, it is assumed that the majority of the country's inhabitants not only have a clear understanding of the rights, privileges and benefits to which they are entitled, but equally understand how these rights might be achieved. In a highly dualistic society such as South Africa's, this prescript inevitably favours those who have knowledge of the extent to which their rights may be ensured through litigation and, equally importantly, those who have the resources to pursue this course.

The case studies discussed below describe the responses of two communities in Cape Town to adverse administrative and political decisions and illustrate the fact that poor and under-resourced communities are at a distinct disadvantage when attempting to challenge the hegemony of the state through peaceful means. For most communities, therefore, a recourse to protest action (with the latent potential for violence) remains the only viable option. As a point of departure, it is necessary to provide a brief contextualization of the space economy of Cape Town and the lived realities of different segments of its population.

The space economy of Cape Town

Cape Town is the oldest urban settlement in South Africa, having been established in 1652 as a refreshment station for ships of the Dutch East India Company sailing from Europe to the East. As a seaport, Cape Town has always exhibited a more metropolitan character than other cities in the country, with a heterogeneous mix of people of European, African, Asian and mixed race. It has nevertheless also always been geographically divided by race and, to a less obvious extent, by class. As a legacy of apartheid, categories of race and class still tend to coincide. As a consequence of the rigid policies of racial segregation that were in place less than two decades ago, and notwithstanding the emergence of a black middle class, the majority of Cape Town's citizens still live in racially homogeneous suburbs. As Young observes in that regard, 'Processes that produce and reproduce residential segregation are obvious forms of social, economic and political exclusion ... Residential segregation enacts or enlarges many material privileges of economic opportunity, quality of life, power to influence actions and events, and convenience' (Young 2002: 196). Furthermore, as Laloo suggests, the property rights of affluent (and predominantly white) South Africans shape relations of power in the broader society and this, by implication, also influences their political standing with the state (Laloo 1998: 441). Significantly, however, unlike their counterparts in many economically advanced countries such as the United States (Mott 2004), the poor in South Africa do not form part of a racial minority and constitute both the largest class and the bedrock of the ruling ANC party.

The Green Point Common Association

The first case study relates to the aggregated communities that are situated around Green Point Common, some five kilometres from the centre of Cape Town. Although the area has become more racially integrated in the past two decades, its dominant demographic profile remains white and middle class.[2] At issue for the community at large was the proposal to construct a major new stadium for the 2010 FIFA World Cup on Green Point Common, which is currently zoned as public recreational space. Not only would the development turn the spotlight of the world on Cape Town, but it was estimated that it would bring some US$1.2 billion into the city in terms of infrastructure grants from the central government and revenue from tourism and other multipliers associated with the soccer tournament.

Responsibility for the construction of the stadium fell to all three levels of government: the national government, which would cover major infrastructural costs, the provincial government, which was responsible for granting planning permission, and the municipal government, for overseeing the construction process. The decision to locate the stadium on Green Point Common, as opposed to either of two other potential sites, was taken by the municipality of Cape Town at a time when the ANC was in power. Importantly, Green Point was also the preferred site of the world soccer governing body, FIFA, and this fact assumed greater significance as events progressed.

Following the announcement of the preferred site for the stadium, a collection of interest groups met to discuss their concerns about the proposed construction. These ranged from the loss of public open space to adverse environmental impacts, concerns about additional costs to local ratepayers and an influx of undesirable people into the area. This loose coalition was subsequently formally constituted as the Green Point Common Association (GPCA). According to its website, the GPCA was 'a community-based not-for-profit group, comprised of organisations, ratepayer associations, sports and recreation clubs and concerned citizens from the greater Green Point and Cape Town communities' (GPCA 2006). Through the sharing of knowledge, the coalition's stated aims were to keep 'the general public and special interest groups abreast of events affecting the Green Point Common ... [and] to encourage good public governance and vigilant compliance with public policies, legal processes and procedures' (ibid.).

From the outset, the GPCA actively sought to mobilize public opinion against the stadium's construction in Green Point. In an early victory, the city's newly elected Democratic Alliance (DA) party mayor, who was also the leader of the main national opposition party, placed a moratorium on the planning of the stadium, citing irregularities in the procedures followed by the previous ANC-led council. This decision led to strong protest from both the national and provincial governments, which cited the national interests involved in hosting the 2010 FIFA World Cup and the potential threat to them if the process of construction was delayed. Following a series of discussions with the provincial government, the City of Cape Town eventually backed down and gave the stadium its full support. The eventual alignment of the views of the city and provincial governments was driven by two major imperatives: in the first instance, a rapid decision to proceed with construction of the stadium was required if the project was not to be lost to Cape Town; in the second instance, the programme of construction held the promise of national funding for infrastructural development and a major inflow of revenue into the city.

Despite having lost the city's support, the GPCA continued to mobilize and threatened to mount a legal challenge against the construction of the stadium. In particular, it encouraged its members to lodge complaints against the provincial government's Record of Decision, which had accepted the findings of a questionable environmental impact study and had given planning permission for the project to proceed. These initiatives presented the threat of a protracted legal struggle. While the GPCA did not, ultimately, succeed in halting or diverting the construction of the stadium, it was successful in extracting concessions from both the municipal and provincial governments as a condition of the withdrawal of its challenge. These included a commitment to retaining the common as a recreational area; a commitment that the stadium would not be surrounded by a village which might subsequently be sold off as housing; the allocation of alternative municipal ground to a local golf club to compensate for land lost in the construction of the stadium; and a commitment by the city to compensate the club for a loss of earnings and to cover staff costs until such time as it was again fully operational (Dentlinger 2007).

The Coalition for Langa Community Concerns

Langa township, which was established in 1927, was one of only three areas in greater Cape Town in which African people were officially permitted to reside during the apartheid era. Although a proportion of the population were defined as permanent residents, a large proportion (perhaps the majority) were considered migrant labourers who would eventually return to designated ethnic homelands in the eastern part of the country. During the 1960s and 1970s Langa comprised low-cost houses for the relatively small number of families living legally in Cape Town, together with an array of single-sex hostels to which large numbers of migrant workers were consigned. Gender imbalances were consequently extreme and the area manifested many of the characteristics of a labour camp. Apart from a government-run beer hall, a police station, a school and a clinic, there were very few facilities available for the community. With the progressive unravelling of the apartheid policy in the 1980s, increasing numbers of women 'illegally' joined their partners in the hostels and brought a more balanced demographic make-up to the area. The greater sense of community was evident in anti-apartheid protests which took place in Langa during the 1980s. This influx nevertheless aggravated existing housing shortages. Since no informal housing was permitted by the authorities, the offspring of those occupying houses were forced to construct shacks in the backyards of their parents' homes. Some occupants also rented out shacks to newcomers without accommodation.

With the collapse of apartheid in the late 1980s and 1990s and the ending of the influx control laws which inhibited the movement of black people into the cities, there was a large and rapid influx of people into greater Cape Town. As a consequence of the already severe housing shortages in the metropolis, the majority of these newcomers were compelled to live in burgeoning informal settlements on the peripheries of the city. With the passage of time, and as land became scarce in these large informal settlements, desperate newcomers began erecting shacks on the verges of established suburbs such as Langa. The rapid growth of an informal settlement on the outskirts of Langa began in the mid-1990s and rapidly gained momentum. The settlement, known as the Joe Slovo camp (named after an ANC struggle stalwart and the first minister of housing in the Mandela cabinet), skirts the N2 freeway from the airport to the centre of Cape Town.

In May 2005, the national Department of Housing announced the launch of the Gateway housing project as part of a broad programme to eradicate shack dwellings in the major cities of South Africa. Following this, the City of Cape Town, on the advice of the national minister of housing, announced that the houses would be allocated on a 70:30 basis to the residents of the informal settlement and to the backyard dwellers respectively. To the occupants of the backyard shacks, many of whom had been on the municipal housing waiting list for up to twenty years, this allocation was inherently unjust, particularly, they argued, as they had at no stage been consulted on the allocation process, and because many of those in the informal settlement had been there for five years or less. Aggravating this state of affairs, shortly after the announcement of the project a fire swept through the Joe Slovo informal settlement, leaving some eight thousand people homeless. Rather than being permitted to rebuild their homes, these people were placed in temporary accommodation and were informed that they would be the first to be moved into the new dwellings.

With the announcement of the launch of Gateway project, the community of Langa was invited to a public meeting with the mayor at the office of the Tygerberg municipal substructure. The meeting became extremely heated as angry backyard dwellers confronted the mayor with what they believed to be the unfairness of the 70:30 split. Despite their strong appeals for a 50:50 division of housing units, the mayor was reportedly unmoved and gave no indication that a more equitable form of distribution was possible. Following the meeting, those who had participated in the consultative meeting with the mayor established the Coalition for Langa Community Concerns (COLACOCO). Its chairperson was a retired school principal and a resident of Langa of some fifty years' standing. The coalition, also known as the 'backyard dwellers', petitioned the national minister of housing, the member of the provincial executive committee (MEC) responsible for housing and the mayor's office on the need to review the division.

COLACOCO also widened its concerns to include a more equitable distribution of the units being renovated in old migrant worker hostels. It was maintained that these quarters were under the control of a Hostel Dwellers Committee, which allocated the units to their friends and family irrespective of how long they had lived in Langa. The concerns of the backyard dwellers, legitimate as they may have been, inevitably pitted them against both the residents of the Joe Slovo camp and the Hostel Dwellers Committee. Relations with the latter group soured rapidly and the prospects of violent confrontations between the two became very real, when supporters of the Hostel Dwellers Committee marched on the home of the COLACOCO president. The internecine struggles ultimately weakened the case of COLACOCO and they were not able to enforce a change to the 70:30 allocation of housing. Less than three years after it started, the movement dissolved.

Leadership

The leadership of any social movement is ascribed, in that it is generally the agency of a self-selected few which serves to galvanize community concerns and which initiates collective action. In both case studies a series of events, both long-standing and proximate, served to spur individuals to action and to assume positions of leadership. As the orientation of their leaders and the resources at their disposal differed significantly, however, so too did the strategies that they adopted to achieve their goals. Their experiences are of further interest in the extent to which the different communities opted to make use of the formal participatory channels open to them.

The modes of participation open to the Langa coalition were largely limited to formal political channels. These included engagement in ward committees, participation in public meetings and petitioning both senior administrators and political leaders. When these measures failed to elicit any positive outcomes, they resorted to limited protest action (typically handing over memoranda to political leaders) and, in the case of some militant youth, direct action in the form of hostel invasions. Significantly, they placed faith in the interventions of their local ANC ward councillor to intercede on their behalf. The councillor, however, distanced himself from these protests, in large part owing to the fact that he did not want to be seen to be opposing politicians in more senior levels of the governing hierarchy.[3] He also played an active role both in subverting the independence of COLACOCO and in advancing the agenda of the national government.

To that extent, he was instrumental in setting up a project steering committee, ostensibly to bring together all parties with an interest in the Gateway housing scheme. Among those invited to participate in the steering committee were the local government councillors, city officials, representatives of the housing company and construction companies, representatives of the Joe Slovo settlement and non-governmental organizations, among others. In its final composition, the steering committee had thirty members, only two of whom were representatives of COLACOCO. In this context the views of the coalition formed a small minority among a variety of competing voices, some of which were purely technocratic and bureaucratic in nature (for example, the building contractors), and their impact was minimized.

Through the steering committee, the local government councillor was able to present the idea that the 70:30 split was immutable since the decision had been taken by higher authorities. Thus the minutes of May 2006 attest that 'Councillor Gophe clarified the issue pertaining to the 70/30 split stating that the presiding Forum cannot change the decisions taken at higher political level. Local concessions could however be entertained within local negotiations' (LPC 2006a: para. 5.2.4). In this manner, debate on the fairness of the policy was foreclosed, in that the decisions taken by the steering committee were ostensibly based on consensus.

In the context of political opportunity theory, the case studies illustrate the very different options open to different communities attempting to exercise their democratic rights and to influence policies that adversely affect them. In other words, the ability and the means to 'work the system' differed significantly. To that extent it mattered little that COLACOCO was mobilizing to ensure access to housing, a proactive measure to enhance the welfare of their members, while the GPCA was mobilizing to halt or reshape a development project, in an essentially reactive move intended to retain the status quo. The GPCA's ability to marshal information on the prescripts of the city's planning regulations, together with knowledge of the legal redress possible and the demonstrable financial means to follow this route, meant that the government (at all three levels) had to take seriously the challenge they posed. In addition, the individuals mobilizing in opposition to the stadium manifested a far greater degree of homogeneity in terms of socio-economic standing (predominantly white and middle class), levels of education and political affiliation than their counterparts mobilizing in Langa.

While the direct action of some community members in Langa was undoubtedly a product of frustration at the fact that their involvement in the processes of participatory democracy had failed to yield results, it also served to strengthen the resolve of the provincial government to press ahead with its policy and to resist what it termed 'bully' tactics. In the final analysis, the case of Langa illustrates how undifferentiated channels for the attainment of rights, through formal (and non-violent) means, can serve not only to assist some communities more than others, but also to divide and rule poor communities and dissipate their energies in internecine struggles.

In contrast to what might be perceived in official circles as the 'responsible' approach of the COLACOCO leadership, the leaders of the

Joe Slovo community adopted a more confrontational and aggressive approach to the state when confronted with the prospects of relocation out of Langa. Following a futile engagement with the ward councillor, the Task Team responsible for mobilizing the community led a march on parliament and delivered a strongly worded memorandum to the national minister of housing demanding that they be consulted on the future development of their informal settlement. When the minister refused to meet the marchers and sent an assistant to receive their memorandum, a decision was taken to escalate the protest and the community blockaded the N2 arterial highway to the airport. The police were called and in a stand-off rubber bullets were fired, people were injured and others were arrested. The publicity generated by the defiant stance of the Joe Slovo drew the attention of national and international NGOs and the assistance proffered by these organizations culminated in a legal challenge to their forced removal which went as far as the Constitutional Court. Although the court ruled in favour of their removal (on the grounds that this was necessary for the construction of new dwellings), it also instructed that 70 per cent of the new houses to be built on the site should be reserved for Joe Slovo residents.

Litigation as protest

As has been observed elsewhere, the use of litigation has enabled social movements to go beyond the formal mechanisms of participatory democracy and to challenge the state in an arena that was traditionally seen to be at the heart of the establishment (Duarte 2004). This tactic is not new, and it is evident that throughout the civil rights movement in the United States, leaders made use of both the courts and protest activity (Jaynes and Williams 1989; Klarman 2004). While a resort to litigation was reserved in large part to assert the need for fundamental rights on the part of disenfranchised communities, however, it is increasingly being deployed as an integral component in the armoury of social movements mobilizing in defence of a variety of different causes (Hilson 2002).

Historically, the role of courts in a democratic society has been viewed in terms of two competing models. In the first and mainstream model, courts are viewed as the arbiters of disputes between private citizens asserting particular rights (Lobel 2004: 2). In a competing perspective from public law, the judiciary is seen to play an important additional role in implementing social change. According to Lobel, the ongoing debate between these two views of the judiciary's role in a democratic society has obscured a third model of the role of courts. The third alternative perspective, he asserts,

> views courts as forums for protest. Under this model, courts not only function as adjudicators of private disputes, or institutions that implement social reforms, but as arenas ... which political and social movements utilize to agitate for and educate about their legal and political agenda. (ibid.: 2)

Just as studies have reported that the act of protest itself (in the form of marches, demonstrations, etc.) is an empowering one for those participating, so too have others pointed out that a resort to litigation against the state has its own intrinsic value over and above that of enforcing change. As Lobel observes:

> While victory is an important index of success in the first two views of the role of litigation, winning in court is not salient in the forums of protest model. Of course, the litigators and their clients certainly hope, and at times expect to win in court; but their objective is broader than courtroom victory. They primarily seek neither the damages awarded to private litigators under the traditional model, nor the injunction of the public law model, but rather to use the courtroom struggle to build a political movement. The litigation can serve a variety of roles: to articulate a constitutional theory supporting the aspirations of the political movement, to expose the conflict between the aspirations of law and its grim reality, to draw public attention to the issue and to mobilize an oppressed community, or to put public pressure on a recalcitrant government or private institution to take a popular movement's grievances seriously. What is decisive is that judicial relief not be viewed as dispositive: such relief is important but not the driving force of the litigation. (ibid.: 2)

The reaction of the Green Point Common Association to the perceived threat to their lived environment also involved popular mobilization, but the modes of engagement with the authorities were significantly different to those of COLACOCO. While the association did formally engage with the political leadership of the city, as well as with planners, environmental impact analysts and other officials, it was always clear that litigation was a powerful tool at their disposal. According to the chairperson of the GPCA, himself a retired barrister, 'The only democratic defence that is open to us is that of fighting for our lives through the court' (David Polovin quoted in Roelf 2006). He also threatened that the 'entire process will be subjected to a long and drawn out process in the courts ... [and]

no sod will be turned'. It is certain, moreover, that had the association chosen to invoke a court injunction, they could have succeeded in delaying the construction process to the extent that the World Cup Organizing Committee would have been compelled to select an alternative venue outside of Cape Town. Conceding this, a senior official in the office of the provincial premier stated that were the GPCA to opt for litigation,

> Cape Town will have to kiss hosting a semi-final game goodbye ... We will simply not have enough time to fight the case and then start building afterwards. We are now in the do-or-die phase. Construction of the Green Point stadium has to begin right now. Even if the GPCA lose their court case, the time delay will set us back so much that it will be impossible to complete the stadium in time for a semi to be hosted in Cape Town. (Joubert 2007)

It is also evident that the GPCA were more interested in the concessions that they could extract from the state than with actually halting the construction of the stadium in its entirety,[4] and to that extent the threat of litigation was successful as a means to an end. Although the GPCA is currently dormant, it is noteworthy that other social movements have arisen in the Green Point and Sea Point areas, the most prominent of which, Seafront For All, is seeking to block private beach development in an area hitherto open to the public (Fisher 2008). While there is no direct link between this interest group and the GPCA, the success of the latter has clearly served as a model for citizen mobilization in the area. This is evident in the media campaign launched by the organization and in the legal challenge against the property developer and the provincial government being fought in the High Court.

The use of the media

While the resort to litigation was a major factor differentiating the strategies deployed by the two communities, so too was their use of the media. As Oliver and Myers have pointed out, the media are not 'passive channels of communication and nor are they neutral or objective observers or recorders of events' (Oliver and Myers 1999: 39). Knowledge of the media industry and of media processes provides a means for social movements to present their case definitively and to frame their struggle for the public at large. As Oliver and Myers observe, 'Experienced organisers plan events that meet journalistic standards of newsworthiness, write press releases, call reporters, and craft their "sound bites" for the media' (ibid.: 43). By shaping the public discourse in this way, they are able to portray their demands as reasonable and justifiable in terms of their rights as citizens.

While the actions of COLACOCO drew some media coverage, this was not an orchestrated process, but rather an outcome of independent reporting of ongoing community protests. In the early phases of the campaign, steps had been taken to alert the media to the struggle under way, and the chairperson of COLACOCO gave some interviews to local media and appeared on national television.[5] Once the steering committee was established, however, it effectively served to muzzle opposing voices. The minutes of a meeting of the committee held in May 2006 cite the problem of conflicting reports in the media and invoking the MEC for housing.

> The meeting was advised that the MEC is very concerned with conflicting reports being circulated in the media. ... The meeting agreed that none of its members shall liaise directly with the media about issues affecting the social housing programme at Langa. The meeting clarified that representatives are permitted to report only to their constituencies as well as principles on progress achieved, however all media liaison must be directed to the MEC until further notice. (LPC 2006b: para. 3.7)

It is also evident, however, that COLACOCO itself was wary of what it perceived to be misrepresentation of their case, even if this was likely owing to poor investigative journalism on the part of uninformed media rather than any evident bias.

In a contrasting approach, the GPCA actively campaigned to win public support for its case through the media. This included establishing a website with an online blog to elicit public debate, conducting media interviews, issuing press releases and writing letters to the press. This process upped the ante, as it were, and created the impression of a sizeable opposition. It is evident that the media assault achieved three additional objectives. In the first instance, it helped to build coherence among the disparate groups comprising the association, by reinforcing a common understanding of the threats posed by the proposed stadium. In the second instance, it helped to intimidate those within the community, such as local hoteliers, who were favourably disposed to the construction of the stadium. By maintaining a coherent focus, furthermore, the association was able to avoid the divisions that ultimately undermined the actions of COLACOCO. In the third instance, the media coverage alerted FIFA to the possibility of a delay in the construction of the stadium and they, in turn, raised their own concerns with the South Africa government

273

(Mangxamba and Dentlinger 2006), increasing pressure for a settlement of the GPCA's challenge.

Conclusions

Ballard et al. distinguish between social movements in South Africa that aim to promote radical counter-hegemonic change and those that strive to fulfil their rights within the existing democratic system (Ballard et al. 2006: 400). While the former seek to overthrow the existing order, the latter (who constitute the bulk of social movements in the country) struggle to hold the government accountable for their constitutionally enshrined rights. While at a descriptive level there is some validity in this division of social movements, it is based on a narrow reading of the notion of hegemony. Social movements that challenge the right of the state to make decisions on their behalf do not necessarily seek to overthrow the state, but they do challenge the notion that the state knows best and they have withdrawn their consensus from a political order that presumptively naturalizes this understanding. As Kothari points out elsewhere, despite the fact that most struggles and demands are directed at the state, 'the mass of people are still committed to the state even though the state has fallen prey to interests that have no commitment to, or even empathy from the people' (Kothari 2005: 13).

Viewing the struggle for rights as a challenge to the hegemony of the state in determining the parameters for citizens' engagements provides a better understanding of why some social movements that opt for peaceful measures are more successful than others. Given that social movements with knowledge and resources are able to take on the state on in its own terms, as it were, they are more likely to succeed than those that follow more conventional political channels for redress where the state is indeed hegemonic.

In neither case study was there any recognition on the part of the state of the legitimacy of the demands of the communities involved, and in both instances their protests were portrayed as irresponsible, unreasonable and against the public good. That a compromise was reached with the GPCA was therefore not a reflection of the state's acceptance of the validity of their claims, but an indication that the state had been forced to make concessions to avoid both losing face internationally and the possibility of significant financial loss. By the same token, in the zero-sum game of state–citizen contestation, no steps were taken to assuage the demands of the backyard dwellers by constructing alternative housing for them elsewhere in Langa, rather than in the Gateway project (something

274

COLACOCO had proposed). To that extent, the case studies illustrate, somewhat starkly, that challenges to the hegemony of the state cannot be advanced on the basis of moral rectitude, by following the right channels, or solely on the basis of rights enshrined in the constitution.

This reading of events posits an essentially adversarial relationship between state and citizens and suggests that the state will concede to popular demands only when forced to do so. Assuming the independence of the judiciary, a resort to the courts does, in a sense, move the struggle on to neutral terrain on which the state is no longer hegemonic and on which it is subject to the very legal systems from which it derives its own legitimacy. Recognition of this reality is to be seen in the increasing number of social movements that have resorted to litigation either through their own resources, as in the case of the Treatment Action Campaign, which successfully campaigned for antiretroviral drugs for those living with HIV/AIDS (Pieterse 2008), or through amicus briefs, as in the case of the Joe Slovo community, who challenged their removal from Langa in the Constitutional Court.

For those social movements that lack the resources to take on the state through the courts, by far the majority, the only remaining option is to take to the streets in protest. As McAdam et al. (1996: 14) point out, for such movements, 'The successful use of "proper channels" would seem to depend upon control over precisely the kinds of conventional political resources – money, votes, influence with prominent others – that social movements tend to lack.' In such circumstances, they maintain, social movements 'have little choice but to use their ability to disrupt public order as a negative inducement to bargaining'. To that extent, social movement protest has increasingly become an integral part of the political landscape in many countries in the South, and it coexists with, and in some instances supplants, formal institutional channels for engagement with the state. In this scenario, formal political processes are becoming increasingly irrelevant for the poor majority (see Mohanty in this volume for a discussion of social movements in India), although most do not actively seek to overthrow the prevailing political order. Far from representing the interests of dissident groups (as suggested in much of the new social movement literature), social mobilization and the social movements to which they give rise in the South are, in effect, becoming a conventional vehicle for the attainment of democratic rights for ever increasing numbers of citizens.

Notes

1 This is evident in the fact that despite widespread protests nationally, the ANC was returned to power with a substantial majority in the 2009 elections.

2 According to the 2001 census, 75 per cent of the 10,000 people who lived in the constituency of Sea Point, in which Green Point Common is situated, were white and middle class.

3 The councillor, who has now defected from the ANC to the newly formed opposition party, the Congress of the People, conceded as much in an interview (personal communication with Councillor Xolile Gophe, 7 March 2009).

4 Personal communication, David Polovin, chairperson, GPCA, 4 March 2007.

5 Personal communication, Siphiwo Tindleni, chairperson, CO-LACOCO, Langa, 10 February 2007.

References

Ballard, R., A. Habib and I. Valodia (eds) (2006) *Voices of Protest: Social Movements in Post-Apartheid South Africa*, University of KwaZulu Natal Press.

Bond, P. (2000) *Elite Transition: From Apartheid to Neoliberalism in South Africa*, London: Pluto.

Daniel, J., R. Southall and J. Lutchman (2005) 'President Mbeki's second term: opening the golden door', in J. Daniel, R. Southall and J. Lutchman (eds), *State of the Nation, South Africa 2004–2005*, Cape Town: HSRC.

Delaney, S. (2007) *Amandla! Protest in the New South Africa*, Freedom of Expression Institute, 15 May, www.fxi.org.za/content/view/83/, accessed 22 January 2009.

Dentlinger, L. (2007) 'Ratepayers to cough up R140m more for stadium', *Weekend Argus*, 24 February.

Duarte, M. (2004) 'Protesting through law: the emancipatory power of law at the service of social movements', Paper presented at the annual meeting of the Law and Society Association, Renaissance Hotel, Chicago, IL.

Fisher, S. (2008) 'Battle to save the seafront', *Mail and Guardian*, 7 October, www.mg.co.za/article/2008-10-07-battle-to-save-the-seafront.

GPCA (2006) *Who We Are*, Green Point Common Association, www.greenpointcommon.co.za/pages/about.asp?subnav=1, accessed 24 May 2009.

Hilson, C. (2002) 'New social movements: the role of legal opportunity', *Journal of European Public Policy*, 9(2).

Jaynes, D. and R. Williams (1989) *A Common Destiny: Blacks and American Society*, Washington, DC: National Academies Press.

Joubert, P. (2007) 'No easy green light for Green Point', *Mail and Guardian*, 26 January.

Klarman, M. (2004) *From Jim Crow to Civil Rights: The Supreme Court and the Struggle for Racial Equality*, New York: Oxford University Press.

Kothari, R. (2005) *Rethinking Democracy*, Delhi: Orient Longman.

Laloo, K. (1998) 'Citizenship and place: spatial definitions of oppression and agency in South Africa', *Africa Today*, 45(3/4).

Lobel, J. (2004) 'Courts as forums for protest', bepress Legal Series,

Working Paper 213, law.bepress.
com/expresso/eps/213.

LPC (2006a) 'Minutes of the N2
Langa Project Committee Meeting
17 February 2006', Langa Housing
Offices, minutes on letterhead of
Cape Town Community Housing
Company.

— (2006b) 'Minutes of the N2
Langa Project Committee Meeting
11 May 2006', Langa Housing
Offices, minutes on letterhead of
Cape Town Community Housing
Company.

Mangxamba, S. and L. Dentlinger
(2006) 'Get cracking, Fifa boss
tells SA', *Cape Argus*, 7 December.

McAdam, D. (1982) *Political Process
and the Development of Black
Insurgency, 1930–1970*, Chicago,
IL: University of Chicago Press.

McAdam, D, J. McCarthy and M. Zald
(1996) 'Opportunities, mobilising
structures, framing and processes
– towards a synthetic, comparative
perspective of social movements',
in D. McAdam, J. McCarthy
and M. Zald (eds), *Comparative
Perspectives on Social Movements:
Political Opportunities, Mobilizing
Structures, and Cultural Framings*,
Cambridge: Cambridge University
Press.

McCarthy, J. and M. Zald (1977)
'Resource mobilization and social
movements: a partial theory',
American Journal of Sociology, 82(6).

Meyer, D. (2004) 'Protest and political
opportunities', *Annual Review of
Sociology*, 30, August.

Mott, A. (2004) 'Increasing space and
influence through community
organising and citizen monitoring: experiences from the USA',
IDS Bulletin, 35(2), April.

Oliver, P. and D. Myers (1999) 'How
events enter the public sphere:
conflict, location and sponsorship
in local newspaper coverage of
public events', *American Journal of
Sociology*, 105(1), July.

Pieterse, M. (2008) 'Health, social
movements, and rights-based
litigation in South Africa', *Journal
of Law and Society*, 35(3).

Piper, L. and R. Deacon (2008) 'Party
politics, elite accountability and
public participation: ward committee politics in the Msunduzi
Municipality', *Transformation*,
66/67.

Rasool, E. (2005) *Premier Calls
for Legitimate Actions to Draw
Attention to Legitimate Grievances*, Issued by the Office of
the Premier, Western Cape
Provincial Government, 23 May,
www.info.gov.za/speeches/2005/
05052412151001.htm.

Roelf, W. (2006) 'Residents may
sue to stop stadium plans',
South African Press Association,
12 April.

RSA (1996) *The Constitution of the
Republic of South Africa, Act 108 of
1996*, Republic of South Africa.

Tapscott, C. (2008) 'The challenges of deepening democracy
in post-apartheid South Africa',
in F. Saito (ed.), *Foundations for
Local Governance: Decentralisation
in Comparative Perspective*, New
York: Springer.

Tarrow, S. (1989) *Democracy and
Disorder: Protests and Politics in
Italy 1965–75*, Oxford: Clarendon.

Terreblanche, S. (2002) *A History of Inequality in South Africa
1652–2002*, Scottsville: University
of Natal Press.

Tilly, C. (1978) *From Mobilisation to
Revolution*, Reading: Addison-
Wesley.

Williams, G. (2004) 'Towards a

repoliticization of participatory development: political capabilities and spaces of empowerment', in S. Hickey and G. Mohan (eds), *Participation from Tyranny to* *Transformation?*, London: Zed Books.

Young, I. M. (2002) *Inclusion and Democracy*, Oxford: Oxford University Press.

About the contributors

Angela Alonso is a Professor in the Department of Sociology, University of São Paulo and Coordinator of the Environmental Conflicts Area, Brazilian Centre of Analysis and Planning. She has written books on environmental conflicts in Brazil and the Brazilian reformist movement in the nineteenthth century, as well as a biography of the leader of the Brazilian abolitionist movement. Currently she is a Guggenheim Fellow and a Visiting Fellow at the MacMillan Center in Yale University, researching the ideas and strategies of the movement for the abolition of slavery in Brazil.

Carlos Cortez Ruiz is Professor at the Universidad Autónoma Metropolitana (UAM) in Mexico, where he teaches postgraduate studies on rural development. He acts as coordinator of an interdisciplinary research programme on human development that puts emphasis on social strategies for sustainable human development. His work emphasizes methodologies that combine research and action in complex intercultural contexts and that enable the development of capacities for social change through social networks that have an impact on public policies and on the accomplishment of rights. Using this perspective, he has written on social action, citizenship, rights and methodologies of action-research and public policies in Mexico.

Valeriano Costa is an Associate Professor in the Department of Political Science at the State University of Campinas, São Paulo. He has been an Associate Professor since 1998. Since 1999 he has been a researcher of the Environmental Conflicts Area at CEBRAP, where he took part in several research projects on environmental conflicts in Brazil and the history of the Brazilian environmental movement. Between 2003 and 2005 he worked on the evaluation of administrative structures of Brazilian state governorships for a programme that finances public modernization projects. Formerly he worked as an Associate Researcher in the Center of Contemporary Cultural Studies (CEDEC) in the city of São Paulo, Brazilian transition to democracy, decentralization of public policies, and the reform of the public administration at the federal level of government. He is co-author, with Fernando Abrucio, of *Reform of the State in the Brazilian Federative Context* (1998) and has been involved in research on the Brazilian environmental movement and mobilization in Brazil.

Arilson Favareto is a sociologist, with a PhD in environmental sciences and a Professor at the Centre of Engineering, Modelling and Applied Social Sciences – Federal University of ABC Region (UFABC), Brazil. He is also a researcher-collaborator at the Brazilian Centre of Analysis and Planning (CEBRAP).

Débora Alves Maciel is an associate researcher at CEBRAP (Brazilian Centre of Analysis and Planning) and a member of the Study Group on Law and Policy of the CEIPOCUNICAMP (Center for International Studies and Contemporary Politics University of Campinas – Sao Paulo). She was Professor of Sociology at the Faculty of Law of São Bernardo do Campo/São Paulo and currently she is Professor of Sociology at the Federal University of São Paulo (UNIFESP). She has undertaken research on the formation and trajectories of the Brazilian environmental movement; the access of the environmental conflicts to the Public Prosecutor; the political and judicial mobilization of the legal professional (prosecutors and attorneys, cause lawyers). Currently she is studying the forms and dynamics of legal mobilization of social movements and civil organizations in Brazil since the 1990s. She has a PhD in Sociology from the University of São Paulo (USP).

Simeen Mahmud is currently Research Director at the Population Studies Division at the Bangladesh Institute of Development Studies. She studied statistics at the Dhaka University and medical demography at the London School of Hygiene and Tropical Medicine. Her past research has focused on demographic estimation, the relationship between women's work, status and fertility and demographic transition in conditions of poverty. Her current research focuses primarily on women's work, pathways of women's empowerment, participation and mobilization for citizenship and rights.

Lyla Mehta is a Research Fellow at the Institute of Development Studies, University of Sussex. She is a sociologist and her work has focused on the gendered dimensions of forced displacement and resistance, rights and forced migration and the politics of water. Since 1991, she has conducted research on displacement and resistance in India's Narmada Valley. She has engaged in advisory work on issues concerning displacement, gender, dams and development with various UN agencies and the World Commission on Dams and has also been active in advocacy and activist work on these issues with NGOs and social movements in Europe and India. She has authored *The Politics and Poetics of Water: Naturalising Scarcity in Western India* (2005), edited *Displaced by Development: Confronting Marginalisation and Gender Injustice* (2009) and co-edited *Forced Displacement: Why Rights Matter* (2008).

Ranjita Mohanty is an independent scholar based in New Delhi, and works as a consulting sociologist with national and international organizations. She has a doctorate in sociology from Jawaharlal Nehru University, New Delhi. She was a Fulbright Senior Research Fellow (2006-2007) at the Anthropology Department, University of North Carolina, Chapel Hill, USA. Her research addresses the grassroots issues of development and democracy within the social science perspective. Her abiding interest is in studying the politics of the powerless, and the contestation and negotiation of power that takes place between civil society and the state. She has directed the research programme at the Society for Participatory Research in Asia (PRIA) for close to a decade, and has many years of association with Citizenship DRC. She has co-edited two books: *Does Civil Society Matter? Governance in Contemporary India*, and *Participatory Citizenship: Identity, Exclusion and Inclusion.*

Lubna Nadvi is a teacher in the Politics Department at the University of KwaZulu-Natal, Durban. She has research interest in African and South African politics, comparative politics, including Middle Eastern and Asian politics, gender and feminism, political Islam, social movements and civil society, HIV-AIDS, and international relations. She is also a long-standing activist with the social movements forum(s) in Durban.

Ndodana Nleya is a PhD candidate and Assistant Researcher at the African Centre for Citizenship and Democracy at the School of Government at the University of the Western Cape. He holds an MSC in water resource management from the University of Western Cape. He previously worked in various portfolios in industry in Zimbabwe before pursuing an academic career.

Eghosa E. Osaghae is Professor of Comparative Politics and Vice Chancellor of Igbinedion University Okada, Nigeria. His research interests include ethnicity, nationalism, federalism and the politics of statehood in Africa. He has published extensively on these subjects in books and journals.

Laurence Piper is Professor of Political Studies at the University of the Western Cape. His research interests include new democratic institutions

and practices, especially in the developing world.

Vera Schattan Coelho is a senior researcher at the Brazilian Centre of Analysis and Planning (CEBRAP), where she coordinates the Citizenship and Development Group. She has a PhD in social science. Her interests centre on the processes of democratization and development taking place in Brazil and other countries and the tensions that arise from the attempt to combine the democratization of social relations with development. She has led various comparative studies in the areas of new forms of citizen participation, deliberation and consultation to improve social policies and democracy. She is author of numerous articles on health policy, pension reform and participatory governance and is editor of *Pension Reform in Latin America*: *Participation and Deliberation in Contemporary Brazil* (with Marcos Nobre) and *Spaces for Change* (with Andrea Cornwall).

Nardia Simpson is an Australian qualified lawyer with a Masters of Philosophy in development studies from the Institute of Development Studies, University of Sussex. Her interests include legal sociology, land tenure, informal justice institutions and access to justice. She has worked in the areas of property and environment law, as a lecturer in human rights and development, and as a consultant for UNIFEM. She is currently based in New Delhi, where she advises multilateral organizations and the government of India on social infrastructure and public–private partnership.

Linda Waldman is a social anthropologist with experience in African poverty and the related issues of gender, racial classification, ethnicity and identity. She obtained her PhD at the University of the Witwatersrand, South Africa, where her research focused on indigenous identity and nationalism among the Griqua of South Africa. She joined the Institute of Development Studies as a Fellow in the Knowledge, Technology and Science Team in 2004. Her recent research activities include an examination of how environmental issues are integrated into Poverty Reduction Strategy Statements and a comparative study of asbestos-related disease and its legal, medical and socio-cultural dimensions in South Africa, the United Kingdom and India.

Index